Arthur Henry Beavan

Marlborough House and its Occupants

Present and past

Arthur Henry Beavan

Marlborough House and its Occupants
Present and past

ISBN/EAN: 9783337152512

Printed in Europe, USA, Canada, Australia, Japan

Cover: Foto ©ninafisch / pixelio.de

More available books at **www.hansebooks.com**

MARLBOROUGH HOUSE

AND

ITS OCCUPANTS

PRESENT AND PAST

BY
ARTHUR H. BEAVAN

ILLUSTRATED WITH DRAWINGS BY HOLLAND TRINGHAM, R.B.A.
AND PHOTOGRAPHIC VIEWS
TAKEN BY THE SPECIAL PERMISSION OF
HIS ROYAL HIGHNESS THE PRINCE OF WALES, K.G.

" *A largess universal, like the sun,
His liberal eye doth give to every one.*"

London:
F. V. WHITE & CO
14 BEDFORD STREET, STRAND
1896
[*All Rights Reserved*]

PRINTED BY
KELLY AND CO. LIMITED, 182, 183 AND 184, HIGH HOLBORN, W.C.,
AND KINGSTON-ON-THAMES.

PREFACE.

CHARLES DICKENS once remarked that Prefaces, though seldom read, were continually written; chiefly, he conjectured, for the benefit of posterity.

Yet the few who do glance at these compositions have probably noticed the half-apologetic tone often pervading them, some authors considering it necessary to explain at considerable length why their books were written at all.

There is, however, a certain kind of topic, so indisputably popular, as to require no literary "apologia pro vita sua," even though the pen that writes thereon be a faltering one.

With such a subject—Marlborough House and its illustrious inmates—it has been my privilege to deal in the following pages, whose contents will, I feel confident, commend themselves, by virtue of their inherent national interest, to every loyal person throughout Her Majesty's wide dominions.

I have respectfully to thank His Royal Highness, the Prince of Wales, for his kindness in permitting drawings and photographs of Marlborough House to be taken for this work; and H. I. M. the Empress Frederick of Germany—always the Patroness of Literature—for her gracious assistance.

I have also to tender my thanks to His Highness, Prince Edward of Saxe-Weimar, K.P., for much interesting information respecting Queen Adelaide; to General H. Lynedoch Gardiner, C.B. for many particulars relating to

Prince Leopold's occupancy of Marlborough House; to His Grace, the Duke of Marlborough, for permitting the records at Blenheim Palace to be examined; and to His Grace, the Duke of Wellington, for allowing the original sketch of his illustrious ancestor's funeral car to be reproduced.

I desire to acknowledge my indebtedness in various ways to Sir Horace Rumbold, Bart., K.C.M.G., H.M.'s Minister Plenipotentiary at the Hague; to the Hon. F. C. B. Ponsonby Fane, K.C.B.; to J. Taylor, Esq., C.B., of H.M.'s Office of Public Works; to H.M.'s Commissioners of Woods and Forests; to Francis H. Miller, Esq., Superintendent of the Royal Victoria Yard, Deptford; to H. C. Maxwell Lyte, Esq., C.B., Deputy Keeper of the Public Record Office, and his obliging secretary, James J. Cartwright, Esq.; to Dr. Richard Garnett, C.B., Keeper of Printed Books at the British Museum; to the Astronomer Royal, Greenwich Observatory; and, lastly, to my wife, whose secretarial services have been invaluable.

ARTHUR H. BEAVAN.

CONTENTS.

PAGE

CHAPTER I.

The Entrance and Approach from Pall Mall—The Offices—The Kitchen—The Stables—The Grounds and Garden   1

CHAPTER II.

The Large Drawing Room—The Indian Room—The Studio, or Painting Room—The Tapestry Room—The Staircases—The Entrance Hall—The Equerry's Room—The Room of the Ladies-in-Waiting   25

CHAPTER III.

The Royal Household Dining Room—The Basement—The Plate Room—The Saloon—The Prince and Princess's Warrant Holders   44

CHAPTER IV.

The Large Dining Room—The Derby Day Dinner at Marlborough House   60

CHAPTER V.

The Princess's Reception Room, Boudoir, Bedroom and Dressing Room—Music at Marlborough House   .   71

CHAPTER VI.

The Prince's Dressing Room and Ante Room—The Prince's Private Sitting Room—The Royal Visitors' Rooms—The Young Princesses' Rooms—Miss Knollys' Room—The Fire at Marlborough House, 1865—The Top Floor   89

CHAPTER VII.

How Marlborough House was Settled upon the Prince of Wales—The Household and Domestic Arrangements—The Princess's Household 105

CHAPTER VIII.

The Home Life of the Royal Family at Marlborough House—Sketches of some of the Household Officials 120

CHAPTER IX.

Notable Balls, Fêtes and Garden Parties at Marlborough House 141

CHAPTER X.

Some Notable Dinners at Marlborough House—Some Remarkable Pageants in Pall Mall 164

CHAPTER XI.

Personal Characteristics and Anecdotes of the Prince and Princess of Wales 180

CHAPTER XII.

Some Interesting Ghosts round and about Marlborough House—A Glance at Pall Mall, and a vision of its dim Past 205

CHAPTER XIII.

Facts Historical, Antiquarian, and Architectural concerning Marlborough House—Modern Alterations and Additions, and a suggested New Site for Marlborough House . . 224

CHAPTER XIV.

The Duke of Wellington's Funeral Car at Marlborough House—The Vernon Collection at Marlborough House . . 247

CHAPTER XV.

Past Occupants:—Prince Leopold 259

CHAPTER XVI.

Past Occupants:—Queen Adelaide 282

CHAPTER XVII.

Past Occupants:—The First Duke and Duchess of Marlborough—Conclusion 298

Illustrations.

	TO FACE PAGE
PORTRAIT OF H. R. H. THE PRINCESS OF WALES (*Frontispiece*)	
THE GARDEN FRONT OF MARLBOROUGH HOUSE	15
THE LARGE DRAWING ROOM	25
THE INDIAN ROOM	30
THE SALOON	48
THE LARGE DINING ROOM, SOUTHERN END	61
THE INDIAN ROOM, SOUTHERN END	110
THE LARGE DRAWING ROOM, EASTERN END	124
THE GARDEN PARTY AT MARLBOROUGH HOUSE JULY 5TH 1893	160
PORTRAIT OF H. R. H. THE PRINCE OF WALES	185
KIP'S BIRD'S EYE VIEW OF ST. JAMES PALACE AND MARLBOROUGH HOUSE	236
THE DUKE OF WELLINGTON'S FUNERAL CAR	251
H. R. H. PRINCE LEOPOLD	263
H. M. QUEEN ADELAIDE	284
THE FIRST DUKE OF MARLBOROUGH	303
THE FIRST DUCHESS OF MARLBOROUGH	304

NOTE.—The Photographs of Marlborough House have been taken by Mr. W. E. Gray, 92, Queen's Road, Bayswater, W.

MARLBOROUGH HOUSE

AND

ITS OCCUPANTS—PRESENT AND PAST.

CHAPTER I.

THE ENTRANCE AND APPROACH FROM PALL MALL —THE OFFICES—THE KITCHEN—THE STABLES— THE GROUNDS AND GARDEN.

As the heavy gates at the entrance to Marlborough House swing back with much clatter to allow some vehicle to emerge into Pall Mall, passers-by naturally pause, in their desire to obtain a peep at the Prince of Wales' London residence. But all they can see is a narrow carriage-drive, apparently terminating a little way down near a plain red-brick building; a pavement on the left, edged with dwarf shrubs; and a solitary gas-lamp projecting from an angle of the lofty building adjoining. If quick to observe, they may also perceive that the roadway is bounded on the right by the rear of a low building, commonly supposed to be in some way connected with the German Chapel, or Marlborough House, but which is really independent of either, being the dwelling-place of the park gatekeeper, and the St. James' Palace turncock.

At the side of one of the sentry-boxes flanking the entrance gates, where all the year round the Queen's Guards keep watch and ward, is a door kept ajar by a leathern strap, and so ponderous that considerable dexterity is required to push it back and enter with any sort of dignity.

Once within, a gate-porter, clad in Royal livery—urbane, but befittingly conscious of his responsible position—issues from a curious little lodge behind the door, and asks the nature of your business; or, in the event of his temporary absence, one of the numerous policemen always on duty, comes forward and attends to you. Should you desire to enter your name in the Visitors' Book, you are politely shown into a small room close by, where, in a substantial volume lying open upon the table, you add your signature to that of many other callers. But, if bound for the Comptroller of the Household's department, you are at once directed to the plain red-brick building before mentioned. If you are a perfect stranger, however, you are probably ushered into the office of Police-sergeant Payn, by whom you are closely questioned, and—all being satisfactory—are permitted to proceed, when you quickly discover that the carriage-drive does not end as it appeared to do, but turning sharp to the left, passes a stone and brick screen, and, by way of a tolerably spacious quadrangle, terminates at the porte-cochère of Marlborough House.

This quadrangle is formed by the main building, its various offices, and the unsightly backs of sundry clubs in Pall Mall. Terra-cotta boxes of antique design filled with dwarf rhododendrons, mask the base of the walls, and five shapely bay trees in large wooden boxes stand like sentinels in front of the porch.

The business offices are arranged upon an excellent system, and are pervaded by a refined, reposeful atmosphere, only disturbed by a certain element of expectation on the part of the visitor, who knows that at any moment he may come across the Prince or some of the higher officials.

Two courteous messengers, Gwillim and Bruce, have charge of the ante-room, where several commissionaires are also in attendance. There the letters, telegrams and parcels constantly arriving and being despatched are dealt with, and all enquiries are first made.

A corridor with tesselated floor, and walls adorned with some fine engravings after Landseer—dogs and deer that can hardly be looked at without instantly recalling the soft breeze of the moors and the scent of the heather—overlooks, from its five windows, the courtyard, and gives access on the left to a small room, where Mr. E. Bryant, the junior clerk, has under his care one of Remington's improved type-writing machines, fitted to what is called a "drop cabinet," an arrangement enabling it to be lowered quite out of sight when not in use, and converted into a writing-desk.

Adjoining is a comfortable apartment furnished with every appliance for writing, where are many ponderous ledgers for the entry of departmental transactions. Along the walls are oaken presses, wherein documents of all kinds are carefully filed, while framed illuminated addresses to the Prince of Wales from various Masonic Lodges look down upon the person of Mr. G. D. Long, who, under Lord Suffield, has clerical charge of all pertaining to the Royal stables.

Then comes a cosy waiting-room, and beyond it —across the ante-room—the sanctum of Mr. F. Morgan Bryant, private secretary to Sir Dighton Probyn, and chief clerk in these offices, upon whom devolves the great responsibility of "keeping the books." And here I may remark that the oldest established City firm can hardly surpass the exactitude and method with which every transaction is recorded at Marlborough House. So well is the indexing arranged, that at a few minutes' notice any letter or paper relating to years back can be produced, and this is what few counting-houses with the best of systems can boast of. Behind Mr. Bryant's writing-table hangs R. Caton Woodville's well-known Jubilee picture of the Prince and Princess of Wales. Everything is in absolute order, and should his Royal Highness make an unexpected descent into these regions, his clerical staff are ready for him.

There are clerks and clerks!—from the highly-favoured official at the Treasury or Foreign Office, who sits in a gorgeous apartment overlooking the park—the Clarence Bulbul of Thackeray's imagining —rejoicing in a salary of £2,000 a year and residing at South Kensington or Belgravia, down to the City drudge at £1 a week, living at Camberwell or Hoxton. But the clerks at Buckingham Palace, Windsor Castle and Marlborough House are a class by themselves. The utmost discretion and fidelity are required of them, and never do they betray their trust. Facts and circumstances of the highest moment pass to their knowledge, most inadvisable to disclose or even hint at; and, in spite of the " pumping " to which they are subjected by relatives and friends, they steadfastly resist the temptation to talk of the sayings and doings of Royalty. Their periods of service are always long as, once duly installed, they seldom or never leave save from failing health. Thus, Mr. Baskcomb, who lately retired, had been twenty-one years at Marlborough House, while Mr. Bryant took office in 1879.

Sir Francis Knollys' room is next to Mr. Bryant's, and just across the passage, by way of the corridor in the main building, is the apartment where the Comptroller of the Household reigns supreme. It is some 30 ft. in length, and not unlike the "parlour" of a first-class bank. From its windows can be easily noted the arrivals and departures at the main entrance, and its occupant is in instant communication not only with the office by means of a labyrinth of speaking-tubes, but with His Royal Highness, who has in his sitting-room a moveable frame about a foot long, containing six or eight electric buttons, with the names of such personages as the Comptroller, etc., etc., inscribed thereon, whom he can summon in an instant. This convenient arrangement can be carried from one part of the room to another and the Princess is provided with a similar apparatus. Marlborough House is now connected with the general system of Post Office telephones—a great convenience ; and the rooms of the Prince and Princess of Wales, Sir Dighton Probyn, Sir F. Knollys, and the House-Steward, are also in direct communication one with another by means of the switch-board in the messengers' room.

To the Comptroller's room the Prince often comes to discuss important matters with Sir Francis Knollys and Sir Dighton Probyn. It is *par excellence* the business-room of Marlborough House, and if its walls could speak, their revelations would be of deepest interest. Like the other offices, it is comfortably furnished, for use and not for show.

A large block of plain bricks and mortar facing the offices across the quadrangle, is devoted to the domestic department of Marlborough House, where first in size and importance comes the lofty kitchen —35 × 25 feet—fitted with every modern appliance and convenience. There is only one kitchen, conveniently situated, however; in this respect, unlike the *culina* at Buckingham Palace, whence the various dishes have to be conveyed a distance of nearly a quarter of a mile before they arrive at the Queen's private apartment on the north side, necessitating the use of charcoal-heated hot-closets, which are placed outside Her Majesty's dining-room.

At Marlborough House it is highly interesting to take a peep at the culinary department when some grand banquet is in course of preparation. Passing from the main building down a flight of steps and through swinging glass doors, the kitchen is reached, where at the farther end is a large fire-place with spits whose capacity for holding joints seems unlimited. On one side of the range is a huge oven, and on the other a splendid gas-grill with bars that, by means of a lever, can instantly be raised or lowered. Occupying the centre of the room is a spacious oaken table, whereon one sees sundry saddles of lamb being prepared for the ordeal by fire. In another apartment are arranged the most tempting-looking dainties—*chaudfroid* of ortolans, quails, *filets de truite*, etc., etc.; and in the confectionery room, some lovely composition in sugar, clear as crystal, and pervaded by an exquisite shade of green, reminding one of some beautiful production of Salviati.

At the rear of the kitchen, the domestic offices extend eastward, and afford space for several larders, china and confectionery rooms, steward's offices, etc., in short, for every convenience required in the running of a large establishment.

Separated by a narrow passage leading into the garden, are the stables. They were built by Messrs. G. Smith and Co. from Sir James Pennethorne's design, in the year 1859, at a cost of £25,000, under one of the provisions of the Act of Settlement of Marlborough House upon the Prince of Wales in 1850, whereby it was enacted that Her Majesty's Commissioners of Woods and Forests should—subject to the direction of the Treasury—provide suitable coach-houses and stables on ground belonging to Marlborough House, and for that purpose should apply out of the proceeds, arising from the sale of the old stables and coach-houses formerly belonging to Carlton Palace, a sum not exceeding £5,000.

Considerable correspondence passed between the Treasury, the Woods and Forests, and the Prince's representative, as to the exact disposal of these old materials. But eventually, as this proposed arrangement proved inconvenient, the sum of £2,100 was paid over to the Prince of Wales in lieu, and accepted in full satisfaction, of his claim under the Act.

These stables stood at the back of the present County Council offices in Spring Gardens, in what was called Carlton Ride, and were not pulled down until the year 1862, the southern boundary wall of the ride, and a porter's lodge on the south side of it, remaining until 1865.

On the site of the present mews stood a fine riding-school belonging to George, Duke of Marlborough, which, in a plan of 1784 attached to the surveyor's report on Marlborough House, appears as standing at right angles to the present kitchen wing, and extending to the north-east 231 feet. It was 43 feet wide—commodious as the one at Buckingham Palace.

Although on a scale necessarily inferior to Her Majesty's stables in London or Windsor, those of the Prince are fairly spacious, considering the area available. About forty or fifty horses are kept here during the season, with perhaps a dozen or more at Mason's Yard, Duke Street. Space being restricted, most of the animals have to be accommodated on a floor above the coach-houses, to which access is easily obtained by an inclined roadway. There are, of course, permanent quarters for the coachmen, grooms, etc., where all that can add to their health and comfort is considered.

In front of the building is a quadrangle covered over with glass, shaded in summer by striped awnings, where the various carriages are got ready for use, and undergo a thorough cleaning after their excursions in town. Coming and going as they are throughout the day, and often far into the night, neither men nor horses have much idle time on their hands.

The state-coach, used only on the grandest occasions, has a compartment to itself, and is almost exactly like the Queen's, except that the arms emblazoned thereon are those of the Prince of Wales and not of the Sovereign. It has nearly the same amount of gilding and rich fringe on the hammer-cloth, which said "bravery," if wetted by a shower of rain, entails no little labour upon the cleaners.

Amongst the most interesting carriages is the "Russian," a gift from the late Czar. Somewhat resembling a sociable, it is roomy and comfortable, and lined with dark blue morocco. It is rather a favourite vehicle at Marlborough House, and has sometimes been seen in the Park. Then there is the Prince's brougham—a skilful production of Hooper's—fac-simile of one of Paris manufacture formerly used by His Royal Highness and given by him to the Duke of York after the death of the Duke of Clarence. In its way the British-built brougham is quite a gem, lined with dark blue—as are most of the carriages, either in cloth, morocco, or silk rep— and contains a small clock, as well as every convenience that the heart of the most confirmed smoker could desire. It has a simple and effective means of communicating with the driver, superseding a somewhat complicated electrical apparatus which the Prince did not care about; and incandescent lamps are used for illuminating purposes, Not to be overlooked is the pretty Victoria once so frequently observed in the "drive," its two greys, Chelsea and Brief, together with a supplementary pair of the same colour, but older, being upstairs.

Several roomy fourgons stand in the courtyard ready for service; also two large private omnibuses, and a plain brougham devoid of arms or crest, in fact, so commonplace-looking as to attract no attention in the streets; wherefore, it is occasionally used by the Princess, when shopping, etc.

There are, in all, some forty-five stalls and twelve loose boxes in the building, the names of the horses—mostly bays—being inscribed on enamel tablets overhead. All the fittings are up to date, and in perfect order. The ventilation is very good, and, needless to say, everything about the place is spotlessly clean and scrupulously neat, including the inevitable plaited straw bordering.

Emperor, a fine black charger, ridden by the Prince at the trooping of the colours, is, perhaps, the handsomest horse in the stable.

Birkenham draws the Princess's brougham. Marky, a chesnut, used to be ridden by Her Royal Highness; but horse exercise, she has for some time past left to her daughters.

With great regularity, every animal in the stables is taken out for exercise early in the morning; and as they are used in turn for carriage-work, they seldom get frisky, so that an accident such as happened some years ago to the young Princesses —of which the following is the correct account— occasioning much alarm at the time, is not likely to occur again.

Accompanied by Mademoiselle Vauthier, their governess, the three Princesses were out driving on the afternoon of July 11th, 1881, when just as they had passed through the Arch, something startled Westminster, one of the fine bays attached to the landau, and he commenced to kick; in so doing he hit his companion, Servia, severely on the stifle, considerably upsetting his nerves, and without a moment's warning the pair began to gallop furiously down Constitution Hill. Luckily, George Osborne, the coachman, kept his presence of mind and concentrated all his energy towards the keeping clear of obstructions. In this he was only partially successfull, for as they tore along the Mall, a slight collision took place with Colonel Wilbraham's brougham. With great pluck the footman somehow contrived to get down from the box, and, jumping into a hansom cab, followed, in order to be in readiness when the end came. The young Princesses, though much alarmed, maintained an admirable composure, the absence of which might have complicated their serious position. Osborne would have continued along The Mall, and so on to the Horse Guards Parade, but there was something in the way, and he had to attempt the sharp turn through Marlborough Gate. This was safely accomplished, and as the horses evinced some signs of slackening speed, there seemed a chance of being piloted safely into Pall Mall, or—failing that—into St. James' Street, where the ascent must have stopped the runaways. But such was not to be. As the traffic in Pall Mall was too dense to admit of turning to the right, Osborne went up St. James' Street, where, in trying to avoid a cab, the projecting splinter-bar caught in the lamp-post almost opposite to the entrance of the Thatched House Club, and brought everything to a standstill without overturning the landau. "We were all well, though frightened,' says Mademoiselle Vauthier (now Mrs. Johnson), "were lifted out of the carriage, went into the club, Sir Dighton Probyn was sent for, and we all walked back to Marlborough House."

Some days after this occurrence, George Osborne was presented by the Prince and Princess of Wales with a valuable scarf-pin and other articles of jewellery, in recognition of his plucky conduct, and received their cordial thanks, accompanied by a hearty hand-shake from each member of the family. A short time ago, Osborne should in the ordinary course have retired from active service on a pension but the Princess would not hear of it, and he is now permanently installed as Her Royal Highness's own special coachman, a post of honour he well deserves, and bears with becoming modesty.

Generally smoking a cigar or cigarette, and attended by Lord Suffield or one of the equerries, the Prince of Wales sometimes strolls into the stables after breakfast to inspect any new purchase that may have been made, when he is sure to notice, though slow to remark upon, anything in the slightest degree out of order in his equine establishment.

In a room with black and white tiled floor is an interesting display of harness. That used on state occasions hangs up in glass cases, and is most elaborately adorned with gilt bearing the Prince's well-known crest. Similarly protected from damp, are other and plainer sets, all beautifully blacked and polished. A few remarkable-looking saddles— one of crimson velvet upon a frame of solid silver, another of blue velvet, and others specially made for the Princess—some whips with handles exquisitely chased in gold and silver, and sundry hunting-horns around which family associations still linger, complete the list of objects most worth looking at.

By the kindness of the Prince, accredited persons furnished with tickets of admission from the superintendent, are permitted to go over the stables, the best time being the afternoon, when the necessary cleaning-up is completed.

THE GARDEN FRONT OF MARLBOROUGH HOUSE.
Taken by special permission of H.R.H. the Prince of Wales.

Facing page 15.

In the first lease granted to the Duchess of Marlborough, it was expressly stipulated that the garden of the old Friary should not be built upon ; and to this is probably due the fact that, situated as it is almost in the heart of London, it is still so spacious and convenient. With good judgment, the Prince has elected to eschew elaborate flower-beds and other obstructions ; and but for a handsome bordering of geraniums, etc., which duly makes its appearance along the raised terrace-walks, and some groups of flowers filling up the stone vases here and there, together with the circular bed exactly in front of the "garden-entrance" to the house, nothing is to be seen but "flat lawn," delightfully shaded by elms, chesnuts, and evergreen oaks of quite respectable age, thus giving plenty of room for numerous guests to roam about. Here, "the dust and din and steam of town" is almost forgotten, and in this safe retreat wood-pigeons securely nest, starlings fly about intent on providing for their offspring, and the song of the thrush is often heard. The grounds are almost entirely protected from the vulgar gaze by trees on every side ; so, too, is the house, except on the south or Park side, whence in summer a peep of the upper rooms may be obtained. But towards the end of October, when the trees are bare of leaves, an observer looking northwards across the ornamental water in St. James' Park, can obtain a capital view of Marlborough House, backed by the ornate roof and flagstaff of the new Oxford and Cambridge Club.

On each side of the garden entrance stands a small field-piece bearing the following inscription :

"Brass-mounted gun rifled on the 'La Hitte' principle, taken September 13th, 1882, mounted on the right of the entrenchments Tel-el-Kebir presented to H. R. H. the Prince of Wales by Admiral Lord Alcester, G.C.B."

Here, also, as on the north side of the house, bay-trees in boxes give variety to the frontage.

When the Marlborough Gate road was designed and made through the Palace precincts from Pall Mall to St. James' Park, by the Board of Works in 1856, a strip of land remained over and above the requirements of the new thoroughfare ; so it was assigned to the garden of Marlborough House, adding to its western boundary a piece of land 272 feet long by 83 in width, and the old wall was then brought into its present line.

In this portion of the grounds is an artificial hillock approached by a slightly winding path, on whose summit, a little above the level of the wall, is a kind of platform provided with chairs and benches, appropriately called the Princess's Mound. Here, after the Trooping of the Colours at the Horse Guards on the Queen's birthday, the Princess of Wales and other members of the Royal family, listen to the massed bands of the Grenadiers, Scots Guards, and Coldstreams in Friary Court, before the *déjeuner* at Marlborough House. When "God save the Queen" is played, the Royal party rise from their seats, and little Prince Edward of York's cap is gravely removed from his head. 'Tis a pretty sight.

In a retired spot at the eastern corner of the garden, is a summer-house furnished with tea-tables and chairs—some of homely wicker work, and others cosily cushioned. At the back, against the wall, are a stuffed peacock and pea-hen, the former perched upon the topmost rung of a miniature ladder. Hereabouts, in past years, the youthful princes and princesses were in the habit of disporting themselves on tricycles along the broad gravel walks, and, no doubt, drank tea together in the arbour, unrestrained by the presence of tutors and governesses.

Sheltered by a neighbouring grove of trees, is a touching evidence of the Princess of Wales' well-known love of animals—four tiny tombstones side by side, whereon are the following inscriptions:

"TINY."
The favourite dog of Her Royal Highness the Princess of Wales. Died March 16, 1861. Aged 18 months.

"MUFF."
The favourite dog of Her Royal Highness the Princess of Wales. Died 14 May, 1865. Aged 2 years.

"JOSS."
The favourite Japanese dog of Her Royal Highness the Princess of Wales. Died 10 July, 1864. Aged 2 years.

"BONNY."

The favourite rabbit of Her Royal Highness the Princess of Wales. Died June 8th, 1881.

Perhaps most conspicuous is the grave of "Boxer," once the property of the late Colonel O. Montague, a friend of the Prince and Princess. Poor Boxer strayed into the preserves near Virginia Water, and was unfortunately shot dead by a keeper. The Prince and Princess were so distressed that they had the poor dog's remains sent up to London, and accorded the honour of sepulture in their own garden, where above the grave the sad tale is thus recorded:—

"POOR LITTLE BOXER."

"Here, scarce a league from St. Paul's historic dome,
Where the broad elm trees shade a royal home,
Lies a true friend to man, a dog; what man
Could more win love or more enhance his fame?
Through the parched desert and the midnight fray
When his fond master led the glorious way,
He bravely followed, and with mute caress
Cheered both his labours and his idleness.
A miscreant slew him—None was near to save,
Let kindly tears bedew his honoured grave."

Nor is this pathetic incident without precedent. In the year 1714, a Mr. Robert Molesworth, afterwards created a Viscount, caused the body of a favourite greyhound to be sent from London to Edlington Wood, near Doncaster, and there buried beneath an altar-shaped monument, with a suitable inscription ; the dog having been the means of saving his life by pulling at his coat and preventing him from entering an outhouse just at the moment when a robber, lying there concealed, shot dead a servant advancing thither.

And is there not at Victoria Gate a well-kept dogs' cemetery with more than forty graves, marble adorned and bright with flowers ? Who can say nay to the pretty custom of paying a kindly tribute to our canine friends, when Royalty itself has led the fashion long ago ? A nation, said to possess fifty-five dogs to every thousand inhabitants, and willing to pay, on occasion, so much as £1,000 for some famous pedigree St. Bernard or collie, can surely enter into the pathos of the scene witnessed at the funeral of Major-General Stotherd—who, it may be remembered, died very suddenly at Camberley last year—around whose coffin stood his three dogs, guarding, with characteristic fidelity, the remains ot their beloved master.

There are no conservatories or hot-houses at Marlborough House ; the glass structure leading from the drawing-room into the garden being more in the nature of an ornamental portico. It is used as a lounge and smoking-room, and looks very pretty with its floor of blue and yellow tiles, its couches covered with turkey-red twill, convenient tables, easy chairs, blue and white vases, and white marble fountain filled with ferns and lycopodium—

whereon a tinkling moistening spring ever falls.
The door opening into the room within, is draped
with turkey-red and white curtains, and on each
side is an Indian figure—black and bare-headed—
playing upon a pipe. This conservatory, as it is
called, is a favourite place for the Royal family
to be photographed in; though recently it has
been their practice to be taken in one or other of
their private rooms. Some of its contents were
formerly in a Turkish mandar'ah or reception-room
which the Prince had on the first floor, where the
Royal visitors' bed-room now is. It contained
souvenirs of H. R. H.'s Eastern travels—amber
mouth-pieces, embroidered tobacco bags, chain-
armour, helmets, daggers, swords, etc., and a frag-
ment of Egyptian hieroglyphics; in the centre was
a fountain, and there were the usual luxurious
couches inseperable from divans. The Princess is
an adept in photography, pursuing the popular art
chiefly at Sandringham, and preferably in the open
air. Her Royal Highness is quite capable of taking
excellent portraits, and if every "Royalty" were
like her in this respect, they could, by taking one
another's likenesses, probably solve the much vexed
question discussed in the *Times* last November,
between editors and professional photographers,
when, as usual, the law upon the subject turned out
to be anything but clear; yet the newspaper con-
troversy elicited at least one fact, viz., that if the
photographer receive payment for his work, he has

no right to apply for the copyright without a written permission from his employer, who is obviously the real proprietor. In the case of Royal personages, the exacting of fees is particularly objectionable, as it may be assumed that they pay for their photographs, and do not, as a rule, give the required documentary "permit." It must be admitted that Royalties stand on a rather different footing from the rest of mankind as regards the photographs of themselves exposed for sale; and it is surely opposed to the good of the realm that any persons should practically obtain a monopoly of selling the Sovereign's likeness, or that of the different members of her family. A remedy for this unsatisfactory state of things might be an amendment of the Copyright Acts as applied to photography, removing Royalties altogether from their provisions, and enacting that, in their case, copyright privileges should not under any circumstances be granted.

However, to return to the garden. At Marlborough House no attempt is made to rear plants or flowers, as at Sandringham, where, in the splendidly-kept houses, bananas and pine-apples ripen, and vines and peach-trees yield large returns; while in the forcing-houses are always to be seen a fine array of crotons, poinsettias and orchids, to say nothing — when in season—of masses of lily-of-the valley, the " daphne indica," of which the Princess is so fond, and the 200 feet of frames wherein violets are produced in immense quantities.

Everything of this kind — the thousands of bedding-out plants required for the terrace borders, the profuse indoor floral and plant decorations, down to the choice button-holes placed every day ready for the use of the Prince, and the chief officials—has been provided since the year 1877 by Wills and Segar, with whom there is a contract at so much per annum, with an extra allowance for balls, etc.

Since the Prince of Wales first came into possession, the garden has been the scene of many a brilliant assemblage—the most important of which I shall describe hereafter—though none perhaps have been more interesting and picturesque than the meeting together of the members of the " Royal National Pension Fund for Nurses," in which admirable institution the Princess takes the greatest interest. Its object is to encourage all nurses in the British Empire to save each year, if possible, from one-eighth to one-sixth of their earnings, thus providing " at the lowest possible cost to themselves, an allowance during incapacity for work caused by sickness or accident, and a certain income for their declining years."

Somewhat late on a certain fine afternoon last July (1895), Piccadilly and St. James' Street presented an unusually gay appearance as groups of these hospital nurses, attired in varied and becoming uniform, with flowers in their hands, made their way back from Marlborough House, whither many of them had not long before been conveyed in private omnibuses, and where on their arrival they had been drawn up in military companies, four abreast, in front of the conservatory, every nurse wearing the armlet designed by the Princess—a band of red with a white border (the Danish national colours) and a red lozenge in the centre containing Her Royal Highness's coronet and monogram embroidered in white. Then the Princess of Wales handed to each a certificate bearing upon its face a figure of an angel of sympathy and a fac-simile of her own signature. When the proceedings, that is the speeches, were over, the company had tea in a large tent, Their Royal Highnesses going about amongst them, exchanging pleasant observations, etc. After tea, the finishing touch was given to the happiness of the nurses, by the Princess herself. Whispering a few words to the Prince and to Sir Dighton Probyn, Her Royal Highness advanced to one of the many tables covered with flowers, and taking therefrom a spray of lovely roses, smilingly gave it to one of the nurses, at the same time intimating that the others might help themselves to these beautiful souvenirs. No further encouragement was needed—in a few moments all the floral decorations disappeared, to be afterwards commented on by the large crowd waiting outside for the nurses' departure.

Here it may be remarked that the Prince has

always been uniformly considerate in all matters relating to medical etiquette, obeying with the utmost diligence the wishes of his appointed physicians, of whose services, unfortunately, he and his family have often stood in need. His Royal Highness has never departed from the orthodox systems, but with his well-known liberality of view, has numbered amongst his most intimate friends the late Dr. Quin—the celebrated homœopath—whom he used frequently to visit at Victoria Mansions, and whose witty sayings he greatly appreciated.

The above kind of hospitable entertainment is one in which the Princess is pre-eminent; and, as the chairman of the weekly board of the Royal Free Hospital said, when the Prince and Princess went there last year to open the new buildings :

" Those who managed the Royal Free Hospital had for forty years been building a temple, not so magnificent as the temple of Diana, but designed for the glory of God, and the healing of the sick, and they were glad to place the name of Alexandra in the final section of that great institution in remembrance of a royal, gentle, and gracious Princess, whose nobility of character, kindness of heart, and tender sympathy for the sick and suffering poor, was known not only to them, but to the whole world."

CHAPTER II.

THE LARGE DRAWING ROOM—THE INDIAN ROOM—THE STUDIO OR PAINTING ROOM—THE TAPESTRY ROOM—THE STAIRCASES—THE ENTRANCE HALL—THE EQUERRIES' ROOM—THE ROOM OF THE LADIES-IN-WAITING.

THE conservatory leads direct from the garden into the great drawing-room—a noble salon, 65 × 25 feet—formerly three distinct rooms, the handsome groups of pillars against the wall marking the original divisions. Coming suddenly out of the bright sunshine, it is somewhat difficult to distinguish things clearly; but when Brown, the obliging " tapissier," raises the gracefully-festooned pale silk blinds of the four windows overlooking the garden, one observes that the scheme of decoration is white and gold, that the ceiling is picked out with colours relieved with gold, and that the ivy-leaf design on the triple pillars is very handsome.

Covering the polished oak floor, is a splendid " Axminster," supplemented by Persian rugs; the walls are panelled in crimson silk, projecting wherefrom are ormolu girandoles fitted for the electric light. Over the fireplace at each end of the room is a beautiful white mantelpiece surmounted by a mirror, and near that on the left, are two grand pianos side by side, with covers of magnificently embroidered elephants' trapping. Externally plain, these instruments in the hands of a skilful player, send forth sounds as enchanting as ever greeted the ear of Mr. Vanderbilt, who is said to have recently paid £3,000 for a piano bought for his new Fifth Avenue House, the stool itself costing another £40; or of Mr. Macquand, the banker, of New York, who has a piano that cost £5,000, yet only in keeping with the scale upon which his mansion is furnished; for, if report be true £30,000 has been expended on one of his rooms alone, the smaller chairs being £400, and the easy-chairs £600 a-piece.

These noble pianos of the Princess are Broadwoods, and technically described as "three hundred guinea concert grands." They were selected for Her Royal Highness by the late Sir Charles Hallé, and deservedly occupy the place of honour in this establishment, being representative of what exclusively British art can accomplish, and the perfection to which the mechanism of pianos has been brought since the days, one hundred and sixty-four years ago, when Burkhardt Tschudi set up the sign of "Ye Plume of Feathers," in Great Pulteney Street, a privilege obtained from Frederick, Prince of Wales, no doubt through the influence of Handel, who, like Haydn and Mozart, played upon harpsichords of his make. King George III. gave Tschudi's successor, John Broadwood, a special appointment, so that the old firm may well pride themselves upon having, for five successive reigns, had dealings with the English Court.

The Princess's Erard harp—no longer in use—at one time stood behind these pianos, and some years ago, when Her Royal Highness gave afternoon teas here, the most delightful little impromptu concerts were held, whereat the voices of Jenny Lind, Patti, and other prima donnas were not infrequently heard.

Her Royal Highness often invites budding pianistes and singers to perform before her, and receives them in this room, though on special occasions they are taken up to her boudoir.

From a small easel at the back, a life-like presentment of the Dowager Empress of Russia appears to keep watch and ward over the two pianos, and against the wall is a large carved Indian screen containing charming photographs of the Royal children. In fact, there are family portraits everywhere, the most noticeable being in a handsome four-fold Chinese ebony screen, whose panels are adorned with costly Japanese silk of diminutive pattern and neutral tint. On a stand close by, is a wedding present from far-off Australia—a service of pure gold; and near one of the groups of pillars is an East Indian set of ornaments of the same precious metal. A Chinese folding-screen in a carved frame, displays some fine embroidery and arranged at intervals against the wall on velvet-covered pedestals, are four pieces of statuary, half-life-size. Near to the one representing a veiled child, is a white and gold portfolio, belonging to the Princess, bearing her initial, " A."

All the chief pieces of furniture are white and gold, upholstered in crimson silk, the fine ottoman in the middle of the room being of crimson silk too. Wherever this stately fabric is used, Spitalfields looms have been the medium of production. Most of the smaller articles vary in colouring, and some of the chairs and couches are covered with embroideries brought by the Prince from India.

Quite the most beautiful objects in the room are two Louis XVI. cabinets mounted in ormolu, with ivory plaques in centre panels and inlaid with various woods. They cost £300 a-piece, and a fine Dresden vase stands upon each. The occasional tables and writing-tables, matching this exquisite pair of cabinets, are also very handsome.

A finishing touch is given to the beauty of this splendid room by the introduction, wherever possible, of lofty palms, Kentias, and Latanias, whose graceful fronds droop caressingly over the beautiful objects they partially veil.

On entering the famous Indian room from the western door of the drawing-room, and glancing round at the cases full of lethal weapons, we recall, as follows, the words of a popular novelist. " In India there is always the flicker of the sword, whether it be the weapon of steel in man's hands, or the sword of pestilence, matters not, there it is ;

but here in England we forget it, and hide it behind bricks and mortar and much speaking."

By no means hidden away, however, is this, perhaps the finest collection of Indian arms and rare objects of art ever brought together.

It will be remembered that during the visit of the Prince of Wales to India in 1874, he was presented by the native princes and chiefs with a vast number of rich gifts, all of which were carefully packed, safely received on board the *Serapis*, and brought to Portsmouth. With his usual thoughtfulness and foresight, the Prince, before leaving India, cabled home instructions for the transfer of these valuable presents to the Indian Museum at South Kensington, where the public might have an opportunity of inspecting them. From 1876 to 1881 they were shown at various centres, including Paris in 1878, and now have found a resting-place at Marlborough House and Sandringham.

On account of its representative character the importance of this collection is great, independently of its intrinsic value, which may be estimated at any sum ranging from a quarter to half a million sterling. This can be the more easily realised when the cases are lighted up at night, and rubies, emeralds, diamonds and sapphires on sword, dagger-handles, belts and scabbards, flash back the brilliant rays of electricity.

The room where these treasures are gathered together was formerly the library, and was furnished in walnut and gold with coverings of green and gold silk ; but when most of the books contained in the cases were removed to Sandringham the furniture was remodelled to suit its present use.

Receiving all the sunlight obtainable through its five windows, looking south and west, and situated, as it is, mid-way between the state drawing-room and the painting and tapestry rooms, this apartment is a great favourite with the Princess of Wales. Here it is that dinners are given, when the party consists of more than four or five guests, yet is not sufficiently large to necessitate the use the principal dining-room.

The walls are covered with maroon figured velvet of Eastern design, the windows being curtained with the same. On the floor are Indian carpets and rugs. Chairs of carved English oak, upholstered in cloth of gold, brought by the Prince from India, couches in the same material, but somewhat lighter in tone—exquisite colours on a white ground—with cushions, as a rule partly concealed by gorgeous elephants' housings of green and gold velvet, are grouped about, and a large divan in the centre covered with Indian embroidery, produces a distinctly Oriental effect.

In the windows facing west, are glass-topped tables, full as they can hold of medals, keys, and trowels, chased and engraved. Should the Prince ever have to earn his living as a mason, there are trowels enough to serve not only for his lifetime, but for that

of several generations to follow. All these objects are, of course, mementoes of the laying of foundation-stones and the opening of public buildings.

A particularly handsome vase, the gift of the Czar Alexander II. of Russia, stands near these trowels, on a pink marble pedestal; and, displayed in a prominent position, is a magnificent shield, said to have cost £20,000.

In a corner of the room, covered by an elephant's trapping, is a horizontal grand piano in a rosewood case, by Brinsmead, presented to the Princess of Wales by the Grand Lodge of Freemasons in 1888. Upon it repose many cylinders of solid silver, containing addresses received by the Prince during his Indian tour.

How many such documents, elaborately engrossed and illuminated, recording the undying loyalty and devotion of corporations, municipalities and public bodies all over the kingdom, must not His Royal Highness have received in the course of his life!—all neatly packed in cases or embroidered rolls; source of boundless admiration to many a provincial town or city, as the mayor, aldermen and town clerk affix their signatures, fondly imagining, maybe, that when the Prince hands the precious burden to one of his suite it will—along with others—find its way to some drawing-room table at Marlborough House, and there remain. These documents are certainly well looked after, and duly appreciated, and I know the exact spot honoured by their presence, but I must elect to maintain a sphynx-like silence on the subject.

Obviously the feature of the Indian room is the collection itself. This is contained chiefly in carved pollard-oak cases arranged along the walls of the apartment, and which are very fine, the oak being relieved with gold and the lower panels inlaid with boxwood. Most effectively are the contents illumined by means of electric light, which, upon pressing an outside button—a method suggested, I believe, by the Prince himself—reflects from invisible points upon the different objects.

"The sword," says the late Sir Richard F. Burton, "is not only the oldest, the most universal, and the most varied of weapons, but it is the only one which has lived through all time."

Roman legionaries we know found steel weapons of the finest temper in the Spanish Peninsula, and we are told that the weapons of the Celtiberians were so keen that no helmet or shield existed that could not be cut through by them. We are not surprised, therefore, to learn that the blade of many a celebrated Indian sword came from the West, and did not originate in the glowing land where they set it in precious metals encrusted with gems. Nor is it to be wondered that the weapons of European manufacture taken from England by the Prince for presentation in India, were much appreciated by the native rulers and tributaries. Terrific is the force that can be put into a skilfully directed blow from one of these samples of the "white arm," well exemplified in a story told me by Henderson, the well-known professor of swordsmanship, who was present at the battle of Chillianwallah, in the year 1849. It was to the effect that towards the termination of the fight, as our troops were reluctantly retiring, a Sikh by his defiant attitude towards an Irish soldier, seemed to challenge him to leave the ranks and engage in single combat. Nothing loth, the Celtic hero rushed upon him and thrust his bayonet right through his foe; but, though mortally wounded, the Sikh instantaneously, with his razor-edged tulwar, cleft his opponent's head in two, both combatants falling dead at the same instant.

This Indian collection has been most carefully classified and catalogued, but no mere recital of its items would convey an adequate idea of its beauty and comprehensiveness. There stands prominently out, however, in one's recollection of it, a certain gold tray from Mysore, in Southern India, a splendid piece of workmanship, and a wonderful example of modern decorative art. There are enamels worth their weight, not in *gold*— for they are composed of that metal—but in Bank of England notes. They come from Jeypore in Rajputana, and although the cost of the presents made to His Royal Highness by each native prince was supposed to be strictly limited to £2,000, in this case the restriction was skilfully evaded by pricing them at that nominal sum—though the real value was probably not much less than £25,000.

But perhaps the most exquisite object in the Jeypore collection is a golden inkstand, shaped like an Eastern gondola, and literally glowing with reds, greens and blues.

One of the dishes is the largest of its kind ever produced, and took four years to make. Then there is an enamelled atardan, or scent-holder ; also a cup, saucer, and box, all alike blazing with imperishable hues.

Some of the brass figures in the collection are very quaint. One group represents soldiers on horseback, swaggering in most comical attitudes. These are from Peddapuram, near Vizagapatan.

Amongst the arms in the cases is a glorious sword with blade mounted throughout in half-relief with hunting scenes. Another has its scabbard literally covered with floral designs in hard gold. An ivory gun-stock is carved *à merveille*, with groups of wild animals ; and four gun-barrels — perfect examples of damascening — sorely tempt us to break the Tenth Commandment.

A full account of this wonderful exhibition—for such it in truth is—appeared in the *Times* of June 22nd, 1876 ; but to be thoroughly appreciated it must be seen and contemplated for hours together.

From weapons of destruction to the peaceful productions of industry is a pleasant transition. Therefore, on our way to the tapestry room—

approached by a short corridor from the Indian room—we take a peep at the Princess's painting room, quite a small apartment, that was originally a passage leading into the garden. Its floor is covered with matting, the windows are curtainless, a couple of easels and a chair or two complete the furnishing, and there would be nothing of interest in its appearance were it not for the presence of a few sketches and paintings by our beloved Princess. Here Her Royal Highness sometimes sees great authorities on art, whose criticism and advice she always welcomes. The late Lord Leighton, whom she not only esteemed and admired, but regarded as a "much valued friend," was a frequent visitor. Twelve o'clock is the usual hour for visits of this kind, but neither here nor in the adjoining tapestry room—known also as the " Princess's sitting-room " —does Her Royal Highness pass much time, her favourite apartments being upstairs.

Of the antiquity of the beautiful art illustrated so charmingly on the walls of the tapestry room there can be little doubt. When the Tabernacle was being made in the wilderness, ten curtains of fine twined linen, blue, purple and scarlet —the work of a cunning broiderer— were commanded to be prepared; while tapestry hangings, whose iron rings and poles may still be seen at Pompeii and Herculaneum, covered the Roman walls between the pillars in the atrium.

As regards our own country, alas! a taste for this,

the highest form of art-needlework, seems to defy revival. Only the other day, the "plant" of the Royal Windsor works, whose productions often rivalled Gobelin and Beauvais fabrics, was dispersed abroad—the looms going to Aubusson. Thus the second attempt to resuscitate an almost extinct industry failed for want of proper support, two hundred years having elapsed since the first effort was made at Mortlake to re-introduce the manufacture into England. Why such a noble adornment for the walls of large mansions is not universally adopted is a mystery! unless it be that the advanced woman of the day, well versed in the "fads" of modern hygiene, has decried it as insanitary, harbouring dust and microbes.

A very handsome Chinese silk carpet covers the floor of this room, in the middle of which is an ebony table of rare workmanship, mounted in ormolu. The chairs are variously upholstered. Dwarf book-cases of mahogany and gold, surmounted by lovely vases and bronzes, contain the Mitchell bequest to Her Royal Highness—a choice collection of books valued at £10,000. Although the room is crowded with pretty furniture, bric-à-brac, etc., etc., its crowning beauty, after all, is the exquisite old silk tapestry on the walls, representing Scriptural subjects—a gift to the Princess from her Majesty, the Queen. One can picture the *religeuses* sitting day by day for many a year patiently working at their labour of love in some old convent with its high-walled garden, where lilies, tall hollyhocks, and useful herbs contended for possession of the well-kept borders, and spicy odours from clove carnations filled the wan air.

A "jib" door, as it is technically called—hard to find when in a hurry—leads from the tapestry room into the corridor, at the point just opposite the Comptroller's official retreat. This part of the house is always more or less in the gloom, architectural difficulties preventing any direct light from reaching it, and, moreover, the corridor, though but sixty feet in length, is inconveniently narrow and cramped for so large a mansion. Two graceful female figures in niches—the "Bathers"—by Mr. John Gibson, R.A. are its sole adornment.

At the foot of the west, or the Prince of Wales', staircase—situated between the tapestry room and the saloon—is a great malachite vase, eight feet in height, mounted on ormolu.

The corresponding flight of stairs on the farther side is called the Royal visitors' staircase; and adjoining is the Princess' lift; also another, used for luggage.

Both these staircases, by no means spacious—are of black marble, covered with rich Axminster carpet, the bannisters being of wrought iron, relieved with gold.

On the walls of the west staircase are portraits of the great Duke of Marlborough, his brother, Lord Churchill, and Prince Eugene of Savoy, also representations of the battle of Ramilies, May 23rd, 1706, when Marshal Villeroi was completely defeated. In leaping a wide ditch, Marlborough's horse fell, and he was violently thrown to the ground. His aide-de-camp, Captain Molesworth, instantly offered him another, whose stirrup Colonel Bingfield, the Duke's equerry, held. As the great Commander mounted, the Colonel fell back dead, a cannon-ball having taken his head clean off—and this dreadful scene is here represented.

All these paintings were restored in 1889 by Mr. John Richards, R.A.

On the Royal visitors' staircase is depicted the battle of Malplaquet, one of the most stubbornly-fought of Marlborough's battles, which ended in the retreat of the French, who were in perfect order, and had neither lost colours nor prisoners. Prince Eugene was wounded in this engagement, fought September 11th, 1709, as was also his opponent, Marshal Villars, so severely as to necessitate his leaving the field.

Midway in the corridor, facing one another, are two not particularly wide doorways, one leading to the saloon, the other to the entrance hall. The latter is not remarkable in any way; it is perfectly plain, and the walls are bare, save for one or two paintings. But the absence of antlers or other adornment is redeemed by the presence of Thorwalsden's splendid marble group—"Adam and Eve"—a gift from the King of Denmark.

Marlborough House.

On either side of the outer hall, and commanding a good view of the quadrangle, thus enabling their occupants to note all who come and go, are the rooms set apart for the ladies-in-waiting, and the equerries. In the latter's apartment—quite plainly furnished—are some interesting pictures, and two objects which vividly recall the intense excitement in England fourteen years ago, when the news of the naval operations in Egypt came to hand. On revolving stands, are two 10-inch spherical shells, fitted with silver plates recording the fact that they were fired from the forts of Alexandria during the memorable bombardment of July 11th, 1882, and presented by the Admiral as a souvenir to the Princess of Wales. The incident connected with them was as follows :

In July, 1882, the bombardment of Alexandria having been forced upon Admiral Sir Beauchamp Seymour by the obduracy of Arabi Pasha, at daylight on the 11th, the fleet under his command was under weigh, and at 7 a.m. the signal was given to open fire on the forts ; and shortly afterwards, a second gun proclaimed a general action. H. M. S. *Alexandra* led the van of the outer attacking force, and at 9 a.m., one of the 10-inch spherical shells, now at Marlborough House, came through the ship's side, penetrated the torpedo lieutenant's cabin, and striking against the massive iron combings of the engine-room hatchway, rebounded, after knocking a few rifles out of the arm-rack, and, rolling a little further on, stopped—hissing and spluttering—close to the hatchway, up which Chief-Gunner Israel Hardy was at that instant coming. What followed must be told in the words of this gallant seaman :

"A large tub of water, used for local and immediate extinction of fire in action, being close to me, and seeing that the fuse was still burning, I seized it instantly and placed it in the tub, this having the effect of drowning the fuse. The second 10-inch shell came crashing through the Staff-Commander's cabin, and, hitting the inside of the hatchway, fell into the Admiral's cabin and rolled along the passage way, the powder of the bursting charge running out of the fuse hole, there being no fuse in this one. My opinion is, that the fuse of this shell could not have been set in sufficiently firm, and so must have been knocked out in passing through the ship's side. This shell was also placed in the water with the other, and the powder on the deck destroyed by water."

Chief-Gunner Hardy was presented with the Victoria Cross at Malta, on November 14th of the same year, which signal mark of distinction Her Majesty the Queen was graciously pleased to confer upon him as an evidence of her sense of the daring displayed by him on that occasion.

These identical projectiles were sent to England, and after being polished and set in their stands at the Royal Arsenal, Woolwich, were appropriately presented by the Admiral to the Royal lady, who, some years before, at Chatham, had bestowed upon the noble ironclad her own name.

On one side of the fireplace is a clever and spirited water-colour by Melton Prior. Near it is an aquarelle by H. Chevalier, of a grand polonaise being danced at a ball in the Winter Palace at St. Petersburg on the occasion of the Duke of Edinburgh's marriage. Above the mantelpiece hangs an oil painting by A. de Prades, 1882, of Fairplay (by Paganini out of Astræa) four-year-old, winner of the Household Brigade Cup and of Kempton Royal Steeplechase, 1882. To lovers of the turf, especially those who have a taste for reminiscences and do not disdain to study the past as the true guide to the future, another picture here —that of Baronet painted by J. N. Sartorius—will be invested with particular interest. Baronet (by Vertumnus) was the property of the Prince Regent, and was ridden by the celebrated Sam Chifney, senior, in the year 1791. Beneath the painting it is recorded that he won the Oatlands at Ascot, besides King's Plates at Winchester, Lewes, Canterbury and Newmarket.

Those were the days when a King's Plate of £100 was thought well worth running for, and when the noble sport was conducted under difficulties that few of the present generation can credit or understand.

The Chifney rush, the slack rein, and the peculiar style of finish, was diligently transmitted to his son, to whom he began to give lessons at a very tender age, when he weighed but three stone, and who afterwards became as famous as his father. Chifney, senior, it was who rode the Prince Regent's Escape, in those two races at Newmarket in 1792, which brought about His Royal Highness' retirement from the " Heath." He had been jockey to the Prince from 1784 to 1804, and he died at the age of fifty-two within the rules of the Fleet Prison.

Looking at Baronet's portrait, one's thoughts naturally turn to the sporting career of the Prince of Wales. His good fortune, luck—call it what you will —in yachting, has passed into a proverb; though the *Britannia's* great success has, doubtless, arisen from the fact that, unlike many other large cutters, she is a good all-round boat in any weather, and that since she commenced her racing career, she has been commanded by one of the cleverest skippers anywhere to be found, with a crew, as near perfection as possible.

On the Turf, however, His Royal Highness has had to wait a considerable time before the fickle goddess would condescend to smile upon him; unlike his great-uncle, who at the outset won the Derby in 1788, and in the course of four years, secured the Judges' verdict in his favour in one hundred and eighty-four races. But perseverance and good judgment have met with their reward, and for all his disappointment, the Prince must have been amply consoled last year at Manchester, when the son of St. Simon and Perdita II. carried Calder to victory two lengths from Green Lawn, and a tremendous roar of cheering, repeated again and again, proclaimed the fact that the cup would go to Marlborough House; and at Ascot, when, amidst a brilliant assemblage, Persimmon and Florizel II. won in succession the "County Stakes" and the "Gold Vase," followed up three days later —an Italian sky looking down upon one of the biggest crowds ever seen at the Royal meeting—by the winner of the latter becoming victor in the "St. James' Palace Stakes."

Beyond the entrance-hall is the room used by the Ladies-in-waiting—as regards size, a duplicate of that of the Equerries, but more daintily furnished, with some pretty water-colours brightening the walls. Here the Lady-in-waiting may receive her friends, or grant an interview to persons calling on special business, before they are ushered into the presence of the Princess.

Next is a roomy apartment, still called the "school-room," where the Royal children used to have their lessons, now used as a receptacle for discarded furniture and general odds and ends, also for the unpacking of presents previous to their inspection by the Prince and Princess.

CHAPTER III.

THE ROYAL HOUSEHOLD DINING-ROOM—THE BASEMENT — THE PLATE-ROOM — THE SALOON — THE PRINCE AND PRINCESS'S WARRANT-HOLDERS.

WE are now at the east side of the house—having as it were travelled round it from the south and west —and enter the Royal household dining-room, an exceedingly comfortable "salle à manger," twenty-five feet square. When large parties are given in the adjoining state apartment, this is utilized as a serving-room, on which occasions the equerries and ladies and gentlemen of the household have to dine a little earlier than their usual hour, seven o'clock, so that the room may be got ready. Sir Dighton Probyn, Sir Francis Knollys, the Equerries, Mr. Holzman, the Lady-in-waiting, Miss Knollys, and the ladies and gentlemen in attendance on any Royal visitors in the house have their meals in this room. Their breakfast-hour is from 9.30 to 10 a.m. —Mr. Holzman, the librarian, generally being the first to put in an appearance—and luncheon from 2 to 2.30 p.m. The furniture is of handsome mahogany, plain in design. Occupying a prominent position, and bearing the inscription " Presented to my friend, the Prince of Wales," is a fine oil-painting

—nearly life-size—of King Oscar II. of Sweden, in unimpeachable black silk stockings, and wearing the Order of the Garter.

Few people, looking superficially at the exterior of Marlborough House, would imagine it to possess such spacious basements as it does. In fact, they are unusually commodious. Beneath the tapestry-room and the painting-room is a large, comfortable servants' hall; and under the saloon, drawing-room and entrance hall are excellent wine-cellars, superintended by the wine-butler, with his under-butler, cellarmen and bottlers. There are also a furnace-room, a housekeeper's store-closet, florist's and china-rooms—the two latter being under the school-room. Beer, the national beverage, "tho' stale, not ripe, tho' thin, yet ever clear," has a special cellar beneath Sir Dighton Probyn's office, and on the garden side, under the Indian-room, the footmen are accommodated. Beyond are the linen-room, store-room and still-room, and underneath the Royal household dining-room and a portion of the state dining-room, are several good pantries for silver-cleaning, washing-up, etc.

Like other great mansions, Marlborough House possesses a plate-room. It is absolutely fire-proof, illuminated by electricity, and guarded with unceasing vigilance. The floor is tiled, and there is a good-sized fire-place. Round the walls, reaching from floor to ceiling, are mahogany cases about a yard deep, glass-panelled, and fitted with patent locks. In the centre is a magnificent case matching the others, of the thickest plate-glass, around which one can walk, as at the Tower while inspecting the Crown Jewels. It was constructed in the Silver-Wedding year to receive the large number of presents lavished upon the Prince and Princess. Being strictly utilitarian, it is lined with plain blue cloth, and not with the traditional velvet of jewellers and silversmiths, and now contains some of the valuable gifts that year after year Their Royal Highnesses have acccepted, besides the plate in ordinary use, and the special dinner-services, one of which is probably the finest in existence. Here may be seen presentation-services (breakfast, dinner and tea), elaborate centre-pieces, richly chased salvers, caskets, flagons, tankards, bowls, vases, racing-cups and yachting prizes won by the *Britannia* at Cowes and elsewhere — silver trowels, candelabra, keys inlaid in silver and gilt, candlesticks, beautiful models of buildings and animals, dainty specimens of Indian art-work in the white metal, statuettes, gold and silver cups, old silver spoons, silver-gilt salt-cellars, tea and coffee services, Christening gifts, birthday gifts, wedding presents and Christmas and Easter presents.

So extensive is the collection that it necessitates the constant employment of three or four men to clean and keep it in order. Certainly it merits a prolonged description, but there is so much to be seen elsewhere that one cannot linger here however fascinating the glittering sight.

In the season, when the Prince and Princess are in residence, there are about eighty-five servants employed at Marlborough House, besides some forty more connected with the stables. This large staff is splendidly cared for and admirably managed. All are eligible for a pension after ten years' service, but they usually remain much longer, those who have been in the Prince's employment twelve years mentioning the fact almost apologetically. Thus, although the rate of wages paid is not much above the average, their position is in many respects an enviable one.

In the steward's room, the housekeeper—who sits at the foot of the table, the steward, of course, being at the head—pages, valets, wine-butler, dressers, and all the upper servants, together with those attendant upon Royal visitors, breakfast together at 8 o'clock, dine at 1.30, and have tea at 5 o'clock. Supper is nominally at 9 p.m., and is an excellent one, many of the dishes coming direct from the Royal dinner-table. Those who have meals in this room are waited upon by men in black livery.

Supper in the servants' hall, where the serjeant-footman presides, is at the same hour, tea is at 5 o'clock, dinner at 1 o'clock, and breakfast at 8 o'clock. All those servants not included in the "upper crust" division, are accommodated here, and most plentifully and comfortably provided for.

In the days when Marlborough House was designed by Sir Christopher Wren, it was necessary that an architect should take into account the social customs of the time. This is why so many houses of the period, say, from the year 1700 to the end of the eighteenth century, were built with very spacious halls opening out into the streets. At Devonshire House, for instance, one of its largest apartments was originally the vestibule; and old Montague House possessed a noble marble-floored and pillared hall.

Thus, for the great Duchess, Sir Christopher Wren had to provide a waiting-room of ample proportions, for the accommodation of the crowd of politicians, broken-down officers, authors, actors, and suppliants for favours and advancement, who were certain to assemble there.

Autre temps, autre mœurs. Therefore, when Marlborough House was enlarged and altered for its occupancy by the Prince and Princess of Wales, and a porte-cochère and entrance hall added to the original front, the old vestibule was converted into a saloon, a truly noble *salle - de - réception* thirty feet long by thirty wide, not very large, but admirably proportioned. At one end, a narrow gallery connects the Royal private apartments with the visitors' rooms on the first floor. There are no windows, but good light is obtained through a domed skylight. The top of the light is covered with lead, painted inside with

allegorical representations of the Arts and Sciences.

I am inclined to think that this is one of the handsomest rooms in London. Indeed, it would be hard to find another anywhere, whose general arrangements are more harmonious ; and such an indescribable atmosphere of by-gone times pervades it that were one to draw to the heavy portières, and, alone in the fading daylight, let imagination exercise its full power, one could almost see the Duchess herself returning from an interview with Queen Anne ; or—aged before his time, the grim spectre of paralysis hovering over him — the illustrious John Churchill, greatest of English Generals, who had raised his country to a height of glory never obtained since the days of Poictiers and Agincourt, but who in his declining years was so beset with detraction and envy, that neither here nor at Blenheim could he find the rest so nobly earned and so earnestly desired.

On the upper part of three of the saloon walls, are Laguerre's paintings of the immortal battle of Blenheim, August 13th, 1704, and Marshal Tallard surrendering to Marlborough, in whose travelling carriage he left the scene of his utter defeat, after having had the mortification of witnessing his five squadrons of the gens-d'armes fleeing before the Carabiniers under Colonel Palmes, and the final cavalry charge of eight thousand sabres, Marlborough at their head, bearing down with irresistible force upon ten thousand of the enemy, scattering them like chaff before the wind.

After the death of William IV. when Marlborough House was being got ready for Queen Adelaide, in 1838, these pictures, with those on the staircase, having become rather dilapidated—or, as it is said, because the Dowager Queen did not like them—were effectually concealed behind a covering of stucco, or some such material, happily of a preservative nature, and their very existence was forgotten.

Many years later, in 1859, Prince Edward of Saxe-Weimar was discussing with H.R.H. the Prince Consort the alterations then in progress at Marlborough House, and happened to mention these paintings, which he (Prince Edward) well remembered. The Prince Consort was at first incredulous, and dismissed the subject, but Prince Edward returned to the charge, assuring him that his statement was correct, and offering to prove it. Accordingly, a small portion of the stucco was removed, and, to the Prince Consort's great astonishment, the existence of Laguerre's battle-pieces was effectually demonstrated.

During the same year the Hon. Sir Spencer C. B. Ponsonby Fane may also claim the merit of having discovered these well-nigh forgotten works of Art. Sir Spencer—unaware of Prince Edward's knowledge—suspecting that something lay behind the whitewash and colouring, cleared away a portion, and laid bare the pictures beneath. They were then restored and cleverly touched-up in accordance with Laguerre's designs, so far as they were known.

As regards the painting of the battle of Ramilies on the principal staircase, some years afterwards, in 1889, the Prince of Wales came across the original engravings in the Royal Library at Windsor Castle, and at once perceived that some errors had crept into the pictures at Marlborough House while being restored by Mr. Richards, R.A., for which he was clearly not to blame. So His Royal Highness gave instructions to have nearly the whole repainted in strict accord with the old impressions, and Laguerre's work now looks as fresh as when first created.

But the concealment of these paintings is only a further illustration of the remarkable difficulty there is in arriving at the actual truth of anything after a few years' lapse of time.

Covering the entire area of the saloon there is a splendid carpet, technically called an Axminster—and, by-the-way, it was near the picturesque little town of that name, on the borders of bosky Dorset and Devon, "deep-meadowed, happy, fair, with orchard lawns," that John Churchill, Duke of Marlborough, first saw the light.

Time has softened the bright hues of this right Royal production—a present to the Prince on the occasion of his wedding—but it accords wonderfully with the tapestry on the walls, and the groups of

4*

cabinets, chairs, couches, etc. There is a curious feature about it, usually unobserved. It has in the centre an extremely ornamental star, slightly—about a foot—out of the straight, that is to say, the carpet cannot be placed in the exact middle of the room, owing to the projection of the massive fireplace, which prevents it being laid quite on the square.

Rivalling the works of Titian or Rubens, superb panels of Gobelin tapestry take the place of pictures on the walls of this beautiful room, producing an indescribably lovely effect. Much of it was presented to the Prince by Napoleon III. and, with one exception, belongs probably to the period of Louis XIV., when the immortal romance of Cervantes, was still, comparatively speaking, in its *première jeunesse.* Here are depicted Sancho Panza, Don Quixote, and the chief characters in that dramatic and wonderful piece of fooling.

Serving as a foil to this, and occupying almost the entire length of the western wall, is a piece of tapestry representing the slaughter of the Mamlukes at Cairo, when under the rule of Mahmud II. This is, of course, a modern production from the famous French atelier, and—like the older work—is a gift from the late Emperor.

Those who know Cairo, will recollect the parapet of its Citadel, and the narrow passage below it; pointed out as the scene of Mahommed Ali's massacre of the Mamlukes, in the year 1811. There had been a frightful slaughter of the Beys and their

Mamlukes in 1805, when these unfortunates, falling into a snare laid for them by Mahommed, in a part of the main thoroughfare of Cairo called the Beyn-el-Kasreyn, suddenly found themselves between two fires. Some escaped, but others took refuge in the mosque of El-Barkookeeyeh, where they were slaughtered in the most brutal manner. All this was but a kind of rehearsal of what was to follow; for, undeterred by the recollection of their betrayal, the Mamlukes walked quietly into a similar trap laid for them by the wily Governor of Egypt, six years later on, unsuspiciously accepting his invitation to be present at the ceremony of investing his son with an exalted military command. After being hospitably received in the Citadel by him, they slowly descended the steep, narrow road leading to the great gates. But as soon as the last of them had passed into this defile, the gates were closed, and the Governor's troops having, meanwhile, manned the walls and the summits of the surrounding houses, poured volley after volley upon their defenceless victims below. A few of the Mamlukes attempting to fly, managed to scale the walls, only to be made prisoners, and afterwards killed in cold blood. Four hundred and seventy Mamlukes are said to have entered the Citadel, and but one—a Bey — is, traditionally, supposed to have escaped by forcing his horse to leap over the ramparts, himself alighting uninjured on the ground beneath. The very spot is, to this day, shown to wondering and credulous tourists of all nations.

On each side of this painting in needle-work, is a Florentine lamp of carved wood, upheld by an ebony arm, thrust as it were through the wall. In shape, these lamps resemble the fixed lanterns on the taffrails and stern galleries of men-of-war in the last century. *On dit* that H. I. M. the Empress Frederick—whose appreciation of art is well-known—at once fell in love with them, and made up her mind to immediately order similar ones from Italy.

Not far from each of these quaint lamps is an ornate black and ormolu pedestal, supporting a bronze, and on tall stands immediately below are marble busts — one, of the Queen of Denmark, the other, of the King of Greece. Everywhere there is fine statuary, its beauty emphasized by the surroundings of palms (Latania-Borbonica). On one of the cabinets stands a life-size terra-cotta bust of the Princess of Wales—an excellent likeness.

Opposite the great Mamluke tapestry is a beautifully sculptured fireplace of purest white marble. The Queen-Anne overmantel is framed in carved oak and gold, and bears on the frieze of its middle panel the date, April, 1863, being the year when the Royal couple took possession of Marlborough House.

Against the north wall are two Louis XIV. cabinets, exquisitely inlaid in coloured woods, with richly gilt ormolu mounts, and several lovely ivory medallions.

Very artistically grouped are the couches and chairs, some having modern frames filled in with Gobelin tapestry of the Empire style, a present from the Emperor Napoleon III., as was also the tapestry screen. The old Gobelin on the square Louis XVI. chairs, is illustrative of Æsop's fables. Generally speaking, the more solid furniture is upholstered in this costly fabric, but the smaller pieces vary considerably, and have been purchased by the Princess from time to time. Two of the four doors are draped with heavy blue velvet portières, with tapestry borders.

Like Her Majesty the Queen, the Princess—and for that matter, the Prince, too—is quick to notice if any piece of furniture or ornament is moved from its usual place, and at once seeks an explanation. A carefully prepared plan exists, with the position of the various articles marked thereon, thus immensely facilitating their replacement after cleaning operations.

In connection with furniture, it has been said with truth that both the Prince and the Princess have ever since their marriage done their utmost to encourage home manufactures in every department, and—with the exception of Eastern Art work, the tapestry, and the Sèvres china—everything in Marlborough House may, broadly speaking, be said to be of British make. The journals of the day describing the preparations for the coming wedding in 1863, stated that "in the furnishing and decorations of the state apartments at Marlborough House, English art and English manufacture have been duly patronized. Spitalfields and Manchester have supplied the silk and damask, and Wilton the Axminster carpets, while the furniture has been made entirely in London workshops."

Furniture-making and silk-weaving—two of the handicrafts of thirty-three years ago just referred to—are still the chief industries in the East-end. In the last century, the latter gave occupation to some 60,000 people in the district.

As a matter of fact, the old-established firm of Holland & Sons have always had the honour of "upholstering" for the Prince and Princess both at Sandringham and in London, and their beautiful cabinet-work can more than hold its own with anything made abroad.

Our Royal family's constancy to British manufactures came well to the front three years ago, when, by express orders, the trousseau prepared for Princess May was exclusively of British make—East-end looms producing the pearl-white satin ; Ireland, the exquisite poplin ; and Scotland, the useful tweeds and tartans, and it is said that the entire trousseau for Princess of Maud of Wales will be made in England.

A perusal of the list of the Prince and Princess's warrant-holders present at the Annual 9th of

November dinner, will show to what extent London tradesmen are patronized by their Royal Highnesses. And if any one be desirous of witnessing a scene of enthusiasm and loyalty, he had better contrive to be present the next time the holders assemble to enjoy the Prince's annual present of venison and to drink his health with honours.

These warrant-holders occupy rather a peculiar position in the economy of London life. Over some insignificant-looking shop in a shabby neighbourhood, may be seen the Royal Arms or the Prince of Wales' feathers, but it does not follow that the proprietor is in possession of the certificate bearing the signature of Lord Colville of Culross, or Sir Dighton M. Probyn, which alone entitles him to be denominated a warrant-holder. He may, perchance, once have served some of the servants at Marlborough House when on board wages, and therefore imagines himself a "Purveyor to the Royal Household"; or he may be a butcher, who, at Christmas time, having purchased a royal "prize-taker," has been requested, according to a kindly custom, to provide a joint thereof for the Royal table; or he may have put the Arms up simply as an advertisement, in ignorance of the pains and penalties thus entailed. These may be something terrible, for aught he knows to the contrary—so ignorant are most people on the subject—" something lingering" as says the Mikado, "with boiling oil in it." But, as a matter of fact, the "Patents,

Designs, and Trade Marks Act" of 1883, imposes a fine on summary conviction, not exceeding twenty pounds, upon any person assuming or using the Royal arms without authority.

To lessen the illegal use of the Royal Arms, the "Incorporated Association of Her Majesty's Warrant-holders"—originally established in the year 1840 under the style of the " Royal Tradesmen's Association"—have recently done much service by pointing out to erring tradesmen, in a quiet and unobtrusive manner, the risk they run. That the Association's action is quite justified is shown by the fact that, in the metropolis upwards of six hundred cases were recorded of the Royal sign having been put up without authority.

Needless to say that the Prince deals only with the best firms. Strict enquiries are made concerning them, and if taken into favour, they must supply the household for one year satisfactorily before they are even eligible for the warrant. Then, after a certain lapse of time, they can apply for the privilege, which is granted under very clearly defined conditions, the diploma embodying the name of each individual member of the firm to whom it is issued. In the event of change of partners, bankruptcy, or death, the warrant has at once to be returned. A too prominent display of the " Feathers " over an establishment, is not considered to be in good taste, neither is the use of the certificate as a mere advertisement encouraged ;

the latter is therefore frequently seen only inside the premises. The Royal warrant is rightly looked upon as a great honour. "We all of us," said Mr. Algernon Graves, at one of the annual meetings of Her Majesty's Warrant-holders, "lay great store on our warrants. It is a species of 'Peerage for Trade.'"

Annually the loyal warrant-holders celebrate the Prince's birthday by illuminating their premises, and by dining together in true British fashion—a custom of thirty-seven years' standing. Last year they met to the number of 300 at the Whitehall Rooms, Northumberland Avenue, when, after a splendid banquet—the tables profuse with beautiful floral adjuncts—a list of loyal toasts was received with the utmost enthusiasm deepened by the receipt of a telegram—read out by the Chairman, Mr. Algernon Graves—from Sir Francis Knollys, expressing his thanks for the loyal message he had just received from their President. In the menu, the *pièce de résistance* or rather *d'honneur* is invariably venison from two fine bucks sent by the Queen and the Prince of Wales. The wines are always excellent, and at dessert, the good old fashion of drinking port wine prevails.

CHAPTER IV.

THE LARGE DINING-ROOM—THE DERBY DAY DINNER AT MARLBOROUGH HOUSE.

AMONGST all the countless entertainments given on the evening following the national carnival on Epsom Downs, not one is so well organized and perfect in its way as the Derby Day Dinner annually given by His Royal Highness the Prince of Wales to the members of the Jockey Club, in the large dining-room at Marlborough House. For many years the late Lord Wilton had been in the habit of giving a big dinner to the members of the club at his house in Grosvenor Square on the Monday preceding the great race; and on his death, in the year 1885, the Prince continued the practice with the happiest results.

On no evening in the year are the favourite dining-resorts of Londoners so crowded as on the Derby Day, nor does any function of the season bring with it so much responsibility and taxation of resource to restaurateurs and public caterers generally. The "Savoy," the "Grand," the "Metropole," the "Bristol," the "Continental," Spiers and Pond, the "Cafe Verrey," Blanchard's, etc., clubs without number, private houses, and Coleherne Court in

particular, where Mr. Edmund Tattersall's Derby Dinner is looked upon as an institution—all are on their mettle to provide fittingly for the celebration of the Blue Riband Day.

In the state *salle des festins* at Marlborough House, the long table, with its covers laid for over fifty distinguished guests, is a fine sight; but before entering into details thereupon, it will be as well to say something about the surroundings.

As the *invités* enter from the drawing-room at the east of the building, they see before them a noble seven-windowed apartment over fifty feet long, with an ornate marble mantel-piece at either end, over which places of honour hang copies of Winterhalter's famous pictures of Her Majesty the Queen and the late Prince Consort.

Immense Kentia palms in ornamental bowls stand on each side of these paintings, and in some of the windows are rare exotics in pedestal-supported vases.

Ornamental bracket groups of candle-shaped electroliers against the walls, show up the pictures to advantage, and there are more large ones here than in any other state apartment.

Over the two north doors are oval-framed portraits of the late Emperor Frederick of Germany and the Empress Frederick, who, herself an accomplished artist, has contributed the other two over-door pictures of charmingly-painted flowers.

From the South Sea House in Threadneedle Street, recalling the time when

> "Statesmen and patriots plied alike the stocks,
> Peeress and butler shared alike the box,
> And judges jobbed and bishops bit the town,
> And mighty dukes packed crowns for half-a-crown,"

came the portraits of the first three Georges, and there used to be also a painting of William IV.

The panelled ceiling is very handsome, white, slightly relieved with colour; the walls are hung with claret silk of a pattern copied from some old silk damask at Hampton Court; while the curtains are of silk damask of the same colour, specially made by Fry and Sons, Dublin—having in the centre the Royal Arms, filled in with scroll-work. A Turkey carpet, resplendent in all the colours of the East—blue and white predominating—covers the floor.

Not being over-crowded with furniture, the servants have plenty of room to move round the splendid table, which has on rare occasions been so arranged and enlarged as to accommodate seventy or eighty guests. Very comfortable-looking are the chairs, upholstered in royal scarlet leather. There are a good many Minton vases about, and between the candelabra on each mantel-piece is a very pretty clock. Tall glass screens temper the hospitable glow from the glorious fires kept up in the winter, although Marlborough House is heated throughout with hot-air pipes from the basement. Beneath a fine piece of unframed tapestry occupying the middle of the east wall, is a remarkably handsome sideboard made by Holland and Sons. Like the rest of the furniture, it is of mahogany and gold, with the Arms of the Prince and Princess carved thereon in gilt. On grand occasions, the back is taken away, and its place supplied by a buffet constructed to display to the best advantage the magnificent plate for which Marlborough House is famed.

At small dinner-parties—as stated in Chapter II.—the Indian room is used, tables being set there of different shapes, round, square, and sometimes horseshoe, according to the Prince's desire. But it is only in this stately hall, that the very important banquets are held. All strictly private and family dinners are given, as we shall see hereafter, in the reception-room on the first floor.

Not only is the Prince of Wales the most charming of hosts, but he is an "excellent judge of the finer efforts of the cuisine," and entertains with refinement and elegance both at Sandringham and Marlborough House.

It has been well said that gastronomy commences with our birth, and continues until the point of death, when the last drop or morsel is taken to alleviate the pangs of anguish. Appertaining to all mankind, it alike directs the banquets of kings and the suppers of peasants. Its study, therefore, is derogatory to none, and one of the loveliest of high-born duchesses—now many years dead—did not consider it beneath her dignity to compose and send down to her cook the menu of each day, equal to the inspiration of any master in the art.

A dinner at Marlborough House in 1896 is a revelation of what high-class cookery can achieve. The Prince has in his chef, M. Menager, a practical, and no merely theoretical, disciple of the illustrious trio, Ude, Boucher, and Carême. He is well known in his profession, and came to the Prince of Wales from a certain establishment in Berkeley Square, where General Ellis was in the habit of dining, and who subsequently brought him to his Royal Highness's notice. His staff consists of two cooks, a confectioner, and eight or nine kitchen-maids.

Some of M. Menager's compositions are artistically very fine. Upon many personages, however, of the highest distinction, this Gallic refinement of the culinary art is apt to be unappreciated, if not altogether thrown away. Is it not a fact that one of Her Gracious Majesty's favourite dishes at both luncheon and dinner, is the roast beef of old England in its various forms? At the great dinner given by the Queen at Buckingham Palace on the eve of her opening Parliament in person, January 26th, 1841, shortly after the birth of the Princess Royal, the menu contained amongst its relevés, *filets de bœuf piqué braisé aux pommes de terres* and amongst the first entrées, *bords de pommes de terre garni de palais de bœuf*, while upon the magnificent buffet were roast beef and boiled round of beef. Did not George III. prefer boiled leg of mutton and turnips to the most sublime composition of his *maître d'hotel*? Was not Napoleon the Great inordinately fond of *crepinettes de cochon*? a most horribly indigestible dish. Did not the great William Pitt, who hated entrées, consume in preference to anything else enormous slices of bread-and-butter, or huge hunches of bread-and-cheese when he got the chance in his retirement at Walmer?—and after all Pitt was not far wrong. As the *Daily Telegraph* once said: "Look at us. Here we have been eating it all the days of our life, and it comes up smiling at five o'clock every afternoon. Jam may endure for a while, but bread-and-butter is the old and faithful stand-by. Try all the substitutes you can think of, and in the end you have to discard them as unsatisfying. This England of ours might be worse—I think it would be better—without beer. Who shall estimate its social status were bread-and-butter banished for ever?" Then is there not a well-authenticated rumour that Her Royal Highness the Princess of Wales entertains a decided *penchant* for Yorkshire pudding? And, are not the "tripe and onion" and "Irish stew" days in certain West-end clubs, immensely appreciated by the members, who have to put their names down beforehand for these odoriferous dishes?

To return to the Derby Day Dinner. Last year about fifty-four invitations were sent out to the members of the Jockey Club, and of that number, only eight were unable to obey His Royal Highness's command. Those present included the four Royal Dukes—Saxe-Coburg and Gotha, Cambridge Connaught and York; the Princes Christian and Soltykoff; five other Dukes; two Marquises; the Comte de Berteux; seven Lords; two Right Honourables; two Honourables; and ten untitled individuals.

At these dinners, the usual custom is for the guests to assemble in the saloon, where they are welcomed by the Prince of Wales, and should the fortunate owner of the Derby-winner happily be amongst them, he is of course, specially congratulated.

Dinner—generally at 8.30—announced, the distinguished company, wearing evening dress (uniform being eschewed on such occasions), proceed to the large dining-room, and take their allotted places, the Prince sitting in the centre, facing the buffet. So excellent are the arrangements, that in no way are the movements of the small regiment of pages —looking most imposing in their state livery— impeded.

One of these attendants is told off to wait upon each Royal guest, and one to each couple of other invités; so it goes without saying that the waiting is perfect, and that there is never a hitch in the smooth and stately progress of the banquet.

Much thought is bestowed upon the preliminary details. The laying-out of the table is exceedingly good, and does great credit to the wine-butler, or "decker," whose duty it is to arrange everything, under the superintendence of the house-steward, to the satisfaction of the Prince, who does not disdain to watch the preparations.

To the large majority of my readers the office of "table-decker" is perhaps unknown; and as at Marlborough House it is—minus a certain amount of state—the same as at Buckingham Palace, I will briefly describe what transpires at the latter, before the Royal table can be said to be fairly laid. First in order come the "upholsterers," who see that the tables, etc., are properly placed and fit to bear their important burdens. Then the table-deckers arrange the table-cloths, linen on sideboard, napkins and glass, and provide each person with the "staff of life." (The table-cloths are of the finest quality, worked with the Royal Arms, many of them having also the national emblems, the rose, the shamrock, and thistle, embroidered thereon. This applies equally to the table napkins, which are plainly folded into a small square to hold the bread, the fantastic shapes so often seen elsewhere being utterly eschewed). After this preliminary canter, the serious business begins. "Yeomen of the silver pantry" enter and put into position the silver; while the table-deckers fix the wax candles into the branching candelabra, and place the pots of flowers in their vases—some of them quite magnificent, and chiefly of china.

Upon the big dinner-table at Marlborough House, with its exquisite glass and floral decorations, is always placed on this racing anniversary, the superb silver dinner-service ordered for the Prince before his marriage, and executed by Messrs. Garrards', of the Haymarket; its cost at a period when silver was quoted at a much higher figure than at present, may be estimated at from £20,000 to £40,000, but in artistic workmanship the value is fully there. Its principal feature is the centre-piece, a kind of plateau 7 feet 6 inches long and about 2 feet wide, together with two others each 5 feet long, which can be used at the sides or ends. The subjects represented on this magnificent table-ornament are various:—St. George of England, St. David of Wales, etc., the battles of Crecy and Agincourt, Britannia as protectrix of the Colonies, and a symbolical rendering of the Empire of India, etc., and it bears also the Royal Arms of Great Britain and Ireland, together with those of the Prince and Princess of Wales. It is so constructed that no decorations can well be placed upon it—doubtless a shrewd device of the designer, to prevent his graceful work being hidden by flowers.

Of very ancient date is the use of centre-pieces at regal entertainments, none perhaps being more striking than that of the *surtout* or *epergne* belonging to King James I. Pyramidical in form—"it was placed," says the Duc de Sully, "in the centre of the Royal table, which contained most costly vessels, and was even enriched with diamonds."

But the chief ornament at the Derby Day Dinner, is the buffet, to which all eyes turn, and upon whose adornment considerable skill is bestowed. It is furnished with a superb collection of plate—racing-cups, yachting trophies, gold and silver salvers, and other exquisite evidences of the perfection to which the goldsmith's art has attained in this country. These, reflecting back the light from the electroliers, produce one of the finest effects imaginable.

After dinner—during which champagne usually makes its welcome appearance in hospitable magnums—coffee and liqueurs are served, and smoking becomes general, the Royal host—who throughout has been the soul of geniality—setting the example. Obviously there is much sporting conversation—retrospective and anticipatory—plenty of dignified badinage, good stories told, and bon-mots uttered, but, alas! not recorded. Then an adjournment is made to the large drawing-room, where, usually, tables are set for whist—many of the guests devoting their energies thereto until perhaps one or two o'clock in the morning, when the company depart with renewed expressions of hope to their Royal host that the year may see his colours triumphant, both on the turf, and on the element, which, by means of the *Britannia*, he seems to have made specially his own. Here is the menu:—

DINER DU 29 MAI 1895.

POTAGES.

Turtle Punch............ }   Tortue Clair.
Bisque d'Ecrevisses.

POISSONS.

Madeira, 1820...............   Petites Truites au bleu sce. Genoise.
Steinburg Cabinet 1857   Filets de Soles à la Norvegienne.

ENTRÉES.

Cotelettes de Cailles à la Clamart.
Chauds Froids de Volailles à la Renaissance.

RELEVÉS..

Möet et Chandon..........   Hanches de Venaison sce. Aigre Douce.
Mouton Poêlé au Champagne.
Still Sillery, 1846...........   Sorbets à l'Italienne.

RÔTS.

Chambertin, 1875..........   Poussins Rotis sur Cânapés.
Salades de Romaine à la Française.

ENTREMETS.

Asperges en branches sce. Mousseuse.
Crouts aux Fraises à la Princesse.
Chartreuses de Pêches à la Montreueil.
Gradins de Patisseries Assorties.

RELEVÉS.

Casolettes de Fromage à la Russe.

GLACE.

Buissons de Glaces à la Napolitaine.

GAUFRETTES.

Royal tawny Port, 50 years old.
Royal white Port.
Sherry George IV.
Magnums Chateau Lafite, 1864.
Brandy, 1848.

CHAPTER V.

THE PRINCESS'S RECEPTION-ROOM, BOUDOIR, BEDROOM, AND DRESSING - ROOM — MUSIC AT MALBOROUGH HOUSE.

ONLY in modern times has Royalty been able to obtain some approach to real privacy at a distance from, and yet within easy reach of the metropolis. In pre-railway days, Windsor, Kensington, and Kew, were the only places to which the Sovereign could resort when the cares of business were suspended.

With the marriage of Her Majesty Queen Victoria to Prince Albert, a still stronger impulse was given to this natural desire of British Royalty— harassed by ten thousand anxieties—to " fly away and be at rest." Home-life in the country, so precious to the exalted couple, became possible in the Isle of Wight and at Balmoral, and with wise forethought was provided for the Heir Apparent by the purchase of the Sandringham estate.

Admirably did the Queen when writing to King Leopold, express her satisfaction in having secured so delightful a retreat as Osborne. " It sounds so pleasant," she wrote, " to have a place of one's own, quiet and retired, and free from all Woods and Forests and other charming Departments, which really are the plague of one's life." But absolute retirement is, and always will be, unattainable by Royalty.

Not long ago, being privileged by a certain very exalted personage on the continent to explore her magnificent castle, with a view to publishing an account thereof, I was in the most gracious manner allowed "the run of the place," and was afforded every facility for accomplishing my somewhat difficult task. After going through room after room, and admiring the unparalleled works of art, there remained to be explored only the upper portion of the Schloss, containing the private rooms.

"And now, Baron," said I to the high-born court official to whose care I had been consigned, "I have done just half my work. When may I see the most interesting part of the castle, since you have so kindly intimated that I am to go everywhere? For an instant, an expression of perplexity shadowed the Baron's countenance, but quickly vanished, and I proceeded to point out to him how incongruous it would be to publish a description that ignored the greater part of the building. My courteous cicerone saw the force of the argument, and at once made the necessary arrangements for my viewing everything.

After looking into the plate-room, kitchen, wine cellar, linen-room, and all the working part of the large household, I found myself within the sacred circle of the strictly private apartments. I saw the couch whereon an Empress reposes. I saw the antique bed where an Emperor sleeps like any other mortal. I saw the most beautiful of boudoirs. I saw the *chambre à coucher* of more than one charming and accomplished princess; and I noticed on a dressing-table—well, in fact, I noticed all that there is of refinement and fashion in this kind of apartment in the mansion of any well-bred lady throughout Great Britain; and—that is all!

I recollect being told that there were fourteen bath-rooms in this spotlessly clean abode of Royalty, and, no doubt, had I afterwards recorded this fact, it would have been duly appreciated by the public. Had I been of the more intelligent—I mean the gentler—sex, I might have catalogued with ready pen, the essentially feminine contents of these dainty sleeping apartments; but I merely passed through them, and allowed myself to carry away only a general impression of what they were like.

But, as in the case of Marlborough House, I know my feminine readers will not be content unless given a peep into that part wherein the Princess holds supreme sway, I feel sure their Royal Highnesses will grant me absolution, if I, for a few moments, with most loyal feeling, draw back some folds of the concealing curtain.

On returning from a drive in the Park, the Princess of Wales, disappearing from public gaze behind the gates of Marlborough House, alights at the principal entrance, where two fine specimens of the genus "Jeames de la Pluche" aid her descent from the landau, the gentleman-in-waiting, or other member of the household in attendance, receiving H.R.H. in the hall. A walk of a few yards takes her to the lift familiarly bearing her designation—and in a few seconds she is in her own special domain on the first floor. She can at once obtain access to her dressing-room, either by way of the gallery—before mentioned as running along the upper part of one side of the saloon—or by the east corridor through the reception-room, the first of her own particular suite of apartments.

In the illustration of the garden-front of Marlborough House, the position of these apartments may be easily identified, as all the windows pourtrayed on the first floor belong thereto and to the Prince's dressing-room, with the exception of three at the eastern end, which appertain to the Royal visitors' rooms.

On the floor of the reception-room, margined with *parqueterie*, is an Eastern carpet of the conventional pattern, described by some humourist as "like nothing in the heavens above, or in the earth beneath, or in the waters under the earth"; but, nevertheless, beautifully harmonious in design and colour, and suiting to perfection the silk damask curtains, and wall-hangings of creamy-hued, figured, tussore silk, brightened by numerous pictures, principally oil-paintings, and some particularly interesting sketches by the Princess.

Most of the furniture is gilt, and very pretty, especially one or two of the cabinets.

This charming *salle de reception* is daily converted into a cheerful breakfast-room, where breakfast is served at from 10 o'clock to 10.30, and when absolutely *en famille*, the Royal party have luncheon and even dine here. The footman places upon the beautiful oval table in the middle of the room, a circular top (folding something like a card-table), thereby considerably enlarging its dimensions; the dainty gilt chairs are pushed away into corners, and, for the time being, cane ones are brought in and put round the table.

Next to the reception-room is the boudoir, where only the Princess's relations and most intimate friends are admitted.

Of course, everyone knows what a boudoir is—a lady's private apartment; a modern rendering of the Saxon "*bour*," "*bur*," an inner chamber or "bower"; or, in up-to-date parlance, a woman's "den," where she, poor, persecuted creature, may hide away, and do what she likes, unrestrained by the presence of that fearful wild-fowl *man;* of which tyrannical species, an unprincipled member had once the audacity to remind his wife that the French derivation of her favourite retreat was *bouder*, to pout, or be sulky.

Commanding a charming view from its balcony over the conservatory, the Princess's boudoir may safely be called the prettiest room in Marlborough

House. Its dimensions are conveniently moderate —25 feet by 23—and since it is here that Her Royal Highness usually sits, naturally it is here that her personal tastes and predilection are most outwardly manifested.

Some of the furniture is modern and some antique; but it is almost all *marqueterie*, and variously upholstered, and generally covered with pretty red silk slips daintily frilled. In front of the fireplace is a delightfully cozy sofa, and lying about in all directions, are fancy cushions, etc., etc., suggestive of perfect repose and *abandon*. In winter, the fire in the hospitable hearth is fed with wood, the logs being kept in one of the iron stands so cleverly designed by Her Royal Highness for this purpose, a sample of which the public had the opportunity of examining at the Exhibition of the Home Arts and Industries, held in the Albert Hall last year. An Indian carpet and rugs cover the floor. The room is decorated in white and gold; the walls are hung with satin damask of a chintz pattern on a white ground; while the curtains are of Indian red silk damask. There are several beautiful inlaid cabinets, and a grand piano covered with an exquisite piece of embroidered work. Of course, the Princess's writing-table is very handsome, and arranged with a shelf containing innumerable family photographs and others. A *bonbonnière*, filled with the latest thing in sweetmeats, is always ready to hand, Her Royal Highness—like Henry III. of France, and his successor, Henry, King of Navarre—being remarkably fond of all kinds of delicate sugary cates.

One of the Princess's chief delights is to bestow bon-bons upon all the children she knows. Well may the little ones speak of her as the sweet Princess!

Being necessarily somewhat crowded, there is little scope in the room for much embellishment in the way of palms, for whose scarcity more than ample amends is made by the profusion of lovely flowers, everywhere seen throughout the Princess of Wales' apartments. Her Royal Highness might, indeed, be fittingly spoken of as Flora, the goddess of Spring-time, carrying with her the emblematical cornucopia, so great is her love of those blossoms "so blue and golden, stars that in earth's firmament do shine."

At Marlborough House in the season, from three hundred to four hundred vases of cut flowers, constantly changed and kept fresh, are used every day in the various Royal apartments, necessitating the employment of two men exclusively for this work. The floral decorations at luncheon and dinner are always elaborate and beautiful, though varying in quantity according to the number of guests. At State dinners they are superb. It is somewhat difficult to decide as to which are the Princess's special favourites—everything, from the lowly wild flower to the regal lily, is welcome to her; but probaby roses, carnations, lilies-of-the-valley, tulips of all colours, and violets command her greatest admiration. The latter—as I have elsewhere observed—are extensively grown at Sandringham for her delectation. But if this modest little plant be destined to develope to the proportions of the big Californian productions, with blossoms large enough to cover a silver dollar, the forcing frames in present use will have to be materially enlarged.

In their lavish use of flowers, the Royal owners of Marlborough House, apart from personal liking, are only adapting themselves to the universal fashion of the day. Nothing is more remarkable than the immense increase of florists' shops in London during the last forty years; and the amount of money expended in fashionable circles upon bouquets, button-holes and table-plants, etc. is prodigious.

Though perhaps not so ardent an ornithologist as the King of Portugal, the Princess has a great liking for birds, and has in her boudoir several canaries, bullfinches and other songsters. These pleasant little house companions have each their turn of favouritism; from time to time the "cabinet" being changed at their Royal mistress's pleasure, when the retiring, but not disgraced, ministers are relegated temporarily to the large "spare" or "new" room on the first floor, where no doubt they muse on their period of short-lived fame, and the uncertainty of Royal favour.

At one time, the Princess had a beautiful blue pigeon, so tame that it was allowed to fly about loose in her rooms. Alas! it went the way of all pets—an untimely grave received it, much to its owner's distress.

In her early married days, Her Royal Highness took great delight in gold fish, which she kept in an ornamental aquarium, and loved to watch their graceful movements. Were she now to resume this fascinating study of the finny tribe, so increased are the facilities for obtaining new and rare specimens from the four quarters of the globe, that she might even keep as a pet the lovely little Paradise fish of China — described by the late Frank Buckland as possessing all the colours of the rainbow — or the equally beautiful Gourami of Mauritius and Penang, with its silvery head and markings of blue.

As to dogs, everyone who has admired Luke Fildes' portrait of the Princess — the original of which hangs in the red drawing-room at York House—must have noticed the dear little Japanese pug, "Facey," nestling in her lap, the reigning favourite at the time the picture was painted, but the statement in one of the Society papers that the Princess's maid held "Facey," conveying the idea that Her Royal Highness did not do so, is incorrect, as Mr. Luke Fildes assures me that it never left the Princess except on one occasion when she was too much engaged to hold it. So much for mere *on dits*.

"Flossie," now alas dead, was formerly a great pet with the Princess, but quite a long list could be drawn up of dogs honoured by Her Royal Highness's attention since she first came to England.

Together with cats, the Princess's dogs used to race and romp about the private rooms almost unchecked by their kind-hearted mistress, though doing a great deal of damage to curtains and furniture, their "bill for repairs," so to speak, at the end of the month, being considerable. The Princess cannot resist taking notice of cats, whenever she meets with them. While strolling about the stud-farm at Sandringham, her attention was called to a small black kitten that had imprudently strayed away, and had returned to find the door of its cottage-home fast closed. By its piteous cries, it appealed to Royalty for assistance, and the Princess, at once comprehending the situation, went to the rescue, and lifting the latch, let the wanderer in, exclaiming with tenderest sympathy, "Ah, the pretty little pussy, the poor pretty little pussy!"

Her Royal Highness is especially fond of Persian cats, and they abound both at Sandringham and at Marlborongh House, giving themselves great airs as is "their nature to." G. A. Henty, who has studied the question deeply, tells us that the feline race has assumed domestic habits under protest, and that although individuals of the species have been made pets of since the days of early Egypt, they have never, throughout all their generations, developed reciprocal feelings of affection, and will rub their sides against the leg of a table with equal manifestation of love, as against their human master or mistress. But this is surely an evidence of perverted taste not possible to a right-minded cat ; so let us pronounce the accusation libellous !

Had the Royal mistress of Marlborough House been born a Roman patrician in the first century of the Christian era, however great her wealth and position, she would have had—as the author of " Pelham " expresses it—a mere *pigeon-hole* of a bed-room, and, like that of the beautiful Julia, her dressing-room adjoining would not have been much larger, and so dimly lighted, from the intentional exclusion of the sun's rays, as to require an eye accustomed to a certain darkness to distinguish the vivid colorings of the walls, the gold flowers embroidered on the curtains that hung before the door communicating with the cubiculum, and the silver basin and ewer close by the dressing-table, which itself stood upon a carpet woven from the looms of the East. While had the Fates ordained that Princess Alexandra of Denmark had lived in the eleventh century, her bed-chamber, though more commodious than that of the Pompeiian, would have fallen far short of the elegance and refinement of the present day; and she would have had to submit to the absurd etiquette of the period which required that a solemn ceremony should take place every evening before the Royal lady retired to rest. Seated in a chair of state, her shoes were taken off, and her hair dressed. Right and left of her, according to their rank, sat great ladies of the Court watching the process; and behind them, wherever they could find places, the maids of honour.

Happily, the Princess belongs to our own time, a period of the highest civilization, when guests at dinner no longer throw bones upon the rush-laid floors, wherewith to regale the dogs, and when sanitation and systematic cleanliness are not quite unheard of.

Recent experiments in Edison's laboratory and elsewhere would seem to discredit the hypothesis that the earths' magnetism has to do with the unquestionable influence of position in sleep. Yet it is a well-known fact that many persons can only sleep well when lying north and south; and a famous French centenarian went so far as to ascribe his longevity to having always taken his repose in that position. Therefore, it is pleasant to think that the arrangements of our Princess's bed-room enable her to put this theory into practice, whereby we hope that she, as a rule, obtains the sweet slumber so often denied to Royalty, though given to the "wet sea-boy perched upon the high and giddy mast."

A velvet-pile carpet subdues every footstep in this room and the adjoining dressing-room. The furniture of beautiful light Hungarian oak inlaid with purple wood and slightly gilded, contrasts charmingly with pretty little inlaid tables and quaint old bureaus from Denmark. These, with screens of various descriptions, comfortable sofas and useful small tables, the unpretentious *armazon de cama*— as the Spanish language euphoniously has it—with its chintz hangings trimmed with lace matching the window curtains, etc., produce a *tout ensemble* extremely light and pleasing. Lastly, there is a plain walnut book-case containing books used by the Prince of Wales during his University career.

Extremely pretty chintz covers the inlaid mahogany furniture in the Princess' dressing-room, producing a particularly bright and charming effect. A dainty mantel border with curtains ornament the fireplace, surmounted by a mirror. The dimensions of the room are 25 × 19 feet (the bedroom being 32 × 25 feet), but a mirror fitted into the angle of the door makes it appear larger. In the two apartments there are no less than six windows, very prettily draped, whereby a London sun loyally does its best in an erratic climate to oblige the Princess, and an extensive view is obtained across St. James' Park to the south, and over the old Palace, Clarence House, and Stafford

House, to Buckingham Palace and the Green Park. Her Royal Highness's wardrobe-room—that indispensable adjunct of Royalty—is on the second floor over the kitchen; that of the Prince being on the other side of the house over the offices. Ordinary people's garments can usually be stowed away in a comparatively small compass; but to be a Prince or Princess entails the possession of such a variety of State-robes and uniforms, that it is hardly surprising to find a large apartment devoted to the housing of them, with every imaginable contrivance for this purpose. In connection with this department, it may be mentioned that the Princess has two dressers and a wardrobe-woman.

Of course, it is in the privacy of her own suite of rooms that the Princess does most of her work, and indulges to the full her particular tastes. In the pre-eminently feminine accomplishment of needlework she excels, and, as everybody knows, she has a decided *penchant* for millinery. As a rule, Her Royal Highness designs her own dresses; that is to say, coloured pictures of the proposed gown are submitted to her, and she, with brush or pencil, alters the picture to suit her own perfect taste. When a gown specially pleases the Princess, she likes to wear it, and does not disdain even appearing in it a second season. Her Royal Highness is quite a collector of old lace, and possesses some most exquisite pieces, many of great value.

The Princess is very clever in designing chair-covers, worked with beautifully-blended shades of silk in a difficult, and but little known, Italian stitch; and on the subject of embossed leather-work, she is an authority.

That Her Royal Highness takes great interest in and encourages domestic industries in every possible way, is obvious, especially at Sandringham, where she has practically created the "Alexandra Technical School"—whereby already much good has been done in this direction — and maintains it out of her privy purse.

The Princess has an easel in her private rooms, and gets through a fair amount of drawing; but painting, either in oil or water colours, she does only in her studio below. Up here, she has her music-lessons—alas! no longer from Sir Charles Hallé.

Both the Prince and Princess have always evinced the deepest interest and belief in "the sweet power of music." His Royal Highness, although no executant himself, has been, as everybody knows, the prime mover in the founding of perhaps, for its age, the most successful College of Music in the world, whose students have not infrequently had the privilege of performing at concerts held at Marlborough House.

Amongst the host of distinguished musicians who from time to time have appeared there, may be mentioned the late Sir Charles Hallé, his wife, and Mdlle. Neruda—all three great favourites—the latter of whom had the honour of instructing the young Princesses in the pianoforte; Sir Arthur Sullivan, Sir Walter Parratt, Sir William Cusins, Professor Bridge, Madame Albani, and Madame Patti. But Her Royal Highness's special pleasure is the very kindly one of listening to, and encouraging *débutantes*, and Miss Ethel Sharpe's experience at Marlborough House might here be related as an example.

On May 31st, 1895, Miss Sharpe went there to accompany the young Danish 'cellist, Herr Henry Bramsen. They were received by Miss Knollys—who, by-the-way, is a good pianiste—and were ushered into the Princess's boudoir, which Her Royal Highness, and the Princesses Victoria and Maud, shortly afterwards entered. Several pieces were played, and the Princess appeared to be much pleased, and desired them to go on playing. Her Royal Highness afterwards talked—chiefly on the subject of music—to both the performers in the most friendly manner. Herr Bramsen could not speak a word of English, and was delighted when the Princess addressed him in his own familiar tongue. During the playing of a very quick movement, Miss Sharpe, in attempting to "turn over" for herself, accidentally let the piece of music fall to the ground. Instantly, the Princess jumped up with the intention of restoring it to its place on the piano, but the artiste anticipated her gracious intentions.

Marlborough House.

After playing about an hour (the instrument used was a 300 guinea Steinway "Grand," in beautiful ebonite case, selected by Signor Tosti), the Princess shook them both by the hand, and thanked them for the pleasure they had afforded her, and said she hoped soon to hear them again. No later than the week following— Sunday, June 8th — they were once more commanded to attend, and after luncheon arrived at Marlborough House, where Lord Colville of Culross cordially welcomed them. Soon after three o'clock they commenced their performance, which consisted of several solos for piano and violoncello, including works of Schumann, Chopin, Grünfeld, Popper, etc.

Amongst those present were the Duke and Duchess of Saxe-Coburg, the Dukes of Hesse and Teck, and the Prince and Princess of Roumania, some of whom came forward and congratulated the artistes. Both the Prince and Princess of Wales remembered Miss Sharpe as being a scholar at the Royal College, when she played several times before them, and presented a bouquet to Her Royal Highness on the occasion of the laying of the foundation stone of the new buildings.

"No words can express," says Miss Sharpe, "the kindness and interest which our dear Princess showed to us. Although our surroundings and listeners were amongst the greatest in the world, yet Herr Bramsen and I seemed quite at home, and no one could help feeling so when in the presence of our Princess. Our appearance that Sunday led to our being asked the following Sunday, and we left with the kind words of the Princess in our ears, saying that she "hoped we would both come again some day, and play to her."

Her Royal Highness is an excellent pianiste, and plays well on the zither, and formerly was a fairly good harpist. She still sometimes amuses herself with the dulcimer, and is looked upon as a highly-cultivated, yet kindly, musical critic.

In the large drawing-room, there are, as I have before mentioned, two "Broadwoods" side by side, and in the Indian room a fine "Brinsmead.' There is in one of the rooms an "Erard Concert Grand"; and in another a "New-Scale Steinway Orchestral Concert Grand"; and, as we have seen, a "No. 2 Grand" by the same maker, in the boudoir. But there are pianos all over the house, including a few of foreign manufacture, one being by Hornung & Möller, of Copenhagen, strictly speaking, however, of German, rather than Danish, make.

Thus, on every side there are evidences of the musical predilections of the Dublin University Doctor of Music and her daughters. Perhaps, it is not generally known that, at one time, the Princess occasionally played pianoforte solos at private gatherings in aid of charitable institutions.

CHAPTER VI.

THE PRINCE'S DRESSING-ROOM AND ANTE-ROOM—
THE PRINCE'S PRIVATE SITTING-ROOM—THE ROYAL
VISITORS' ROOMS—THE YOUNG PRINCESSES' ROOMS
—MISS KNOLLY'S ROOM—THE FIRE AT MARL-
BOROUGH HOUSE, 1865—THE TOP FLOOR.

NEXT to Her Royal Highness's *chambre à coucher*, just described, and reached by a corridor, is the dressing-room of the Prince of Wales. Between it and his private sitting-room is an ante-room, in one corner of which there used to be a spiral staircase leading to the basement. This was found to be inconvenient, and a door has been made through the wall into the office wing, so that the Prince's valet, who sleeps there, can have direct access to His Royal Highness's rooms without going a long roundabout way to reach them. In this ante-room, the Prince sees tradesmen, etc. ; in fact, it serves the purpose of a small and informal reception-room. Several trophies of war adorn the walls, which, like the ceiling, are panelled in dark walnut. Representatives of many a West-end establishment here await the Prince's pleasure regarding some question of upholstery, sartorial art, etc., etc. Should it be some novice, in whom the bump of locality is not largely developed, who has thus to wait upon His Royal Highness, it frequently happens that he is overwhelmed with confusion, when, at the close of the interview, espying a partly-opened door in the corner, he takes it to be the one by which he entered, and backs towards it. "Not that way," calls out the good-humoured Prince, enjoying the joke immensely, "that is my dressing-room," and after several frantic efforts, the distracted individual succeeds in getting clear of the Royal presence, and breathes freely once more.

If by chance, this kind of interview comes off in the dressing-room itself, the act of withdrawing is still more difficult, for the doors when closed look like the rest of that side of the apartment, and are hard to detect. So between the unfortunate man's desire to pay every attention to the Royal instructions, and his anxiety to avoid any *gaucherie* of demeanour, as he endeavours to retire, he has rather a trying time, made more so by the conviction that the merry twinkle in the Prince's eye is not there without good reason.

Blue tussore silk with white spots, a kind of handkerchief pattern, covers the walls of this dressing-room, the furniture being so placed on every side that only the upper part of this drapery can be seen; nevertheless, the effect is good.

A wardrobe is next to one of these masked doors, and adjoining it, another similar piece of furniture. The couch in front of the fireplace resembles a large divan with a head to it. About three feet wide, of brass frame work, and built low, it has a "scroll-head" supporting the all-essential pillows. A peculiar and most artistic coverlet so deftly drapes this lounge—for this is what it really looks like—forming a frill at the foot, that it completely does away with any possible resemblance it might bear to a bed—and no one would suppose it to be such. The rest of the furniture consists of a dressing-table, an easy-chair, and a few ordinary chairs.

Two windows, looking west, are curtained with modern tapestry; and this room—the same size as that of the Princess—is altogether an exceedingly cozy retreat, where the endless change of attire entailed by exalted position can be pleasantly and expeditiously effected.

So rapidly can His Royal Highness array himself in evening dress, that on occasions when he has been detained by business until ten minutes of the hour fixed for a dinner-party, he has been known to effect the necessary transformation well within the time, and to come down to receive his guests, outwardly as cool and unperturbed as Wellington is said to have been before a great engagement in the Peninsula. His Royal Highness has frequently donned *Court* dress — the decorations, etc., of course, being previously attached to his coat—in an equally short time. Only a man can appreciate the excellence of this *tour de force*.

The Prince has two valets and a "brusher"; also a courier, who acts as valet when necessary.

Many years ago, the Right Honourable W. Windham, commenting on the advantages afforded him for study when staying with Mr. Coke—afterwards Earl of Leicester—says "of the modes of existence that vary from day to day, none is to me more pleasing than habitation in a large house. Besides the pleasure it affords from the contemplation of elegance and magnificence, the objects it presents, and the images it gives birth to, there is no other situation in which the enjoyment of company is united with such complete retirement. A cell in a convent is not a place of greater retirement than a remote apartment in such a house as Holkham."

Although it cannot be called remote, the Prince's sitting-room probably affords him the same retirement as was enjoyed by Mr. Pitt's Secretary of State for War in this famous Norfolk mansion just a century ago; for it is curious how entirely every disturbing sound of the great city's life is shut out from a large London residence, especially if it be detached, and a little away from the main thoroughfare. Though so centrally situated—in the midst of a police district embracing some half-million acres, covered with the habitations of close upon six millions human beings — in the very early hours of a summer's day, so quiet is it at Marlborough House that hardly a sound breaks the stillness, save the twittering of birds in the Park, and the faint occasional whistle of some distant railway-engine; quieter indeed than many a lonely country-house, where, when once the sun is up, crowing cocks and barking dogs make sleep impossible.

Situated immediately above the Comptroller's office, and, like it, commanding from its two windows the main approaches to the house and stables, it is overlooked by the Pall Mall clubs; but as this cannot be helped, we must hope that it is congenial to the Prince's sociable disposition to be thus able to study mankind occasionally, as a diversion from strict business.

This *sanctiarium* or "private cabinet of a Prince"—approached through two arched doorways from the ante-room—is a good-sized room —28 × 25 feet—but not too large for comfort, and here His Royal Highness conducts his very vast correspondence. For writing purposes he uses a pedestal table called a "tambour." His Royal Highness, the late Prince Consort, had a similar one made for him, in consequence of having had some of his private letters abstracted from his desk. But this kind of escritoire, shutting with a spring, and which can only be opened by a golden key in the sole keeping of the Prince, precludes any possibility of its contents being tampered with.

Such a thing seems improbable enough, but Disraeli the elder declares, in his "Commentaries" (vol. I.), that Prince Charles, when in Spain with the Duke of Buckingham, wrote home to King James I. that, "by the French Ambassador's means, the Spanish Ambassador has seen all the letters that we have written to you; you are betrayed in your bed-chamber." "This, however," remarks Lord Beaconsfield's father, "was trivial compared with the magnificence of *our* Ambassador's doings at Madrid ; for Lord Bristol declared there was not a letter sent by the King of Spain to any other State, of which James I. had not a copy before it came to the place of its destination. The Earl even got at the papers in the King of Spain's private cabinet and took notes."

All round the walls, which, like the ceiling and mantel-piece, are panelled in dark walnut wood, runs a shelf, shoulder-high, containing the most beautiful and costly art objects, bronzes, and china. There are some small pictures hanging on panels and numerous brackets supporting more ornaments of every description. In fact, the room is absolutely full of *bric-a-brac*. There is also a life-like bust of the late Duke of Clarence, whose favourite dog "Vennie," a kind of silvery grey Irish terrier, is generally to be seen here with the Prince of Wales, who is much attached to it. An Indian carpet covers the floor ; the curtains are of velvet, and the furniture is upholstered in dark blue morocco. Of course there is a sofa, and several delightfully easy chairs, amongst the latter being one with remarkably comfortable curves, specially designed for His Royal Highness by a medical man in Harley Street.

The Prince at one time had in this room a green parrot, of which, it is said, he became possessed in quite an accidental manner. Unlike most of its kind from Brazil, usually difficult to train, it was a capital talker, and when its Royal master, for its delectation used to hold up a small hand-glass close to the cage, the parrot, admiring its own reflection, would call out "Oh! you pretty dear! Do let me kiss you!" or something equally self-flattering. Polly eventually went to Sandringham, where it died.

Although sometimes, the Prince joins the family-circle at the 10.30 breakfast in the reception-room, as a rule he is content with having that meal alone in his sitting-room, when it consists usually of an egg, tea—a beverage of which he is particularly fond—and toast.

In this respect, His Royal Highness is at one with an age, which has proclaimed the consumption of a hearty morning meal to be a lost art—at least on this side of the Tweed—and has pronounced two "square meals" a day, taken respectively at noon and night, sufficient for the generality of "Society" people. At Sandringham, however, when the Prince breakfasts in company with the Duke of York, he sits down to, and probably partakes of, an elaborate repast, in deference, no doubt, to his son's less advanced ideas on the subject.

On this floor, but quite on the other side of Marlborough House, looking south and west, are the Royal visitors' rooms—two bed-rooms with sitting-rooms attached. This somewhat limited accommodation precludes all possibility of house-parties, such as the Prince and Princess delight in when at Sandringham, especially in the shooting season.

In these bedrooms the furniture is in bamboo-style, and principally of pitch-pine, the curtains are silk and the carpet velvet pile. Whenever the King of the Belgians pays a visit to Marlborough House, he occupies the room with the southern aspect, wherein is a brass bed seven feet long. There used to be one measuring but six feet six inches, and the day following its occupation by His Majesty, a man of no slight stature, he made a humorous suggestion concerning his personal dimensions to his Royal host, and a bed with the necessary additional inches was at once obtained.

In the sitting-rooms adjoining, the carpets and curtains are like those of the bed-rooms, and the furniture is of ebonized wood inlaid.

Ascending to the second floor, we find the sitting-rooms and bed-rooms of the Princesses Victoria and Maud, directly over their Royal mother's apartments. Simply, but well furnished in mahogany, their boudoirs are extremely comfortable, with rich velvet pile carpet, chintz curtains, easy chairs, couches, writing-tables, pianos, photographs, engravings, pretty work-baskets and bags, beautiful plants and flowers, and all the endless objects so dear to the feminine mind.

The signature of any one who has disappeared from sight, like Nansen—around whom the darkness and ice of the unknown North Pole has closed, whose sprawling autograph protected by glass may be seen at the Savage Club traced on the green painted wall behind the chairman's seat—is always more or less pathetic. But when the handwriting is that of one who has journeyed to the "undiscovered country from whose bourne no traveller returns," it becomes sacred. Such is that of the late Duke of Clarence, seen in one of his sister's rooms. Entering the apartment one day, he drew off his diamond ring, and with it wrote on the window-pane the date and his name, "Eddy." Shortly afterwards, the present Emperor of Russia happened to come into the room, and, seeing the Duke's work, followed his example by inscribing underneath, the name by which *he* was familiarly known, "Nicky."

Last year, a pleasant surprise was planned by the Prince and Princess of Wales for their daughter, Princess Victoria. By a kindly conspiracy, they contrived that she should be absent on the evening preceding her birthday. No sooner had she left Marlborough House, than a present was swiftly conveyed to her room, and the door securely locked. The next morning the young Princess was delighted

and surprised to find there, one of Bechstein's
mediæval upright pianos in a dark mahogany case
with gilt fittings, a gilt plate thereon, bearing the
inscription, "Victoria. From Papa and Mama,
July 6th, 1895." It was enthusiastically pronounced
to be the nicest piano she had ever played upon, and
as the young Princess is a capital executante, she
should know something about the subject. Signor
Tosti, who is a kind of informal musical director
and adviser to the family, selected this instrument,
and, indeed, several others at Marlborough House,
where he is a great favourite. It will be remembered that this gifted artist was in the habit of going
almost every evening to York House in the old
Duchess of Cambridge's time, and singing to her.

The young Princesses' bed-rooms are very pleasant, and prettily adorned—unpretentiously furnished in mahogany, with the usual couches, easy
chairs, fancy tables, etc., the bedsteads being of
brass. Their Royal Highnesses have each a
"dresser;" they have their own special footmen,
two each—one on, and one off, duty. That the
young Princesses are devoted to their mother
is no secret; neither is the fact that they would
have never been persuaded to leave her, to form
any mere conventional alliance suggested by
state policy; their "hearts must go with their
hands," and this is why the nation's sympathy
spontaneously springs forth and blossoms abun-
dantly as the day approaches for Prince Charles of

Denmark to claim his English bride. Under the admirable training of her mother, Princess Maud has developed all the excellent domestic accomplishments which she shares with her sisters. Moreover, she possesses a buoyant and vivacious disposition, that source of brightness in any home; and, like her father, she is a lover of sport in all its forms. The sailor Prince from "over the sea" has scored a great success in winning so charming a life partner, and must be heartily congratulated. From time to time, shadows have brooded, and clouds have gathered, deepening into darkest night, over the home-life of Marlborough House, since first the voices of Royal children were heard in its old rooms. But the coming union so full of promise, may be the herald of brighter days, and a return of the sunshine and gaiety that seemed at one time always to smile on the home of the Heir Apparent.

On the east wing of the floor just referred to, Miss Knollys has an apartment—sitting-room and bedroom combined, the bed being screened off in one corner. The furniture is black and gold, and the room full of charming screens, photographs, ornaments, etc., and is exceedingly pretty, and the very essence of comfort.

Adjoining is a room, used as a receptacle for odds and ends, but sometimes converted into a bed-room.

Turning back, we come upon three "visitor's

rooms," all with maple furniture inlaid with purple wood.

Close to the young Princesses' apartments, is a room formerly occupied by their governess, Mdlle. Vauthier— "Maddie" as they lovingly called her —to whom they were devotedly attached, and who, after being with them thirteen years, left to be married to the wealthy Mr. Johnson, of Farringdon, Devon, formerly M.P. for Exeter. The wedding took place early in the afternoon of Saturday, July 26th, 1890, at St. George's, Hanover Square, and was honoured by the presence of the Prince and Princess of Wales, and the Princesses Victoria and Maud of Wales. It was one of the weddings of the season. The sub-dean of the Chapels Royal officiated, assisted by the rector of Farringdon; and when it was all over, the bride was most affectionately greeted by the Princess and her daughters. Amongst the innumerable presents were two massive silver bowls from the Prince and Princess, and a beautiful bracelet set with diamonds, rubies, and pearls, from the Princess of Wales.

This floor used to be called the "Nursery floor," and thirty-five years ago was the scene of a fire that originated near the Royal Visitor's room below, and which, had it occurred in the night, might have been most disastrous. The evening "special" of July 4th, 1865, startled its readers by the following announcement:—" Pall Mall was in an uproar this afternoon. H. R. H. the Prince of Wales' kitchen chimney was on fire, and the roof of Marlborough House was alive with footmen and grooms passing buckets of water from the cistern. Among them the Prince of Wales was seen to be working. Shortly, Lord Palmerston, Lord Derby, Lord de Grey and Lord Granville were there, and two fire-engines came. The fire was subdued just before we went to press."

Such was the brief journalistic description of the incident. But Lieutenant Colonel Armytage, Captain of the Queen's Coldstream Guards, who was on duty at St. James' on the day of the fire, has kindly furnished me with a personal narrative.

Sometime after luncheon at the Guards' Club, which overlooks the rear of Marlborough House, Colonel Armytage noticed smoke issuing from the roof above the east wing, where the Royal nurseries were situated. Suspecting something was wrong, he at once ran round to the Palace, and called out the Guard—some twenty-five in number—the emergency warranting this exceptional proceeding. They rushed for the fire-engine, which always stands ready in the Engine-Court of the Palace, and ran it across the road, and by the side-door into the garden. Instantly attaching the hose to the most convenient hydrant, they proceeded to the scene of the fire to render all assistance in their power. There they found His Royal Highness in his shirt sleeves energetically turning water off from taps, which was conveyed by the servants in pails and large jugs on to the roof, where the fire was supposed to be situated.

"I am glad you have come," exclaimed the Prince, to Colonel Armytage, and they both straightway began to rip up with tomahawk-hatchets the whole of the floor, until at last the source of the mischief was traced to the ventilating shaft. An entrance effected to the cock-loft, revealed the exact position of the conflagration, and the hose being skilfully directed, the flames were soon extinguished, not, however, before the staircase was absolutely flooded with the continual stream of water which came pouring down; so that when Captain Shaw—who answered the call to Watling Street with commendable celerity—arrived with his three engines, he could not professionally refrain from exclaiming "Hullo! what's all this mess of water!" the amateurs, in their zeal, having used an unnecessary quantity of this precious fluid. Naturally, the Princess was much alarmed, and her first utterance to the gallant Colonel was, "Is there any danger?" to which question he was then happily able to give a reassuring reply. Together with her infant son, Her Royal Highness was removed to another part of the house, but she could not resist coming back from time to time to see what was going on. Some of the servants in an excess of precaution began to remove pictures and furniture, but were luckily intercepted, or the confusion would have been still greater. It was during the ripping up of the flooring that the Prince nearly fell through the rafters. He was as black as a sweep, and covered with dust from the old flooring, which was in a state of complete dry-rot. After Captain Shaw, who was left in charge, had restored the premises to a state of safety, Colonel Armytage withdrew his men to the Guard-room.

In Captain Shaw's official report, he states, curiously enough, that the premises were not insured, a precaution since fully observed.

To complete the description of the sleeping accommodation at Marlborough House. On the two upper floors over the offices, are bedrooms for the unmarried equerries, the librarian, and the head valet, Mr. H. Chandler, successor to Macdonald, a very smart, intelligent servant, who died a little while ago, and was much esteemed by the Prince.

Above the domestic offices, overlooking the quadrangle, are the bed-rooms of the steward, chief cook, pages, and others.

Lastly, on the top floor of the main building—added to the original structure during the extensive alterations in the year 1870—the Princess's three dressers, the Prince's other two valets, and many other servants are accommodated.

At one room only—next to that of the Duke of York's, on the second floor—do we pause. It is locked. But we know that within its walls, where everything remains just as it was at the time of the

Duke of Clarence's untimely death, are many of the playthings of his childhood, inanimate metal and wood, yet sentient and eloquent with the tenderest associations. What household has not some such reliquary, where tiny shoes and garments, never again to be worn by the nestling that has gone, or some battered toy once caressed by baby hands, moves to agony the sorrowing father and mother. "Never morning wore to evening, but some heart did break," since the days when our first parent mourned for Abel the slain, and David sent up that bitter cry for Absalom.

Pessimistic is the tone of modern writing, and "vacant chaff well meant for grain" is all the consolation that much of our modern philosophy can offer to poor human grief.

> "That each who seems a separate whole
> Should move his rounds, and fusing all
> The skirts of self again, should fall,
> Re-merging in the general Soul,
>
> "In faith as vague as all unsweet :
> Eternal form shall still divide
> The eternal soul from all beside,
> And I shall know him when we meet :
>
> "And we shall sit at endless feast,
> Enjoying each the other's good.
> What vaster dream can hit the mood
> Of Love on earth?"

CHAPTER VII.

HOW MARLBOROUGH HOUSE WAS SETTLED UPON THE PRINCE OF WALES—THE HOUSEHOLD AND DOMESTIC ARRANGEMENTS—THE PRINCESS'S HOUSEHOLD.

AND now, how did Marlborough House come into the possession of H.R.H. the Prince of Wales?

Marlborough House and grounds are, and always have been, Crown property, as we shall presently see; and it is somewhat remarkable to find Mr. John Timbs stating in his "Curiosities of London" (edition of 1885), that in the year 1817 the mansion was *purchased* by the Crown for the Princess Charlotte and Prince Leopold.

On Friday, July 26th, 1850, the then Prime Minister, Lord John Russell, appeared at the bar of the House of Commons with a message from the Crown. Having been called upon by the Speaker, his lordship advanced to the table and said: "Her Majesty, being desirous that the mansion called Marlborough House should be appropriated as the residence of H.R.H. Albert Edward, Prince of Wales, after he shall have attained eighteen years of age, has recommended to her faithful Commons, to *enable her* to make such provision as may most effectually accomplish the said purpose. "In pursuance of Her Majesty's most gracious message, I propose that the House shall resolve itself into a Committee on Monday next to take it into consideration."

In the House of Lords, on the 29th of the same month, the Marquis of Lansdowne read a similar message from Her Majesty, but rather differently worded, recommending the House to *concur* with her in making the settlement. On the following day, their Lordships duly took into consideration the Queen's communication, and the noble Marquis, in moving that the address to the Crown in reply should be unanimously adopted, observed, "that it was only necessary for him to explain that the object of this arrangement was to secure in a suitable part of the metropolis, a fitting residence at a future period for H.R.H. the Prince of Wales. It might be asked why it was necessary to secure such a residence at present? The fact was it had occurred to the Members of Her Majesty's Government, and the suggestion had met with the approbation of Her Majesty herself, that it might be desirable to appropriate Marlborough House, which had been vacant by the unfortunate death of the late Queen Dowager, to the object of displaying the collection of pictures which by the munificence of the late Mr. Vernon had recently become the property of the country. There was a general desire that that collection should be placed in a situation where it could be seen with advantage, and Her Majesty's Government thought that until a National building could be provided for it, Marlborough House might be appropriated for that purpose. But as that was not the ultimate object to which the Crown proposed to devote Marlborough House, it became expedient to secure it by express provision for the future residence of the Prince of Wales. That was the main reason for making this arrangement, but economical considerations which were of great importance at the present moment were also in favour of it."

After a few remarks from Lords Brougham and Redesdale, the Address was put and agreed to, *nem. con.*

On the previous evening, however, the 29th, the proceedings in the Commons were not so uniformly pleasant. The House resolved itself into a Committee to consider the Royal message, and after the Chairman had put the question, a discussion followed in which the financial economist, Mr. Joseph Hume, took a prominent part. He argued that it was premature to make any such arrangement, as the Prince was only nine years old, and that many years must elapse before the Mansion could be used by him. He denied that Marlborough House belonged to the Crown, maintaining that it was originally built for the Duke of Marlborough by the nation, and that it therefore reverted to the nation, and not to the Crown.

Mr. John Bright was of opinion that no necessity

had been shown for settling the question at that particular time.

Lord Seymour explained that the public revenue would benefit to the extent of £800 per annum by the removal of the old stables and the extension of Carlton Terrace. And the Chancellor of the Exchequer argued that the proposed arrangements would be most advantageous to the public, at which remark Colonel Sibthorp exclaimed amidst much laughter, "Oh dear!" A division followed in a thin House. Sixty-eight voted for the resolution, and fifty-six against it, giving the Government the small majority of twenty-two, wherewith to send up the faithful Commons' address to their Sovereign.

All this time the little Prince was quietly pursuing his early studies to the best of his abilities, and was probably unconscious of the business being transacted for his special benefit.

The Act of Parliament, 13 & 14 Vict. Chapter 78, is dated August 14, 1850, and it was thereby made lawful for Her Majesty by Letters Patent under the Great Seal, " to grant, settle, and assure all that Capital Messuage, or Mansion, called Marlborough House, situate near the Palace of St. James' in the county of Middlesex, late in the occupation of Her late Majesty Adelaide, the Queen Dowager, and all out-houses and other buildings, Courts, Yards, Gardens, Grounds, and Appurtenances to the said Capital Messuage, or Mansion, belonging or appertaining, to or in trust for His Royal Highness, Albert Edward, Prince of Wales, in such manner that he may have and enjoy the same immediately after he shall have attained the age of eighteen years, and thenceforth, during the Term of the joint lives of Her Majesty and his said Royal Highness."

The Act—a very short one—proceeds in its final clause to provide for the erection of suitable coach-houses and stables; and for this purpose, empowered the Commissioners of Works to expend a sum not exceeding £5,000, to be derived, if possible, from the sale of the material of the old stables and coach-houses, formerly attached to Carlton Palace.

After the Act of Settlement had received the Royal assent, and Letters Patent under the Great Seal had been duly issued, the historic old house entered upon a career of public usefulness by temporarily housing the Vernon Collection.

In 1859, the sum of £15,000 was voted for fitting the house as a residence for the Prince of Wales, it having become rather dilapidated, and the amount formed an item in the general Estimate for Royal Palaces, 1859-60. As time went on, it became necessary to prepare it for the reception of the Prince and his youthful bride, who took possession in the month of April, 1863 —as inscribed over the fire-place in the saloon— and extensive and absolutely necessary alterations were commenced.

The three reception rooms on the garden front were converted into a noble apartment; the two small rooms and spiral staircases flanking these three apartments were thrown into the two now known as the Indian-room and dining-room. An equerry's room, and one also for the lady-in-waiting, together with a portico entrance, hall entrance and corridor, were added to the north front. Suitable stables were built, and many other improvements elsewhere described, were effected for the future sovereign of Great Britain and his consort.

In addition to these and other necessary works undertaken from time to time by the Crown, His Royal Highness has, since his marriage, expended upon repairs, alterations, decorations, etc. sums amounting to a total of over £50,000, thereby greatly enhancing the value of the property.

Electric lighting has been introduced throughout the house; the offices have been embellished, and everything that could possibly increase the comfort of those around him, has been added by the Prince at his own expense.

This thoughtfulness for others is an instinct with the Prince, and is constantly being translated into kindly actions, not only in connection with the gravest concerns of life, but with homely every-day occurrences. Not long ago, an employé who had served His Royal Highness for many years was temporarily invalided at Sandringham. While thus enjoying a rest from work, a hocky-party on the

THE INDIAN ROOM, SOUTHERN END.
Taken by special permission of H.R.H. the Prince of Wales.

frozen lake came off, in which all the Royal party took part, and the important post of keeping the goal was assigned to the convalescent. At the conclusion of the game, the goal-keeper, chilled by enforced inaction, commenced to pull off his skates behind a tree, but the Prince " spotted " him, and taking him by the arm, "commanded" him to " come and drink some hot wine," which he much appreciated.

Of state, properly so-called, there is none kept up at Marlborough House, though the household is arranged similarly to that of most Royal establishments — which are microcosms, so to speak, wherein each individual has his or her particular duty distinctly defined, thus described by Thackeray : " The King commands the first lord-in-waiting to desire the second lord to intimate to the gentleman-usher to request the page of the ante-chamber to entreat the groom of the stairs to implore John to ask the captain of the buttons to desire the maid of the still-room to beg the housekeeper to give out a few more lumps of sugar, as His Majesty had none for his coffee, which probably is getting cold during the negotiation."

At Marlborough House, the chief officials of the Prince of Wales' household, and the members of his domestic establishment are somewhat as follows, but their precedence one of another it is not in every individual case possible to define with absolute exactness. First in importance, if not actual rank, come the Comptroller, Treasurer and the Private Secretary; then the Lords-in-Waiting, Grooms-in-Waiting, and the Equerries. After whom are the house-steward, the pages, valet, the piper, head-cook, and wine-butlers, the serjeant-footman and the footmen, ushers of the hall, pastry men, upholsterers and carpenters, messengers, housekeeper, wardrobe-women, lady's-maids, dressers, housemaids, who together with the rank and file, male and female, constitute the serving and waiting department of this extensive *ménage*.

The Prince, as a rule, expresses his commands to the Comptroller, who in turn communicates them to the house-steward. But the impulsiveness of His Royal Highness sometimes makes him over-ride etiquette, and, breaking the bonds of routine, he gives his orders direct to the functionary who can the most quickly execute them. On special occasions H.R.H. frequently communicates them personally to the house-steward. This individual's post, it may be readily understood, is a responsible one, and was for many years held by Mr. J. Cross, a tried and trusted servant who had previously been the Prince's personal attendant, when travelling in the east with the late Dean Stanley. After a voyage to Australia in search of health, he has now retired upon a well-earned pension, his place being taken by Mr. J. Blackburn, who at one time was serjeant-footman, and afterwards page. When the Prince goes to Sandringham or elsewhere, the house-steward travels in advance in order to arrange matters. During the day he wears ordinary dress, but when on duty in the evening his livery is like that of the pages, except that his stockings are black silk instead of white. He attends only *big* dinners, however, when he waits solely upon the Prince.

As important, if not more so, is the post of chef, worthily filled by Mr. J. Menager.

His Royal Highness exhibits a refined interest in the daily menu, which, "composed" by the chef is always submitted to him on great occasions—and indeed at most other times—when perhaps the Prince strikes out a *plat*, and inserts one he considers more desirable—his decision invariably being a good one. Upon the menu of the previous day His Royal Highness frequently writes his criticism, for the chef's serious consideration.

Although the Princess takes little or no part in the elaboration of the daily "bill of fare," should she desire a special dish—for even Princesses have their likes and dislikes—her orders are communicated through Miss Knollys or the lady-in-waiting to the page, who conveys them to the chef.

While on the subject of dinners, it may be interesting to those not absolutely familiar with Royal etiquette, to hear that the Prince and Princess always sit at the side of the table in the middle facing one another.

8

Footmen, clad in scarlet coat and vest, blue plush breeches, white silk stockings, and low shoes, convey the dishes from the kitchen, while the pages 'wait.' When an unusually large party is given, outside help is had in, chiefly that of retired Marlborough House servants, who, of course, don the Royal livery. On these occasions—as stated in the account of the Derby Day Dinner—one waiter is assigned to every Royal guest, and one to every two other guests.

Formerly at grand dinners the Prince was always waited upon by his favourite valet, Macdonald, a handsome dark young fellow fully six feet high, clad in picturesque jäger costume. His father had been jäger to the late Prince Consort, and was a splendid-looking man of a stature considerably over six feet. Since young Macdonald's death, however, the Prince has had no jäger, and is waited upon ordinarily by the pages, and—on greater occasions—by the house-steward.

Wherever the Prince dines—whether in the midst of a public assembly, or in the home of an intimate friend—his own servant accompanies him, and attends exclusively to him throughout the banquet, receiving the dishes, etc., from the general servitors, and handing them to his Royal master.

This etiquette is observed towards all the members of the Prince's family. A friend of mine was much struck by the rapt assiduity with which the late Duke of Clarence was waited upon by his servant, at a banquet given by the then Chairman of the School Board, at the Goldsmiths' Hall, in the Jubilee year. By-the-way, the young Prince sat between the Archbishop of Canterbury and Mr. Diggle, and as the time drew nigh for him to respond to the toast of the evening, he turned to the latter—his host— and whispered, "I shall be very glad when I have got safely through with this," revealing a piece of paper concealed under his plate, whereon was written the heads of his speech.

As to the pages, they are a superior kind of footmen, and not necessarily youthful as one is apt to imagine. They wear a dark navy blue coat with gilt buttons, and black trousers, their State livery being a similar sort of coat, black velvet breeches, and white silk stockings with gold garters. They are in attendance in the rooms, and not upon landings and staircases.

His Royal Highness is wonderfully considerate to his servants, by whom he is almost adored. In order to avoid discovering any dereliction of duty on their part (which seldom happens), he takes care that they shall receive an intimation when he is coming their way. This more particularly applies to his visits to the stables. Or should a servant happen to appear fatigued, the Prince at once observes it, and lets him off duty, substituting another in his place.

An interesting member of the domestic household who takes the part of an extra page is the Piper. He wears the Royal Stuart highland costume, and is supposed to (and often *does*) patrol the garden between the hours of eight and nine in the morning, piping to wake the family. He also, when commanded, plays outside the house while the family dine.

An important servant during railway-journeys, is the serjeant-footman. He presides over the "gentlemen's gentlemen," and arranges their liveries, etc. He, with the head-valet, always travels with the Prince, and occupies a small compartment adjoining the saloon, to be readily within call. The only distinguishing feature of his dress, which like that of the other footmen is of Royal scarlet, is a red cord worn round the neck whence is suspended his badge of authority stowed away in his pocket. These two attendants must by this time be adepts in the art of railway-travelling, as their Royal master is incessantly moving about from place to place. As an example, take the month of October last (1895). His Royal Highness returned from Denmark on September 29th, and on October 1st left London on a visit to Mr. C. Beckett, M.P., near Leeds, returning to Marlborough House on the 3rd. Two days later, he travelled to Deepdene, near Dorking, to become the guest of the Duchess of Marlborough and Lord William Beresford, coming back to London on the 7th. The next day, he started off to Newmarket, where he remained until the 11th, and then went to Easton Lodge, Essex, to stay with the Earl and Countess of

Warwick. On October 14th, His Royal Highness left Easton and returned to London, and in the afternoon quitted the metropolis to visit Mr. and Mrs. Vyner at Newby Hall, Yorkshire. On the 19th, he arrived at Sandringham from Newby Hall and returned to Marlborough House on October 21st (Trafalgar Day). The next day, he again visited Newmarket, returning to London on the 26th.

There would be fewer accidents if the precautions adopted when the Prince is travelling were universally applied. For instance, when the General Manager receives an intimation from Marlborough House that His Royal Highness intends journeying, say, to Wolverton, he immediately sends a notice to that effect to every station-master along the line, warning them to keep the line clear. Sometimes, in the case of the Queen, a pilot engine is sent on ahead, or plate-layers are stationed within sight of one another throughout the entire length of the journey, so that a mishap is almost impossible. The speed is usually at a uniform rate of forty-five miles an hour. Since safety is thus, as it were, guaranteed by their presence, no wonder that when the Prince and Princess patronize trains from which the outside public are not excluded, there is a rush for tickets by persons desirous of being conveyed by the same satisfactory means.

These trips, by-the-way, are all duly paid for, and pretty heavy is the item of travelling in the Prince of Wales' annual expenditure. Some people seem to imagine that Royalty travels at the expense of the railway company shareholders, just as others hardly credit the fact that Royalty pay rates and taxes like all the rest of the oppressed and long-suffering army of householders—only heavier.

The Princess of Wales' household is on a modest scale. Nominally—because not now in active service—her Chamberlain is, as everyone knows, Lord Colville of Culross, K.T., who has most worthily filled this honourable and responsible office for many years, escaping by force of his unquestioned merits, the envy and detraction so often directed against a man in his position. In his very early days he was in the army, and for twenty years he worked hard as the Conservative whip. He has twice been Chief Equerry and Clerk-Marshal to the Queen, and was once Master of the Buckhounds.

Then there are the ladies of the bedchamber—"bedchamber women" as they are officially called—and the Princess's private secretary, Major General Stanley Clarke, C.M.G.

One or other of the equerries together with one of the ladies-in-waiting, are always in attendance at Marlborough House during the season; they do not sleep in the house, but come and go as required.

It is upon Miss Knollys—officially one of the bedchamber-women, but in reality Her Royal Highness' companion—that the attention of the public is generally fixed; and with reason, for she is the Princess' *umbra*, and *alter ego*. Miss Knollys is always with the Princess, keeps her diary, receives visitors before they are ushered into the Royal presence, and, being the soul of faithfulness and kindness, has throughout her many years of devotion to Her Royal Highness, done her utmost to make smooth the sometimes stormy path of Royal life.

What is that life at Marlborough House like, say, in the middle of June and July ? And how do the Royal couple ordinarily pass the day ?

CHAPTER VIII.

THE HOME LIFE OF THE ROYAL FAMILY AT MARL-
BOROUGH HOUSE—SKETCHES OF SOME OF THE
HOUSEHOLD OFFICIALS.

MOST of the Royalties of Europe—the German Emperor, the King of Italy, the Queen Regent of Spain, the Kings of Sweden and Roumania, the King of the Belgians, and the Empress Frederick—are early risers. But the Princess of Wales cannot be included in this category.

About nine o'clock, a *chota hazri* is served to Her Royal Highness, who may elect to have her *déjeûner* proper in her boudoir, or with the family in the reception room—and it may be observed *en passant* that the Princess is particularly fond of plovers' eggs, which, when in season, are almost always found on her breakfast table.

There are no hard and fast lines at Marlborough House as to the first meal of the day; it being, in this respect, pleasantly unlike many otherwise excellently arranged houses, where, unless all the members of the family and guests appear at prayers preceding breakfast, the host and hostess look unutterable things.

After breakfast, correspondence has to be attended to—letters containing every kind of application to be considered, and those from relatives and friends to be answered.

The Princess may then do a little painting, some leading artist, perhaps, being consulted thereupon in the studio; or "try over" some new music; occupy herself with embroidery, etc.; hold solemn council on matters of dress; or accomplish some photography, a favourite pastime indulged in, as a rule, in the garden.

About eleven o'clock, when the weather is favourable, little Prince Edward of York—"King David" as he is affectionately called—and his baby brother, Prince Albert Frederick, leave York House in a dark-coloured perambulator, with their white-robed nurse, and, escorted by a stalwart police-officer in plain clothes, pass through the side door by the German chapel, to pay a long visit to their grandmama and aunts. Prince Edward is a dear little child and is made a great pet of by everybody, romped with, kissed, and—as the author of Pickwick has it—"handed about like something in the nature of refreshments."

When the Princess calls at York House, she almost always goes on foot, and dresses so unpretentiously, that even the sentries have been known not to observe her, and have failed to present arms. Sometimes she walks thither alone—followed, of course, by a private detective.

Then, too, there are morning visitors to be received, as a rule, in the reception room; if very intimate, in the boudoir. Later on in the day—though usually in the morning—the Princess may receive some deputation in the saloon; or in the big drawing-room, perhaps a *débutante* pianiste or singer (probably introduced to her notice by an intimate friend, such as the Marchioness of Dufferin and Ava), whom she delights by her kindly encouragement and unstinted praise.

A morning drive is often taken, or some shopping done in the plain brougham; but even this modest excursion is not always accomplished without annoyance, as, somehow or other, the news spreads that Her Royal Highness is in such and such an establishment, and a small expectant crowd collects at the doors thereof.

Luncheon, a bright and cheerful meal served at 2.30, sometimes in the reception-room, sometimes in the Indian-room, is often an elaborate ceremony. The following is the menu of a *déjeûner* given in honour of the Empress Frederick of Germany, when twenty-two persons were present.

Huitres naturel.
Saumon Cisileé Souché.   Sauce Genvoise.
Tournedos D'Agneau à la Vatel.
Chaudfroids de Volailles Parisienne.

Caultons Rôtis au Cresson.
Pigeons de Bordeaux.
Salades de Laitues.

Asperges Froids à l'Huile.

Nectarines au Riz à la Coudé.
Soufflés Glacées à la Leopold.
DESSERT.

Marlborough House. 123

After luncheon, the real business of the day begins; the fulfilment of the endless engagements booked weeks and weeks in advance, which a residence in London must inevitably bring to so exalted a lady. These assume an infinite variety of forms: the presiding over the proceedings of some charitable institution; the giving of prizes to successful competitors of some guild or public society; the laying of a foundation-stone; the opening of a new hospital ward, school-of-art; or—but this is seldom —of some splendid bridge within the Metropolitan area, etc., etc., etc. Then there are annual episodes, such as the viewing of the "Trooping of the Colours" at an early hour from the old official residence of the Commander-in-Chief. Now and again, ceremonials of an exceptional character have to be gone through: an Imperial Institute is opened with great splendour; a Royal wedding takes place; or Her Royal Highness holds a drawing-room at Buckingham Palace on behalf of the Queen. For this latter function, the Princess, with true motherly feeling, superintends the toilettes of her daughters, herself arranging the feathers in their hair, and giving all those finishing touches to their adornment, beyond the ken of the masculine mind. And, by-the-way, this reminds us that in the old days when the Royal children were in the nursery, nothing delighted the Princess more than to have an opportunity of donning a large flannel apron, and bathing her beloved little ones herself. It is also said of the Empress Frederick, that when her children were little, she used to take the greatest pleasure in brushing their hair the last thing before they went to-bed.

But to return. A visit of an hour may be paid to the Horse Show at Islington, which the Prince and Princess seldom fail to patronize, or to the Military Tournament held in the same hall. Or, perhaps, they watch a polo-match at Hurlingham for a short time; or honour with their presence a Fairy Fête at the Botanical Gardens, and give delight to hundreds of expectant little ones, particularly when the Princess, struck by an entry representing her favourite Red Cross Society, in an impulsive moment bestows an extra prize upon some little nursing sister clad in silver and grey, amid shouts of sympathetic applause.

The Princess has intense admiration for all bravery and acts of heroism, and now and again receives in the afternoon persons who have distinguished themselves thereby. In the case of Mrs. Grimwood, Her Royal Highness with all her family, grouped themselves around her in the large drawing-room, and eagerly questioned her, listening with rapt attention to that heroic lady's modest account of her thrilling adventures and sufferings in Manipur, and of her escape bare-footed through the steaming jungle.

Then there are private visits to be paid to intimate friends, and members of the Royal family.

THE LARGE DRAWING-ROOM, EASTERN END.
Issued by Special Permission of H.R.H. the Prince of Wales.

Facing page 174.

Afternoon tea is served usually at five o'clock—in summer time often in the garden under the shade of the elm-trees, one or two guests frequently being present, when plenty of light, desultory talk goes on. Visitors may not call upon Her Royal Highness unless commanded (except to enter their names in the visitors' book); the Princess sending word, even to her intimate friends, when she desires to see them.

After tea, a drive in the Park is often taken—the drive we all know. Then back to Marlborough House to partake, perhaps, of an early, hasty dinner, to enable the family to attend the opera, some *premier* or popular play; though now that the electrophone has been installed at Marlborough House they are able to enjoy this form of entertainment quietly at home. Or the dinner may be enjoyed leisurely and *en famille* at the usual hour of 8.30, followed by music, etc. Or it may be one of State—forty or fifty guests invited to meet some distinguished Royal personage.

Besides the usual social ways of spending an evening either in their own home or that of their friends, there are at intervals State balls to attend at Buckingham Palace by command of Her Majesty; or State concerts, when such singers as Patti, Macintyre, Ben Davies, and Bispham from their rather awkward gallery charm their hearers, and Sir Walter Parratt and his six hundred picked instrumentalists ably overcome the defective acoustic qualities of the beautiful concert-room.

Sunday is a quiet day at Marlborough House, and, as at Sandringham, carriages and horses are used as little as possible, though the Princess always drives to Church, even when attending the Royal chapel close by (seldom patronized by her, however), and which she enters through St. James' Palace by Mrs. Martin, the housekeeper's room, by whom she is conducted to the Royal closet. This is not so much a pew as a small "apartment," wherein so many Sovereigns and Royalties of the reigning dynasty have listened, and often slumbered, while some famous divine has held forth ; and where George III. used to attend early prayers on the coldest of the winter mornings, and beat time with his roll of music while the anthem was being sung

The Princess occasionally goes to Christ's Church in Down Street, and she used to be fond of the service in the German chapel, where she sat amongst the other people in the first or second pew. In the afternoon, Her Royal Highness sometimes goes to All Saints, Margaret Street, where her attendance is made manifest to the initiated—as indeed, at all the other churches—by the presence of the detective at the door. The Princess very much likes the service at St. Anne's, Soho, where she is frequently seen, and of whose "beautiful music" she often speaks with delight. In the evening, the Princess never goes to Church.

It has been remarked that of late no notification of the Prince and Princess of Wales' attendance at any particular London church has been made in the papers. The custom of publishing it was discontinued because it was found that crowds of idle people swarmed round the doors of the church the Sunday following the announcement, in hopes of Their Royal Highnesses appearing, greatly incommoding them on their arrival.

Though the Prince retires to rest at a late hour, he rises about eight o'clock, and has his first breakfast about nine o'clock alone in his sitting-room. The amount of hard work he gets through, and his capacity for transacting the most important business is immense. As to the number of letters he receives, they alone would drive ordinary people distracted. But experience and tact enable him to dispose of his vast correspondence with celerity and exactness. Like that of the Queen, the contents of the Prince's mail-bag varies considerably, though the number of letters delivered during the year at Sandringham and Marlborough House, including those addressed to members of the household, cannot fall very far short of the number with which Her Majesty is accredited. With the instincts of a thoroughly business-man, the Prince—at any rate, in the morning—opens and peruses all letters addressed direct to him, reserving the most important communications for discussion with his trusted advisers, and the purely private ones for his own consideration. With regard to the miscellaneous matter, he turns down the edges of most of it, and writes thereon a few words indicating the kind of reply he desires the officials in the room below to send out.

The nature of the unclassifiable mass of appeals is sometimes ridiculous enough. Some one yearns to know what hymn His Royal Highness likes best, or whether he collects walking-sticks. At one time, frequent requests were made for locks of the Royal hair—a loyal desire which even the tresses of Absalom would not have satisfied. People with grievances write to him expecting their wrongs—often imaginary—to be instantly set right. Letters from all parts of the globe are replied to as courteously and expeditiously as possible, without respect of persons. In fact, the humbler the applicant, the more certain he or she is to receive at least a *gracious* answer, even when the petition cannot be granted. As for "begging-letters" pure and simple, they come in shoals, and are seldom, if ever, entirely ignored.

To the branch post-office at the bottom of St. James' Street, is entrusted the great mass of "mail-matter" issuing daily from Marlborough House when the family are in residence, and, I believe, a slight extension of time is allowed in the despatch of evening mails, for the accommodation of Their Royal Highnesses. At Sandringham there is a regular post-office inside the house, where money orders can be obtained, telegrams and cables sent, precisely as in a public post-office. Of course, it is only for the use of the household.

From ten to half-past ten o'clock, the Prince generally sees his private secretary, Sir Francis Knollys, and afterwards the equerry, to arrange about the carriages, etc., required. The Comptroller of the Household, as a rule, arrives at Marlborough House about eleven o'clock, and is conferred with by the Prince, at some length, on the various subjects brought forward by the contents of the day's letter-bag, on the household arrangements for the day, and on his public engagements, made weeks in advance. Indeed, one has only to observe the doings of the Prince published in the papers day by day, to perceive how completely every minute of his time is occupied.

Hardly is His Royal Highness's conference with Sir Dighton Probyn at an end, before he is due elsewhere—has some business appointment in his sitting-room, or perhaps a deputation to receive in the Indian-room, or a meeting to attend there (on which occasions a small table is previously carried in), etc.

Sometimes the Prince strolls into the stables, accompanied by Lord Suffield or one of the equerries.

Personally, His Royal Highness is most punctual, happily contriving, in Shakespeare's words, to "come pat, betwixt too early and too late," thus not making *painful* his punctuality — the only virtue Sydney Smith managed to render disagreeable, for he not only frequently arrived at dinner before his hostess was dressed, but went so far as to receive the remainder of her guests for her. The Prince, never wastes time himself, and he recognizes its value in others. On one occasion, a mercantile man, who had often been summoned to Marlborough House to give certain technical advice, arrived there, as usual, at the time appointed, and at once sent up his name. After waiting an hour, he was beginning to fear something had gone wrong, when the Prince himself appeared, and good-humouredly exclaimed, "Oh! here you are, B.! Why have you not sent up your name? You cannot expect me to come down on purpose to see whether you have arrived!" B. respectfully explained that his name had been given to the servant long ago; so the delinquent was sent for, and reprimanded by the Prince, who observed with considerable emphasis, " Recollect Mr. B.'s time is money," and might have added Nelson's dictum, " Time is everything. Five minutes makes the difference between a victory and a defeat."

Before luncheon, the Prince sometimes goes out in his beautiful little brougham to pay friendly visits, or occasionally—but very rarely—he may be seen walking up St. James' Street ; or the few passers-by in Ambassadors' Court may catch sight of him going on foot towards York House or Clarence House.

Such an episode as a levée at St. James' Palace brings with it an entire break in the day's programme, and involves a considerable amount of fatigue, borne, however, by His Royal Highness without any visible or outward sign. He has to don his field-marshal's uniform, by no means over comfortable one would imagine in hot weather, and if it be a "collar-day," the full insignia of his various orders, and to stand from two o'clock until four, while a constant stream of gentlemen in levée dress file past him and make obeisance. At the conclusion of this function, the Prince occasionally receives at Marlborough House one or other of the Ambassadors.

His Royal Highness necessarily has to preside at the periodical meetings of the council of his own Duchy of Cornwall. These are held, sometimes in the afternoon, sometimes in the morning, at the offices of the Duchy at Lancaster Gate, the last attendance including the Earl of Ducie, the Earl of Leicester, Lord Playfair, Mr. Charles Alfred Cripps, Sir Nigel Kingscote, Sir Dighton Probyn, and Mr. Holzmann.

Most of us know that the Prince, like the Queen (the Duchess of Lancaster), is the first personage in a particular county; but all do not perhaps remember that the Duchy of Cornwall was originally presented to Edward the Black Prince as a kind of

9*

private estate, which included all the "gold, silver and tin" that might be found beneath the surface of the county. Until the birth of her eldest son, the Queen enjoyed the revenues of the Duchy, when they were made over to the infant Duke. Needless to say that during his minority, H.R.H. the late Prince Consort so admirably represented him in the administration of the estate, that the revenues were considerably increased and the whole property placed upon an improved footing which has continued to this day, although the position of Cornwall—that land of soft climate and never failing flowers—is not so flourishing as it once was.

Or His Royal Highness may have to take the chair at some gathering of quite an exceptional kind—to consider the interests, maybe, of a British school at Athens for the study of Greek archæology, etc. At Marlborough House, he may preside over a meeting of Governors of Wellington College; or a meeting to start a memorial fund for a deceased and popular soldier (as in the case of the late General Sir Charles C. Fraser); or, as President of the Council of the Society of Arts, present the Albert Medal to some fortunate individual. He may act as chairman on the committee of a Lady Hallé, or other testimonial; in fact, there are endless meetings requiring his presidency, besides those of the British Museum trustees, and numberless institutes of which he is Chief. On behalf of the Queen, the Prince may open, at the Imperial Institute, a congress on some such subject as the development of railways throughout the civilized world; or in some poor neighbourhood inaugurate an institution for affording to a working population increased facilities for educating themselves in art and literature. Amongst the innumerable philanthropic schemes which His Royal Highness has personally studied, is that of the "common lodging-house," involving now and again the opening of a block of new buildings. He may pay a private visit in his capacity of Patron—accompanied by the Princess—to one or other of the great metropolitan hospitals; or he may go to the National Portrait Gallery, or inspect some special painting in one of the west-end galleries; or honour some world-renowned firm such as Maple & Co., with his presence. He may deliver an address at the Literary Fund gathering, on "the benefits which the modern world owes to the printing-press"; or he may have to welcome at Charing Cross Station, some foreign sovereign on his arrival in London; or receive some foreign minister accredited to, or retiring from, the Court of St. James; or be present at a *déjeûner* in the Hall of some venerable City Company; or he may put in an appearance at the House of Lords for a short time. Then there are the dinners in aid of funds for the multitudinous charities patronized by His Royal Highness, and once a year the Royal Academy banquet, which he generally attends. In addition to all this, the Prince does not overlook popular exhibitions, and disdains not a trip on the " Big Wheel."

But the foregoing gives an imperfect sketch of the varied and immense amount of work that the Prince gets through every day of his life in London. In short, as the Bishop of Rochester has remarked, " very few people in England can rival the Prince as to the multitude of different interests and varied agencies for good with which, as the year passes, he comes in contact."

His Royal Highness more than earns the welcome relaxation of the opera or theatre, or genial hour spent quite late at a smoking-concert after a dinner more or less formal, say at the " Métropole," given by various regiments, or a banquet in honour of a retiring field-marshal, or—once in a generation maybe—of a popular commander-in-chief.

Above all, I must not forget to mention that when the Grand Lodge holds its meetings in its old Hall —restored and beautified after the fire—His Royal Highness presides. Seated on a throne surrounded by its mystic symbol of a double triangle, supported right and left on the dais by his chief subordinates, the silk banners on golden poles grouped in front, while life-sized oil paintings of many a Royal Grand Master of the past silently look down on the solemn proceedings in which they can no longer participate, and the hidden organ rolls with weird reverberation along the wagon-shaped roof, the Prince, covered with splendid insignia and jewels, stands forth as the impersonation of all the charitable and benevolent instincts of our great Empire, which in the case of English Freemasons, last year found practical expression in their subscription of £65,000 towards the wants of the poor and the afflicted.

No wonder that with such a master nearly the whole of the *personnel* at Marlborough House are Freemasons, and models of discretion and reticence, and that the " Marlborough House Lodge " to the ordinary outside world is securely and thoroughly " tiled."

All the beautiful jewels connected with the Prince's high office as Grand Master, are kept at Marlborough House, and carried backwards and forwards by a trusted official as occasion may arise for ceremonial laying of foundation stones and the like. One evening the gentleman in question had, as usual, charge of the ornaments, previously selected by His Royal Highness; but while engaged with the Prince in earnest conversation, one of these escaped his attention and was forgotten. The Prince did not notice the omission until later on, when perceiving a certain ornament on the neck of a prominent foreign and Royal Mason, the absence of his own was made manifest to him, whereupon His Royal Highness, turning to the officer, with a look of reproachful rebuke simply said, " You know I trusted to *you*, who are responsible for this," and quickly recovering from his slight annoyance, never referred to it again.

Marlborough House.

Before describing in the next chapter a few of the most interesting balls, dinners and fêtes given at Marlborough House during the Prince's married life, I should like to refer to some of the officials who play so important a part in the household of the Prince and Princess.

Sir Henry Ponsonby's death last year drew forcible attention to the enormous amount of work that attendance upon Royalty entails, and to the fact that absolute self-identification with the highest interests of a regal master or mistress, demands the exercise of those special gifts, remarkably developed in him—tact, and good taste.

Royalty, all the world over, is much like some fair garden set out with rare and costly flowers, but environed by a formal and ceremonious ring-fence possessing however, certain legitimate entrances. It is one of the duties of the chamberlains, secretaries, and all court officials, from the highest to the lowest, to see that no unauthorized intruder attempt to force his way through any accidental gap in the barrier, and pleasantly and courteously to let him perceive that though each leaf of the hedge be glossy and comely to look upon, it bears a goodly array of prickles.

Not an entirely enviable position, perhaps, is that of these court officials, but one requiring considerable courage, and we must suppose this is why retired soldiers are so often chosen to fill the more important posts about the Sovereign.

Both Major-General Ellis and General Stanley Clarke are names familiar "as household words" to readers of the movements of the Prince and Princess of Wales, recorded in the daily papers. General Sir Stanley Clarke is secretary to the Princess, and in his capacity of equerry, has on more than one occasion accompanied the Prince on the Continent. His pleasant manners to all, are well known. When at Sandringham, he lives at Appleton House, a quaint old place about three miles from headquarters.

Major-General Arthur Ellis is one of the most active members of the Prince's staff, a thorough man of business, and one of the most accomplished art-critics in London. His beautiful residence at Portland Place, contains an infinite number of *objets d'art*, and is especially rich in Eastern arms of all kinds.

Lord Suffield used to be in the Seventh Hussars. He is a fine horseman, and has been in his day one of the most daring riders to hounds. He is still, as ever, the model of fashion, and the soul of hospitality and good nature. He went out to India with the Prince, with whom he has always been a special favourite.

That which Miss Knollys is to the Princess of Wales, her brother, Sir Francis, is to the Prince— his *alter ego*. No need even to indicate his personal appearance, so familiar is it to everyone. He is the second son of the late Sir William

Knollys—the first Comptroller to the Prince of Wales' household—and, as all the world knows, occupies the most important position of Private Secretary to His Royal Highness, managing the endless matters of detail at Marlborough House, often demanding the most delicate handling, with the clear perception and cool judgment that so strongly characterize him, and for which with other valuable qualifications he deservedly holds so high a place in the Prince's estimation. In addition, he is very kind-hearted, and his opinion on most matters may be depended upon, though of course like all mortals he is liable to error; but who amongst us is exempt? As an American diplomatist once said "He who makes no mistakes makes nothing."

Last of these brief sketches is Sir Dighton M Proybn, K.C.B., K.C.S.I., V.C., who, like Sir Philip Sydney the chevalier soldier, and like Bayyard, is without fear and without reproach. Born in the year 1833, he entered the army in 1849, and served on the trans-Indus frontier from 1852 to 1857. As all recollect, he was ever to the front during the Indian Mutiny, when his famous "horse" continually swept, like an avenging scourge, through the ranks of the mutineers. He commanded the 2nd Punjaub cavalry, and was present at the siege of Delhi. In the year 1889 the Victoria Cross was conferred upon him for distinguished and numerous acts of gallantry throughout the Mutiny. At Agra, when his squadron charged, he got separated from his men, and, being surrounded, slew two of the rebels, and single-handed fought an infantry sepoy, whom he defeated. He also captured a standard in the presence of the enemy. "These" said Sir Hope Grant "are but a few of this young officer's deeds of gallantry." Sir Dighton, when in town, lives at No. 1, Buckingham Gate, whence every morning he walks or takes a hansom to Marlborough House. Luncheon, if he desire it, he has in the royal household dining-room; and when his family are out of town he sometimes makes use of the bedroom always at his disposal at Marlborough House. His delight when at Sandringham—where he resides at Park House, an unpretentious-looking villa just outside the park wall—is to look after the Prince's fine hackney stud, and his judgment is much valued on all equine questions. He always accompanies the Princess when in England, and it is almost superfluous to add that both the Prince and Princess repose the utmost confidence in him. Indeed, no happier selection could have been made than that of Sir Dighton Probyn in the year 1877 to succeed Sir William Knollys in his responsible position as Comptroller of the Household.

People cannot help being struck with one thing that characterizes all the male members of the Prince's Household, and this is their excellent mode of dressing, and the newness of their hats. No one ever saw any gentleman connected with Marlborough House wearing one of Lincoln and Bennett's, or Heath's productions that was in the least degree shabby. Whether, like the colonel in a popular novel of last season, who every day seemed to have on a new one, they purchase 365 hats in the year, is an unsolved problem! But the fact that their head-gear always looks new, is indisputable and interesting.

CHAPTER IX.

NOTABLE BALLS, FETES AND GARDEN PARTIES AT MARLBOROUGH HOUSE.

IN the early married years of the Prince and Princess, it was their custom to give a ball, both on the anniversary of their wedding day, and at the close of the season. They were held in the drawing-room and Indian-room, and when very large the dining-room was made use of too, the orchestra being usually accommodated in one corner of the drawing-room, where it could be heard by all.

A marquee, approached by a covered way, was erected in the middle of the lawn, where supper was served, and two other tents, one on each side, were used for the same purpose.

Probably the most brilliant and interesting entertainment ever given at Marlborough House was the Fancy Ball, July 21st, 1874, rivalling in its completeness, the Queen's Restoration Ball at the time of the Great Exhibition. On this occasion the three large rooms were utilized, and the bands were stationed in temporary structures outside the windows. Opposite the garden entrance was the principal tent, there being another running up against the dining-room.

As in the case of the Queen's Ball, in 1851, the announcement of the coming event created the greatest excitement in fashionable circles, and, punctually at half-past ten o'clock, the favoured guests, numbering nearly fourteen hundred, arrived; singularly few of the invités being unable to obey the Royal command.

Instead of restricting the costumes to one particular period, the Prince and Princess wisely left the choice of dress to individual taste, except in the case of those who were to take part in the special set of quadrilles, whose attire had been carefully planned beforehand, and who assembled in a room set apart for them, while the general company awaited their Royal host and hostess in the saloon and drawing-room.

Lord Colville of Culross, as a cavalier, received and marshalled the guests on their arrival, the magnificence and beauty of whose varied dresses called forth frequent ejaculations of approval.

Presently all eyes turned towards the door through which the Prince and Princess were expected to appear, and, ere long, the strains of the National Anthem proclaimed their presence, and, preceded by six guards of honour, followed by Prince Albert Victor and Prince George of Wales in pages' dresses of white satin doublet, trunk hose, and short cloaks, to the music of a polonaise played with great spirit by the Hungarian band, they slowly passed through an avenue of admiring beholders, who could scarce refrain from openly expressing their admiration. Arriving at the other end of the room, they forthwith opened the ball with two quadrilles danced in succession, the Princess appropriately heading the "Venetian," and the Prince the "Vandyck" set.

Lord Hartington, in grey satin and black velvet, personating to perfection the Venetian grandee, had the honour of having as partner the Princess of Wales, while to the Duchess of Sutherland fell the distinction of dancing with H.R.H. the Prince.

Naturally the lovely and most becoming Venetian dress of the Princess attracted every one's attention. It was formed of an under-robe of pale blue satin, completely covered with gold embroidery and precious stones, while the over-dress was of ruby velvet, embroidered in gold and silver, lined with blue satin. Her Venetian cap of ruby velvet was literally covered with jewels, and it required no great effort of imagination to picture her as presiding over some magnificent reception at the Doge's Palace in the palmy days of the time-honoured Italian republic.

At the Junior Carlton Club there hangs an excellent full-length portrait of the Prince of Wales, cane in hand, by Mr. A. Stuart-Wortley. It is quite in Vandyck style, the pose and dignified bearing being singularly like that of Charles the First, whom the Prince represented at this ball. His Royal Highness's dress faithfully reproduced the great painter's presentment of the martyred King. A short velvet cloak, whereon sparkled a diamond star, set off his costume of maroon satin and velvet, a large black cavalier hat, adorned with a long drooping white feather, looped up with an aigrette of brilliants, high buff boots, long spurs, and sword, produced a most realistic effect, while round his neck hung the blue ribbon and jewelled order of the Garter; the long locks, *de rigueur* in such a personality, curiously altering His Royal Highness's appearance.

The first two quadrilles were, as before stated, danced in succession, but the two following, viz., the "Card" and the "Fairy Tale" sets were performed simultaneously. Lastly, came the "Cavalier and Puritan" quadrille, carefully pre-arranged in every detail of dress, as had been the case with those that preceded. When the Puritan ladies stood up to dance, each with a gallant Cavalier officer wearing the becoming uniform of the Life Guards of that period, their appearance was most bewitching. They wore caps, and muslin fichus over plainly made dresses of pale grey cachemire, short enough to display their pretty little buckle shoes. But their bright smiles and genial demeanour towards their partners completely belied the demure and decorous nature of their attire. The names of these delightful Cavaliers and Puritans were as follows :—

Colonel Baillie and The Marchioness of Bristol.
Colonel Owen Williams and The Marchioness of Blandford.

Marlborough House. 145

Hon. O. Montague and Countess of March.
Mr. Wisham and Lady Walter Scott.
Lord Carrington and Viscountess Folkestone.
Hon. S. Egerton and Viscountess Duplin.
Colonel Ewart and Lady Suffield.
Mr. Johnstone and Lady F. Montague.
Mr. Townsley and Mrs. R. Bulkeley.
Mr. Percival and Miss Princep.
Lord H. V. Tempest and Miss Graham.
Mr. Duncombe and Miss Holford.

All who took part in the "Fairy Tale" quadrille were warmly congratulated upon the strictness with which the old traditions of apparel had been maintained, and the consequent fidelity of their impersonations. H. R. H. the Duke of Connaught essayed, for once in his life, the character of "Beast," but so gently did he "do his spiriting" that he might conceivably have fascinated the lovely Miss Graham, who represented "Beauty." Viscount Mandeville was the "Fairy Prince," and danced with Lady F. Gower as the "White Cat." Lord F. Gordon Lennox as the "Prince," had for his partner "Cinderella," represented by Lady Anne Coke. The Earl of Rosebery, as "Bluebeard," was temporarily mated with "Fatima," in the person of Lady E. Fitzmaurice. And Mr. Albert Grey was a remarkably graceful "Puss in Boots," in company with Lady M. Scott, the "Mary, Mary, Quite Contrary" of our childhood.

10

" The " Card " quadrille was danced by a perfect gathering of Royalties and other notabilities :

    The Duke of Athole and H. R, H. Princess Christian.
    Lord Suffield and Duchess of Athole.
    Mr. A. Rothschild and Marchioness of Queensbury.
    Mr. de Murietta and Miss Scobeloff.
    Viscount Duplin and Mrs. Keith Fraser.
    Hon. W. Gerard and Mrs. G. Forbes.
    Prince Civier and Hon. Miss Gerard.
    Count Montgelas and Donna Carraciola.
    Lord Claud Hamilton and H. R. H. Princess Louise.
    Mr. A. de Murietta and Miss Stevens.
    Viscount Vaurener and Hon. Mrs. Carrington.
    Mr. H. M. Stanley and Mrs. C. Forbes.
    Hon. H. Bourke and Mdlle. Musurus.
    Mr. Farquharson and Lady S. Macnamara.

A somewhat remarkable feature in this ball was that mothers and their daughters danced in the same sets of quadrilles, and it was often hard to determine which of the two generations looked the more beautiful — the magnificent costumes of the Vandyck period, being so specially becoming to a certain maturity of beauty. Never before, perhaps, had so many lovely women been seen at one and the same time in any square dance as in these fancy quadrilles. It was the realization of a poet's dream :—

> " A thousand hearts beat happily; and when
>   Music arose with its voluptuous swell,
> Soft eyes looked love to eyes which spoke again,
> And all went merry as a marriage-bell."

As the participators in these charming *contre-danses* gracefully took up their allotted positions, the on-lookers had an opportunity of studying at leisure their various costumes. Princess Christian, as " Queen of Clubs," carried out her personification in a dress of red velvet and silver tissue. Princess Louise, in blue velvet, represented the " Queen of Hearts." The Duchess of Manchester wore a Venetian costume in white and gold. The Duchess of Leeds, in yellow satin, trimmed with pearls, and wearing a large hat with plumes, looked as if she had just stepped out of an old Vandyck picture. Her Grace the Duchess of Marlborough walked in the family ancestral home in the dress and character of Rubens' wife—black satin, trimmed with lavender, and with a long black veil for a head dress. As a· Spanish lady, the Duchess of Wellington looked very handsome; and the Duchess of San Theodo appeared in a perfectly gorgeous dress such as Titian loved to paint, and personated the Queen of Cyprus.

These are but a few samples taken here and there from the bewildering maze of richly attired feminine humanity, the colours of whose dresses and the reflection of whose jewels, dazzled the eye and enraptured the artistic sense.

One could gaze upon Court beauties of the time of Queen Philippa, Charles VI. of France, and of Charles IX. The period of Louis XVI. was represented by the ever-youthful Marchioness of Aylesbury, in white satin and gold. Lady Diana Huddlestone was Marie Antoinette, a character whom the Honourable Mrs. Stoner had also selected to personate. Lastly, Miss Charlotte Knollys, as Charlotte Corday, completed these reminiscences of the Revolution and the Reign of Terror.

The gentlemen made a brave show, and bore themselves right well, in spite of that secret uneasiness felt by every Englishmen when he puts on other than the orthodox dress of the nineteenth century. In the garb of Queen Elizabeth's Master of the Buckhounds appeared the Earl of Hardwicke. Lord Strathnairn assumed the character of the Great Duke of Marlborough, and the Earl of Shannon was dressed to a nicety as an Irish peasant.

Throughout the evening, Lord Charles and Lord Marcus Beresford, considerably enlivened the proceedings as Court Jesters, in the traditional dress with cap and bells. Mr. Disraeli, then at the outset of his memorable six years' reign as Prime Minister, disdaining fancy dress, wore the official uniform of Her Majesty's Cabinet Ministers, with which he somehow seems always associated. At the conclusion of the special quadrilles, dancing became general to the strains of two bands — Coote and Tinney's, and the Hungarian—placed, as we have seen, in covered stands outside the windows of the Indian-room and dining-room, *i.e.*, at the opposite extremities of the three ball-rooms.

A magnificent supper was served in marquees erected in the garden, and, the night being fine and dry, it was most pleasant to be under canvas. All corners and angles were concealed by lovely banks of the choicest flowers; the supper-table looked simply superb, and the whole scene was quite fairy-like.

Up to a very late, or rather, early hour, dancing was kept up, and the sun had been long risen before the last carriage rolled away from the quadrangle.

> " All night had the roses heard
> The flute, violin, bassoon ;
> Till a silence fell with the waking bird,
> And a hush with the setting moon."

Accurately to recall and describe every entertainment of interest connected with Marlborough House throughout the three-and-thirty years of the Prince and Princess's wedded life, is not within the scope of this work, the exigences of space admitting of references to but two or three examples of the overflowing hospitality of the Royal couple.

Throughout the early part of the year 1863, Marlborough House was still undergoing repairs necessary for its occupation by the Prince and his young bride. But with the characteristic dilatoriness of the British workman, it was not fully finished, nor were the "men" out of the house when His Royal Highness and the Princess came into residence on May 28th of that year.

An evening-party and ball were given on June 29th, 1863, and there were a few small dinner-parties during the season, but no special festivities.

In 1865, on the anniversary of their wedding-day, a dance was given.

On the 3rd of June in the same year, Prince George (Duke of York) was born at Marlborough House, and a few days after the event, Her Majesty the Queen, paid a welcome and motherly visit to the Princess and infant son.

February the 20th, 1867, was the natal day of their first little Princess (also at Marlborough House); shortly afterwards the Princess of Wales became seriously ill, continuing so for some months, and causing great anxiety to everybody. The Queen called frequently, and the King and Queen of Denmark came over to see their beloved daughter. To the great delight of the nation, the bulletins announced at last that a speedy recovery might be expected; and on the 10th of May, the infant Princess Louise was christened in the large drawing-room in the presence of an imposing family circle.

Soon after this, Princess Alice of Hesse arrived at Marlborough House on a visit with her children, but it was not until quite the end of the summer that the Princess of Wales was pronounced convalescent, and able to leave town.

Five years later, on Thanksgiving Day, February 27th, one of the most impressive processions ever witnessed in London, passed the gates of Marlborough House, whose Royal owner had the previous year been stricken down with an all but fatal disease.

During the year 1875, the old mansion resounded with busy sounds of preparations for the Prince's departure on a prolonged tour through the Queen's Indian Empire, whence he did not return until May, 1876. The scene as he left London with the Princess from Charing Cross Station, was most impressive. Her Royal Highness travelled as far as Calais with the Prince, whom she did not again see for many months.

From 1876 to 1887, all kinds of Royalties, foreign Potentates, and notable people, were from time to time entertained at Marlborough House. In the latter year, the Viceroy of Egypt, Tewfik Pasha, was magnificently received by the Prince of Wales, who gave a banquet in his honour. The same year saw the inauguration of the "Derby Day Dinner"—given to the members of the Jockey Club—since become an annual institution.

At an early hour on Saturday, March 10th, 1888, was heard

> " The clash and clang that tells
> The joy to every wandering breeze,"

announcing far and wide the advent of the "silver-wedding day" of the Prince and Princess. Unfortunately, a day or two previously, the sad news of the Emperor Frederick's death had reached England; and thus some of the festivities were postponed *sine die;* and, at the Prince's special desire, the military bands that otherwise would have played in the house, were countermanded. At 11.30, the Queen, who had come up to town from Windsor for a few days, drove over from Buckingham Palace in a carriage drawn by four horses. Her Majesty was accompanied by the Duchess of Albany, and Prince and Princess Henry of Battenberg; the Dowager Duchess of Roxburgh, General Gardiner, and the Hon. Colonel Carrington being in attendance. H. M. the Queen was thus the first to congratulate the Prince and Princess on the auspicious occasion. His Majesty, the King of the Belgians, and the members of our Royal Family, soon followed the Queen's example, and throughout the morning, the entire "staff" of Marlborough House were occupied—as they had been the day previous—in receiving the endless gifts that came pouring in from all quarters—in some cases brought by the donors themselves. Bouquets and baskets of lovely flowers—those most graceful tributes of loyalty and devotion—came in shoals.

All the Ambassadors called, and were personally received by Their Royal Highnesses.

Of course, for the day, court mourning was

abandoned, and the Princess looked charming in a pale cream-coloured costume, trimmed with lace. Her daughters — as usual, dressed alike — wore pretty spring-like costumes.

In the interval between these visits of ceremony and the luncheon at Buckingham Palace, the Royal pair received some of the deputations in the Saloon, to each and all of which the Prince made most gracious and charming speeches.

First in order, came the household servants, presenting a massive and symbolical silver tankard. Then the ladies who had twenty-five years before been bridesmaids to the Princess, brought a beautiful silver casket, which Her Royal Highness must have regarded with feelings of peculiar emotion. Next came the Danish residents of Newcastle, whose gift was an exquisite model of the Princess's old home, the Castle of Fridensborg. As head of the Committee of 365 ladies "personally acquainted" with the Princess, the Marchioness of Salisbury brought a lovely diamond tiara—their united gift.

At 1.30, Sir Henry Ponsonby and other members of the Queen's Household were admitted, and presented a set of valuable silver vases. The Earl of Lathom, representing the Freemasons of Great Britain, gave a beautiful diamond butterfly to the Princess, accompanied by an illuminated address to their Grand Master. Fifty gentlemen — intimate friends of His Royal Highness —

appeared next, with three magnificent "Pilgrim flagons."

Two o'clock struck, and the entire family drove to Buckingham Palace to have luncheon with the Queen, and were loudly cheered *en route*.

No sooner had they returned to Marlborough House, when they had to receive Sir Polydore de Keyser and the Corporation, who brought a silver model of the Imperial Institute, whose foundation-stone had been laid the previous year; the Prince, in accepting this gift, made a most felicitous speech.

In the evening, a splendid banquet was given, remarkable as being the first dinner at which the Queen had been present at Marlborough House during its occupancy by the Prince and Princess of Wales. Her Majesty was accompanied by King Leopold II.; and the guests included all the members of the Royal Family who could possibly attend.

The Queen, who wore mourning dress, was received on her arrival by the Prince and Princess; and at 10.30 p.m. left Marlborough House, escorted by the Life Guards, and made a long detour on her way to Paddington Station through Pall Mall, Regent Street, and Oxford Street, to view the illuminations.

Nearly all the presents were arranged for inspection in the Indian-room on long tables covered with blue cloth, richly embroidered in gold. Both fire-

Marlborough House.

places were completely hidden by exquisite flowers, while the floral gifts, baskets of rarest orchids, and bouquets without end, filled the air with their perfume.

Among the principal donors were :—

- H. M. the Queen — A gigantic silver flagon with snake handle curiously mounted.
- H. R. H. the Prince to the Princess—A cross of glorious diamonds and rubies.
- The young Princes and Princesses of Wales—A silver model of " Viva," their mother's favourite horse.
- T. R. H. the Duke and Duchess of Edinburgh—Sapphire and diamond ornament.
- The Emperor of Germany—A set of very fine China vases.
- The Emperor and Empress of Russia—Ruby and diamond necklace.
- Their Majesties, the King and Queen of Denmark—Two chests containing silver gilt tea and coffee services.
- The King of Greece—A gold punch-bowl.
- H. M. King Leopold II.—Antique silver flagon.
- The Empress Eugénie—An exquisite model of H. M. S. the " Great Harry."
- Prince Waldemar of Denmark—A set of very ancient and valuable silver spoons.
- H. R. H. the Duke of Cambridge—Silver cake basket.
- Their Highnesses Prince and Princess Edward of Saxe-Weimar—A silver cup, and beautiful cushion embroidered in silver.

On the following day, Sunday, the Prince and Princess attended divine service in the afternoon at the Chapel Royal, Whitehall, the sermon being preached by Dr. Magee, Bishop of Peterborough; and thus fittingly closed the celebration of the twenty-fifth anniversary of their wedding-day.

Of all the events that occurred during the year 1889, the principal one was that of the marriage of Princess Louise of Wales to the Duke of Fife on Saturday, July 27th. Being the first wedding in the family circle, it naturally created great interest, and created no little excitement in the household, while to the public generally it was a cause of hearty congratulation.

After the wedding, the bride and bridegroom drove in the Duke of Fife's carriage, by way of Piccadilly and St. James' street, to the bride's old home, where a select garden-party had assembled, and where the numerous and costly presents were displayed. At four o'clock, the happy couple took their departure, the Prince of Wales leading the new Duchess to the open carriage awaiting her in the garden. The Princess showed considerable emotion when saying good-bye to her eldest daughter, and stood fondly and tearfully watching her until quite out of sight.

Up to the year 1880, the garden-parties of the Prince and Princess of Wales (with the exception of their very first one, which was held at St. James's Palace) were given at Chiswick House, lent to them for this purpose by the Duke of Devonshire. It is an historical mansion, well known to society, in which Charles James Fox, and later on, George Canning, died.

An immense picture, 16 feet by 7 feet (unfortunately destroyed by fire in 1879), painted by Chevalier W. Desanges, and entitled "A Garden Party at Chiswick," showed the lawn in front of the two groups of fine old cedars of Lebanon, with the Queen in the centre of a most distinguished company, and altogether gave a very fair idea of what these aristocratic assemblies were like. Subsequently, it was found to be more convenient to give these delightful entertainments nearer to the centre of fashionable life; and, as all the world knows, they are now held annually at Marlborough House, and regarded as the culminating feature in the season's gaiety.

Amongst memorable garden-parties, was one given by the Prince and Princess of Wales in honour of the Shah's visit, which Her Majesty the Queen graced with her presence. It is the custom on all these occasions for the guests to alight at the Marlborough Gate entrance facing Friary Court not passing through the house—a privilege reserved for members of the Royal Family. Perhaps it is not generally known that the officers of the Household Cavalry on duty for the day at the Horse Guards, together with the officers of the Foot Guards, are always invited to these garden-parties, and appear in their uniform, thus adding life and colour to the already brilliant scene.

Lowering were the skies, and falling was the barometer on the morning of July 5th, 1893, and faint were the hopes that the weather would be propitious for the great event of the season — the grand garden-party at Marlborough House on the eve of the Duke of York's marriage with Princess May of Teck. All the dismal meteorological prognostications resulted, however, in nothing worse than a grey, but sultry afternoon; so warm, indeed, that it taxed all the energies of the attendants in the refreshment-tents to satisfy the tremendous craving evinced at an early hour for ices and iced beverages so lavishly prepared for the two thousand excited and expectant guests assembled in the well-shaded grounds to meet the Queen and to do honour to the joyful occasion for which the Prince had summoned them. (The catering for these *al fresco* entertainments is all done at home, except on special occasions such as this, when the resources of Gunter or Searcy are requisitioned for some of the lighter confectionery.) The compact crowd of visitors gathered round the porch through which the Queen was expected to pass down into the garden were doomed to disappointment, as Her Majesty, to avoid the necessity of ascending the steps from the main entrance, had her carriage drawn up outside the offices, and made her appearance in the garden through the adjoining side-door.

She had been preceded by the King of Denmark who escorted the Princess of Wales, and the Queen of Denmark conducted by the Prince.

Her Majesty, after taking a very short walk on the lawn, sat down in front of a beautiful Indian pavilion expressly erected for her accommodation at the western end of the garden, where, surrounded by Royalties, Highnesses, and Serenities, she partook of some refreshment, and subsequently held a kind of informal court, the distinguished company crowding round her to see all they could of what was going on. A touching incident occurred, which must forcibly have reminded the Queen of Lord Rolle's attempt to perform his act of homage at her Coronation. From time to time, there were presented to Her Majesty a number of persons with whom she freely conversed in a most pleasant and lively manner. Amongst them, was Lord Ebury, weighed down by his burden of ninety-two years, but who, in the ardour of loyalty, insisted upon kneeling before the Queen. Her Majesty very considerately forbade this effort, and spoke to him in so kindly a manner that the grand' old peer was visibly affected.

The Queen fluently conversed in their native tongue with two of the Indian Princes, whose gorgeous dress outrivalled that of most of the ladies present. It was remarked with what a particularly cordial greeting the Queen received the respectful salutation of the Marquis of Salisbury, who paid his *devoir* with the perfection of courtly grace and dignity.

Mr. Holland Tringham with facile and faithful pencil has reproduced this historic scene. Many notables of the land are grouped about their Sovereign, in close attendance upon whom stand out in clear relief, the picturesquely-attired Indian servant, and the active figure of Sir Dighton Probyn, whose chief anxiety throughout that memorable afternoon, was to keep a clear passage for the august Lady, whose comfort he was specially charged to look after. Most energetically did he discharge his difficult task. The fashionable crowd became at times rather hard to control, and it is said that, in the excitement of the moment, and fearful lest the Queen should be in the least degree incommoded, he requested innocent Mr. Gladstone and our present noble Premier to " stand back and make more room "! Certain it is that curiosity—excusable, perhaps—on the part of many in this aristocratic assemblage, for the time being eclipsed their good manners. Ladies excitedly jumped upon chairs, and strained their necks to watch the Queen drink tea, delightfully proclaiming their good view of this proceeding to the less fortunate ones below ; and when, at last, Her Majesty moved from one part of the grounds to another, they literally flocked after her with a rush and flutter somewhat alarming, and suggestive of bright insects encircling some attractive regal flower—

The Garden Party at Marlborough House, July 5th, 1893.
Original Drawing by Holland Tringham. By special permission of H.R.H. the Prince of Wales

"Thick swarm'd, both on the ground,
And in the air."

Whether, when the Queen rose to take her departure, the Lord Chamberlain did, or did not, precede her with his wand, and by moral persuasion endeavour to clear the way, must ever remain an undecided point. But that a certain amount of confusion prevailed there can be no doubt.

Two military bands—the Royal Horse Guards Blue, under Mr. Charles Godfrey's care, and the Grenadier Guards, conducted by Mr. Dan Godfrey—played most excellent music throughout the afternoon. The programmes hung up in primitive style upon the elms—reminding one of Orlando's verses affixed to the trees in the forest of Arden for Rosalind to find—included amongst many sweet melodies, Mendelssohn's "Wedding March,' Gounod's "Romeo et Juliette," Verdi's "Aida," and some delightful dance music, composed for King Henry VIII. by Edward German.

In the list of invitations for this grand fête, were the names of every member of the British Royal Family, and every Royalty directly and indirectly connected therewith. Many Eastern Princes, Mahajarahs and Rajahs, Ambassadors and Diplomatists, Peers, and Commons of Great Britain and Ireland, representatives of the Church, State, Army and Navy of India and the Colonies, were assembled within the walls of Marlborough House Garden.

The following collation was served to the Royal party :—

ROYAL TABLE.

Filets de Soles Cendrillon.
Chauds Froids de Poulet Bagration.

Petits Pains à la Russe.
Bonne Bouches Princesse.
Sandwiches Variées.

Gelies Macedoines de Fruits au Champagne.
Glace Vanille et Framboise Café Glacé.
Eton Mess aux Fraises.

Petites Patisseries Assorties.
Les Fruits Variées.

Claret Cup.   Lemonade.
Raspberryade.

Everybody was dressed remarkably prettily, light tints predominating—as at Covent Garden Opera House the previous evening, when white was chiefly worn—and the effect was most pleasing.

Her Majesty was attired in black, save that her bonnet was trimmed with white lace, and white ostrich feather tips. She carried a black sunshade, edged with a puffing of white chiffon, also introduced at the ferrule. Her Royal hostess wore self-grey satin, with frills of creamy lace, and a bonnet of grey lisse, trimmed with a high white aigrette, and embroidered with pearls and silver. Princess May had donned a cream-coloured satin dress, brocaded with groups of tiny red roses, her rustic straw bonnet, with dark red velvet strings, being also trimmed with red roses.

Perhaps the most perfect gown worn that day was

Lady Iveagh's. It was of the palest mauve satin, approaching the peach blossom in delicacy of shade, veiled with silk net, and inserted with bands of silk lace of exquisite design, and of a particularly rich mellow shade of ficelle. The bodice was half concealed by similar lace artistically arranged with bands of insertion. She had on a wonderful little bonnet of pleated pale mauve lisse, trimmed with lace and shaded pansies, and her satin sunshade was covered, like her dress, with lace. Most of the guests wore the cream-coloured rose, historically associated with the House of York.

After the Queen's departure the Princess of Wales, and others of the Royal Family, lingered for some time amongst the delighted guests, and it was fully seven o'clock before the brilliant gathering had entirely vacated the grounds.

CHAPTER X.

SOME NOTABLE DINNERS AT MARLBOROUGH HOUSE—
SOME REMARKABLE PAGEANTS IN PALL MALL.

MARLBOROUGH HOUSE is so associated with hospitality that it is necessary to dwell somewhat at length on the subject of the dinners that have been given there.

"An Englishman in Paris" has told us that Dr. Véron, of the Paris Opera, once said:—" My dear friend depend upon it that it is a man's stomach which found the aphorism 'Qui va piano, va sano, qui va sano, va lontano.' A man ought not to be like a boa-constrictor, he ought not to make digestion a business apart. He ought to dine and digest at the same time, and nothing aids this dual function like good conversation."

The Prince Regent long ago recognised this truism, and assembled around his hospitable board all the wit and talent of the day; as did also Samuel Rogers, the poet-banker, whose entertainments given to his literary friends in his well-known house overlooking the Green Park, were famous for their "feast of reason and the flow of soul."

On June 29th, 1895, a notable dinner was given by the Prince of Wales to the Shahzada Nazrullah Khan, when a distinguished party, numbering in all forty-seven, were entertained, the following being the attractive menu.

PREMIER SERVICE.

POTAGES.
Tortue Claire.
Consommé Printanier à l'Impériale.

POISSONS.
Whitebait Naturel et à la Diable.
Filets de Truite à l'Andalouse.

ENTRÉES.
Escalopes de Volaille à la Richelieu.
Chaudfroids d'Ortolans à la Demidoff.

RELEVÉS.
Selles d'Agneau Printanière.
Jambon de York Poêlés au Champagne.

SECOND SERVICE.

RÔTIS.
Chapons au Cresson.
Cailles sur Canapés à la Royale.
Salade de Romaine.

LÉGUMES.
Petits Pois à la Française.

ENTREMETS.
Timbales de Pêches à la Montreuil.
Soufflés Glacés à la Cardinale.
Riz à l'Imperatrice.
Pètits Gradins de Pâtisseries Variées.

Petites Cassolettes à la Russe.

Glaces à la Napolitaine.
Petites Gauffrettes.

DESSERT.

But, alas! the poor Shahzada's religious scruples forbade his partaking of any item therein, except the *Riz à l'Imperatrice*. Nevertheless, he dined well; for he had brought with him his own cooks and his own provisions; the latter being specially prepared on a charcoal brazier in the open air in a passage situated between the kitchen and the stables, and served to him as he sat at the Prince's table. Wine, of course, he religiously eschewed, but on this occasion the temptation to swerve from his faith must have been great indeed.

In the year 1893, the Prince conceived the excellent idea of giving a series of representative dinners at Marlborough House, and in the space of a few months, eleven came off, all of which, both historically and gastronomically, were most interesting, as the following selection will show.

On Wednesday, February 8th, was given the first of these dinners and represented the Government of the day; the names of some of those present showing with what nice discrimination the guests had been selected :—The Duke of York; The Duke of Cambridge; H. E. The French Ambassador, M. Waddington; H. E. The Russian Ambassador, M. de Stael; H. E. Count de Bylandt, Minister of the Netherlands; H. E. The Belgian Minister, Baron Solvyns; Earl of Rosebery; Earl Spencer; Lord Carrington; The Rt. Hon. W. E. Gladstone; Sir Vernon Harcourt, etc.

DINER DU 8 FEVRIER 1893.
POTAGES.
Tortue Claire.
Bisque D'Ecrevisses à la D'Orleans.
Saumon Ciselé Sce. Genoise.
POISSONS.
Filets de Soles à la Valney.

ENTRÉES.
Côtelettes de Poulets à la Maréchale.
Cailles à la Souvarow.

RELEVÉS.
Pieces de Bœuf à L'Anglaise.
Gigots de Mouton Poilés Sépts Hres. au Champagne.

RÔTS.
Bécasses Rôties Sur Canapes.
Pourlardes au Crisson.
Salade à la Portugaise.

ENTREMETS.
Asperges en Branches, Sce. Mousseuse.
Beignéts à la Viénnoise.
Souffles D'Oranges à la Maltaise.

Laitances à L'Americaine.

Corbeilles de Glaces Variées.
Gradins de Pâtisseries Assorties.

A dinner to the unfortunates in the "cold shades of Opposition" came off on the 22nd of the same month, with a sprinkling of foreign diplomacy, as will be seen from the guest list :—

The Duke of York, the Marquis of Lorne, H.E. the Turkish Ambassador, Rustem Pacha ; H. E. the Austro-Hungarian Minister, Count Deym ; H.E. the United States Minister, R. T. Lincoln ; H.E. the Brazilian Minister, Chevalier de Souza Correa ; the Marquess of Salisbury, Earl Cadogan, the Earl of Mount Edgcumbe, the Right Hon. G. J. Goschen, the Right Hon. J. Chamberlain, etc.

DINER DU 22 FEBRIER 1893.
POTAGES.
Tortue Claire.
Crème D'Asperges á la Sevigny.
POISSONS.
Saumon Ciselé sce. Mousseuse,
Filets de Soles à la Joinville.
ENTRÉES.
Petits Soufflés à la Princesse.
Côtelettes de Becassines à la Perigeux.
RELEVÉS.
Dindes à L'Algérienne.
Selles de Mouton à la Nivernoise.
RÔTIS.
Cailles sur Canapés à la Royale.
Canetons de Rouen à la Rouenaise.
Salades des quatres Saisons.

Asperges en Branches.
Croutés à l'Ananas.
Mousses de Mandarines à la Valencienne.
ENTREMETS.
Casolettes à la Russe.
Melons Glacés à la Victoria.
Pâtisseries Assorties.
DESSERT.

A week later another banquet was given, somewhat difficult to classify, including as it did, representatives of Foreign diplomacy, Court officialism, Church, the Law, Art, etc. Amongst the guests were :—

H.E. the Spanish Ambassador, M. del Mazo; H.E. the Swedish Minister, M. Akerman; H.E. the Danish Minister, M. de Bille; Lord Kensington, the sub-Dean of the Chapel Royal, Lord Esher, and Mr. Alma Tadema, R.A.

Marlborough House.

DINER DU 1 MARS 1893.
POTAGES.
Fausse Tortue à la Française.
Crême D'Epinards aux quenelles.
POISSONS.
Turbots, Sauce Homards et Mousseuse.
Petites Truites au Bleue sce. Génévoise.
ENTRÉES.
Suprême à la Parisienne.
Salmi de Bécasses à L'Ancienne.
RELEVÉS.
Dindes à la Chipolata.
Selles D'Agneau Printanière.
RÔTIS.
Canetons de Rouen à la Rouenaise.
Poulets Fins au Cresson.
Salades à la Portugaise.
Asperges en Branches.
ENTREMETS.
Pêches à la D'Orléans.
Petits Soufflés Glacés à la Cardinale.
Laitances à la Diable.
Glaces à la Napolitaine.
Petites Gauffrettes.
DESSERT.

The next dinner was somewhat on the same lines—the *Corps Diplomatique* being still well to the front, the legal profession more numerously represented, and the " Society " element most pronounced. These are some of those who were able to obey His Royal Highness's commands :—

The Duc d'Aosta, the Duke of Teck, H.E. the Portuguese Minister, M. de Soveral ; H.E. the Roumanian Minister, M. Plagino ; the Italian

Charge d'Affaires, M. Bouteneff; and the first Attachés of several of the Embassies ; the Duke of St. Albans, Baron Rothschild, the Earl of Dunraven, the Earl of Cork, Lord Colville of Culross, Chief Justice Bowen, and Sir F. Jeune.

DINER DU 8 MARS 1893.
POTAGES.
Consommé Printanier à la Doria.
Crême de Pois St. Germain.
POISSONS.
Saumon Ciselé à L'Ecossaise.
Filets de Soles Diéppoise.
ENTRÉES.
Cotelettes de Fois Gras à la Strasbourgeoise.
Ris D'Agneau à la Clamart.
RELEVÉS.
Canetons à L'Espagnole.
Filets de Bœuf à la Piemontaise.
RÔTIS.
Chapons Rôtis au Cresson.
Pigeons de Bordeaux, Salade de Laitues.
Asperges en Branches.
ENTREMETS.
Petites Timbales à la Montmorency.
Ananas en Surprise.
Petites Crêmes Frités à la Victoria.
Glaces à la Venetienne.
Petites Gauffres.
DESSERT.

Perhaps the most interesting of the series was the one given on March 12th, to Mr. Henry Irving, Mr. Bancroft, Mr. John Hare, Mr. William Farren, Mr. David James, Mr. Arthur Cecil, Mr. Kendal, Mr. J. L. Toole, Mr. Charles Wyndham,

Marlborough House. 171

Mr. Beerbohm Tree, Mr. George Alexander and other eminent actors, to meet whom were invited the Duke of Fife, Sir Henry de Bathe, Captain Holford, Sir Algernon Borthwick, Sir Edward Lawson, Sir Horace Farquhar, Sir S. Ponsonby Fane, Mr. A. de Rothschild, General Sir Christopher Teesdale, Sir Charles Hall, Sir J. Monckton, Dr. W. H. Russell, Mr. G. A. Sala, Mr. F. C. Burnand, and Mr. Pinero, etc.

DINER DU 12 MARS, 1893.
POTAGES.
Tortue Claire.
Crème de Coucombres à la Royale.
POISSONS.
Escalopes de Turbots, Crême au Gratin.
Filets de Truites à la Bordelaise.
ENTRÉES.
Noisettes d'Agneau à la Parisienne.
Chaudfroids de Cailles à la Richelieu.
RELEVÉS.
Selles De Mouton à la Duchesse.
Poulardes Poilés à la Regence.
RÔTIS.
Bécasses Rôtis sur Cânapés.
Salade de Legumes.
Asperges en Branches.
ENTREMETS.
Timbales à l'Espagnole.
Dames Blanches â l'Orange.
Petites Casolettes à la Norvégienne.
Corbeilles de Glacés Variées.
Pâtisseries Assortis.
DESSERT.

Two days later, there was a most noble gathering together of gallant soldiers and sailors. In the *menu* figured amongst the *Rôtis, Petits Poussins sur Cânapés*. These *poussins*—a refinement upon the American eight-weeks-old "broiler"—were introduced as a *rôti* into the London *haute cuisine*—where they speedily became popular — by Sir Edward Lawson some ten years ago, he having come across them in Russia. They are not larger than a big quail, and, on this occasion, were a marked success. These little birds came from Sussex, provided by Bayley, the well-known purveyor of Mount Street, and the difficulty was —and always is—to obtain so large a number, say sixty, of a uniform size, one having necessarily to be provided for each guest. There is nothing new under the sun; and the serving up of such small fowl — "weaklings," Charles Lamb would have called them—is strictly classic, for the gourmands of ancient Rome, not content with the great variety of the *genus* "Columbus," used to consume as a special delicacy, field-fares fattened up for the purpose in dark receptacles under the ordinary pigeon-houses.

There were present:—The Duke of Edinburgh, and the Duke of Connaught; Prince Edward of Saxe-Weimar; Admirals of the Fleet, viz., the Hon. Sir H. Keppel, Sir G. Hornby, and Sir E. Commerell; Field-Marshals Sir Lintorn Simmons, and Sir H. Haines; Admirals Lord Alcester, Sir R. Macdonald, Sir G. O. Willes, Sir W. Dowell, the Earl of Clanwilliam, Sir A. McLellan Lyons, and Sir Nowell Salmon; Generals Sir D. Lysons, Sir Donald Stewart, Sir A. Alison, Sir F. Stephenson, Lord Chelmsford, Sir C. Brownlow, and Sir P. S. Lumsden; Lieutenant-Generals Sir Charles Fraser, and Sir Evelyn Wood; Rear-Admirals Heneage, Lord Charles Scott, Stephenson, and Fullerton; Major-Generals Keith Fraser, Lord W. Seymour, Sir Baker Russel, and Lord Methuen; Colonel H. Smith; Captain Hammond, and Sir Dighton Probyn.

During dinner, the band of the 2nd Life Guards, under Mr. L. Barker, discoursed a choice selection of music.

DINER DU 14 MARS, 1893.

POTAGES.
Consomme à la d'Orleans.
Brisque d'Ecrevisses.

POISSONS.
Turbots, Sce. Polignac.
Filets de Saumon à la Cardinale.

ENTRÉES.
Chartreuses de Volailles à la Chevalière.
Chaudfroids de Becassines à la Lucullus.

RELEVÉS.
Estomac de Dindes à l'Imperatrice.
Pièces de Bœuf Braisés, Sce. Persil.

RÔTIS.
Petits Poussins sur Cânapés.
Salade à la Bagrations.

Asperges en Branches.
Profiteroles au Chocolat.
Carolines Vanille à la Molé.
Casolettes de Laitances à l'Indienne.
Biscuits de Mandarins en Belle Vue.
Petites Pâtisseries Assortis.

DESSERT.

It may be of interest to mention that the menu cards at Marlborough House are white, with scalloped edges, their sole adornment being the Prince of Wales' crest in Royal Blue, surrounded by the Garter with its motto, and surmounted by a crown. From a social point of view, these entertainments must have effected a large amount of good, and gastronomically they could not fail to indirectly advance the all-important subject of domestic economy; upon which, Mr. J. C. Buckmaster, presiding last year at the eighth annual exhibition of that useful institution, the Universal Cookery and Food Association, opened by His Highness Prince Edward of Saxe-Weimar, pointed out that in the reign of James II. the art of cooking in this country had fallen to a very low depth, while when George III. sat on the throne, it was little better than in the days of the ancient Britons.

Possibly the shrewd and accomplished chairman took a somewhat pessimistic view of the culinary state in England during the 135 years that elapsed between the death of Charles II. and that of George III. No doubt, in the latter monarch's era, the materials used were plain, and French "kickshaws" universally denounced, and patriotically spurned; but the cooking itself, if not *recherché*, was surely good of its kind. Ladies personally superintended the kitchen department, and were trained in the important and graceful accomplishment of carving, of which art the late M. Pouard, caterer to the Queen's Guard at St. James' Palace, maintained that Englishmen within the last quarter of a century had become profoundly ignorant, in consequence of the prevailing fashion of dining *à la Russe*.

Under the beneficent sway of Antonine Carême —to whose memory the central thoroughfare of the Metropolitan market in Paris has been appropriately dedicated—nearly all the crowned heads of Europe, during their visit to London, were right royally feasted by the Prince Regent, and a style of cooking arose characterized by all the elegance for which the French school has been famed from the days when Fagon, the physician, invented the delicious *côtelottes* that bear the name of Louis XIV.'s wife, up to the culminating period of Louis XVIII., whose *chefs* refined upon the celebrated Chateaubriand steak by serving up to that *bon-vivant* monarch, ortolans stuffed with truffles and roasted inside partridges, leaving it difficult to decide which were the more savoury to devour— the *morceau* within, or its delicately-flavoured envelope.

Before closing this gastronomic chapter, must be mentioned the dinner celebrating the happy event of July 6th the same year. The menu speaks for itself:

LE JOUR DU MARRIAGE DU SON ALTESSE ROYALE
LE DUC DE YORK.

DINER DU 6 JUILLET, 1893.

POTAGES.
Tortue Claire.
Consommé Froid à la D'Orléans.

POISSONS.
Filets de Truites à la Russe.
Cendrillons de Soles à la Norvegienne.

ENTRÉES.
Escalopes de Volailles à la Clamart.
Chaudfroids d'Ortolans à la Demidoff.

RELEVÉS.
Selles D'Agneau à la Nivernaise.
Jambon D'York Poelés au Champagne.

RÔTIS.
Poulets Printanier au Cresson.
Cailles sur Cânapes à la Royale.
Salade de Legumes Bagration.

ENTREMETS.
Asperges en Branches, Sce. Mousseuse.
Soufflées chaudes à la Moderne.
Timbales de Pêches à la Princesse.
Petits Gradins de Patisseries.

RELEVES.
Petites Crêmes au Fromage Muscovite.
Corbeilles de Glacés Assorties.
Gauffrettes.

Along Pall Mall and past Marlborough House have been marshalled all sorts of processions— some of very ephemeral interest, and in no way concerning the occupants of Marlborough House. Two pageants there have been, however—the " Thanksgiving" (February 27th, 1872) and the " Jubilee" (June 21, 1887) — wherein both the

Prince and Princess bore a part never to be forgotten either by themselves or by the nation. Bronzed warriors, returning from service abroad, have marched in serried rank past the well-known gateway of St. James' Palace. Royal visitors *en route* to some grand entertainment have gone that way to the City in order to get a peep at club - land. Political agitators in general, and Labour advocates in particular, have always had a liking for this part of the West End, where, followed by thousands of supporters, they have striven to prove to the idle lounger at his club, and to the Prince himself, the eternal right of the workman to receive the maximum of pay for the minimum of work. Even cab-strikers cannot resist the temptation to parade in front of Marlborough House. Last summer, the traffic there was seriously incommoded, if not suspended, by apparently all the hansom cabs in the metropolis slowly driving in single file up St. James' Street to Hyde Park, in order to call public attention to some private grievance of their own against the railway companies, and by so doing inflicting a very real and unnecessary annoyance upon the innocent pedestrian.

As the snow lay deep throughout the kingdom during that fateful December of 1871, the nation's sympathy, stirred to its very depths, rushed out to the Royal owner of Marlborough House, which it was feared he would never again see.

And when on February 27th in the following year, he drove to St. Paul's Cathedral to return thanks to an all-wise Providence, who had ordained his recovery, the pent-up feelings of the Queen's subjects found vent in such a demonstration as had never before been witnessed. The scene as the carriages went down Pall Mall on their way eastward was unique, as was the occasion.

Then came the Jubilee year when, as the glittering procession passed Marlborough House on its return from the Abbey, there was distinctly visible to the spectators in the houses opposite, a pause of an instant's duration, while the occupants of each carriage, as if by common consent, directed their glance to the Heir Apparent's London house. It is sad to realize that out of the Queen's splendid *cortége* on that memorable day, death has claimed no less than nine Princes, viz. :—

    H. R. H. the Duke of Clarence.
    H. R. H. the Crown Prince of Germany.
    H. R. H. the Grand Duke of Hesse.
    H. I. H. the Crown Prince of Austria.
    H. R. H. the Duc d'Aosta of Italy.
    H. G. D. H. Prince Louis of Baden.
    H. S. H. Prince Victor of Hohenlohe-Langenburg.
    H. R. H. the Duke of Saxe-Coburg and Gotha.
    H. R. H Prince Henry of Battenberg.

Not a single Princess, however, has fallen before the stroke of "the angel with the amaranthine wreath."

Forty-nine years before, on June 28th, 1838, our Gracious Queen went down St. James' Street and along Pall Mall on her way to be crowned at Westminster. As she was passing Marlborough House at about a quarter to eleven o'clock, a short delay took place in consequence of one of the traces of Her Majesty's carriage giving way. This incident was, of course, most gratifying to the people assembled at that particular spot, who had a much better view of the Queen than they would otherwise have had. Advancing along Pall Mall, the procession was witnessed by thousands, many of whom had patiently waited several hours to obtain a glimpse of their youthful sovereign. Every window along the line of route was thrown wide open, scaffoldings were erected at the Oxford and Cambridge Club, providing accommodation for upwards of 600 members, while the Carlton managed to provide for 500. Marshal Soult, we are told, met with a most enthusiastic recognition, and the applause that welcomed the Duchess of Kent and the Duke of Sussex was deafening. But the reception of the Queen baffled description, and the wonder is that any human being could have gone through the ordeal of that wonderful day with so much self-possession and dignity as did Her Majesty Queen Victoria, the central figure of all that great assembly.

CHAPTER XI.

PERSONAL CHARACTERISTICS AND ANECDOTES OF THE PRINCE AND PRINCESS OF WALES.

THAT the future subjects of the Prince and Princess of Wales have an intense and affectionate interest in every conceivable thing concerning them, it is unnecessary to repeat, which is no doubt fostered by the fact that owing to the Queen's partial withdrawal from London, and her comparative seclusion, an immense amount of extra publicity has for many years past fallen to the lot of the Heir-Apparent and his wife.

Consequently the world desires to know all it can about their Royal Highnesses, even at the risk of appearing to intrude upon such well-earned privacy as they may occasionally command.

We can all imagine how delighted the Prince must be to get clear away from the fierce glare of public life. Even at Sandringham, he and his family are not absolutely free from the espionage of strangers. People from miles around assemble on the public road at a spot close to the gate of St. Mary Magdalene Church, merely to stare at the Royal party entering the sacred edifice. If His Royal Highness goes out shooting, there are generally a few well-accredited friends of his tenants watching him with profound interest, while, during the annual " big shoots," often quite a troop eagerly follows him, recording his shots.

In Paris the Prince of Wales naturally gets some kind of rest. But, probably, he enjoys himself most, either on his all-conquering yacht, *Britannia*, or at Homburg. On the deck of his famous 143-ton cutter, he can, with a favouring breeze, " flee from his pursuers." While at the delightful little watering place, nestling at the foot of the Taunus Mountains, the well-dressed and admirably behaved crowds, who, every morning at an uncomfortably early hour, wend their way through the shady glades of the Kurhaus grounds towards some favourite *brunnen*, are too well-bred to incommode or disturb him. Here he can perambulate the streets, enter the shops, mingle freely with the people, and walk about as he chooses, stroll into the pleasant pine forests, feed the great carp that roll lazily about in the lake, look on at some important game of tennis, dine quietly at " Ritter's," or on the terrace in front of the Kurhaus, whence, smoking his cigar in peace, and listening to the strains of the splendid band in the grounds illuminated "*en grand jour*," he can watch the groups of every nationality promenading beneath.

From Homburg the Prince can easily visit his relations, who live in various interesting parts of Germany—at Bonn, Rumpenheim, Darmstadt, and imperial Potsdam. Finally, an hour's drive takes him to Friedrichshof, the Empress Frederick's lovely Renaissance castle, where he can enjoy quietude and privacy to his heart's content. One thing only, even *he* may not do, either at Homburg or at Friedrichshof —he may not walk on the lawns. Grass, as "made in Germany," may be looked at and admired, but apparently will not bear treading upon. This, to the natives, is a well understood fact, but to an Englishman it is bewildering, and rather aggravating, and he frequently finds that a serious breach of good manners has been unintentionally committed.

Such was my unfortunate lot, when last I had the honour of an interview with H.I.M. the Empress Frederick. While conversing with me in her beautiful grounds, H.I.M. stood on the exquisitely kept quartzite pathway, occasionally stirring its tiny particles with her sunshade. I remained on the lawn, and abstractedly from time to time thrust the point of my umbrella into the turf. Not a shadow of displeasure crossed the face of the august lady, and I was as graciously dismissed as I had been received. But later in the day her Director laughingly told me that no one—not even the Empress's eldest brother himself—is supposed ever to put his foot upon the sacred turf, and only that I was a visitor presumably ignorant of Teutonic ways, I should at once have been commanded to come off it. Hazarding, the remark that "surely grass is grass all the world over, and in England at least, thought to be improved by a moderate amount of use," I was silenced by the all-sufficient reply that it was "not so in the Fatherland."

I have since thought that I ought to be thankful that this offence did not occur at Potsdam, or it might have constituted an act of *lèse-majesté*, and consigned me to a fortress such as Spandau or Ehrenbreitstein for a lengthy period.

A well known physiognomist has formulated the axiom that full blue eyes are generally associated with a cheerful and happy disposition ; that they evidence a candid and generous nature, and belong to those who make the best of unpleasant circumstances ; that they indicate a talent for, or a great appreciation of, music, painting, or acting ; also a preference for rich colours and highly decorative surroundings ; and that they hint at strong feelings, love of children, and a general fondness for pleasure.

Lavater may not always have been particularly happy in his guesses at character, but I think he would have had good reason to claim the above as a remarkable vindication of his theory, in its application to H. R. H. the Prince of Wales.

Those who know the Prince best, could also bear ample testimony to his less generally known powers of endurance, his capacity for business, and his great tact. None of us are without faults, and of course the Prince, too, has his imperfections and peculiarities ; but to these we are bound in loyalty and respect to be "a little blind," as we are to his many virtues "very kind."

How greatly does manner depend for its success upon tact!—that subtle quickness of perception and readiness of action which enables its possessor to do the right thing at the right moment, to select the one word that best expresses his meaning, and to put painful things nicely. During last season, the Prince had occasion to describe a poorhouse, and made use of the term " union," for doing which some rather unkind remarks were made by sundry people of the Gradgrind type, to whom a workhouse is an institution for work and nothing more. The Prince, no doubt, was perfectly aware that the very poor are keenly sensitive, and prefer to hear the milder expression used when their relatives or friends happen to be inmates of that last refuge of the destitute.

For business details of every nature, the Prince seems to have a natural aptitude. To the numerous International Exhibitions of which he has been chairman—notably that of the "Colinderies" and the one at Paris in 1878, when he so ably presided over the British Commission—he has always given close and unremitting attention, issuing orders and superintending everything with the utmost zeal. Had not His Royal Highness been born in the purple, he would have raised himself by these qualifications to a high position as one of England's merchant princes.

HIS ROYAL HIGHNESS THE PRINCE OF WALES, K.G.

Original Drawing by Holland Tringham. By special permission of H.R.H. the Prince of Wales.
Facing page 172.

Liberality is part and parcel of the Prince's nature, of which examples without end might be quoted. Rarely does a well-authenticated appeal to his charity fail to meet with a response, while his active co-operation in the efforts constantly being made to ameliorate the condition of the "submerged tenth," is well known.

In his yachting career, the Prince's generosity is conspicuously evidenced. Last year, the *Britannia* won nearly every race for which she was entered, and as, in addition to the trophy itself, the money prizes offered ranged from fifty to a hundred pounds, no small amount was realized. His Royal Highness in almost every case gave the whole to Captain Carter and his crew, besides their usual wages, in recognition of their services. Thus, at the Weymouth regatta, when *Ailsa* was once more defeated, the sum of £20 went to the skipper, and £2 to each of the forty men comprising the crew.

Of the Prince's cheeriness, a single example related will suffice. During one of the shooting-parties at Sandringham, when, singularly enough, the Prince's personal attendant was named Prince, there was the usual brief pause for "refreshment" at half-past one o'clock. Presently the Prince enquired of Jackson, the head keeper, why they were waiting. "We are waiting for Count Gleichen, your Royal Highness," replied Jackson. Just then, the Count emerged from the covert with anything but military alacrity. " Forward, Grena dier Guards!" shouted out the Prince in his merriest voice. This command from his own colonel acted like a charm on the tired sportsman, who quickly changed his whole bearing, and marched to the front in a manner befitting an officer in so crack a regiment.

To attempt to describe Their Royal Highnesses' well-known appearance, would border on the ridiculous. In fact, it has been recently calculated that some two million photographs of the Queen, and Prince and Princess of Wales, not including innumerable lithographs and engravings, are produced annually, and find a ready sale in all parts of the globe. But, although, next to that of Her Majesty, the Prince's is the best known physiognomy in the world, *tout le monde* has not been privileged to hear him speak, nor to watch the various expressions of his countenance.

Most charming and genial is the Prince's smile, but the expression of his face in repose is somewhat grave, at times even stern, and does not always relax when speaking in public, though seldom retained in private conversation. Stern can he be when necessity arises, and, no doubt, under provocation, is tempted to "say a swear"; but, the storm once blown over, no cloud of resentment is left behind—the offence is soon condoned, and, as a rule, buried in oblivion.

His Royal Highness's voice is quite unmistakeable; his pronunciation, I should be inclined to describe as syllabic, for instance, the word " interest," would probably be pronounced "in-ter-est."

The Prince's memory of faces is proverbial ; and of his gracious readiness to acknowledge his recognition of them, I need only give one instance. When at Norwich last year, whither he went to unveil an episcopal throne in the old cathedral to the memory of the late Bishop Pelham, His Royal Highness, on leaving the choir, recognised in the stalls Canon Heaviside, his old mathematical tutor, who had been prevented by weight of years and infirmities from joining in the procession preceding the ceremony. Immediately the Prince greeted him with the greatest cordiality, and conversed freely and affectionately with him.

His Royal Highness the Prince of Wales possesses the valuable faculty which the great Napoleon boastingly claimed for himself. He can *faire vibrer la fibre populaire*—suit himself to the times. His action in the Venezuelan business, and the direct impulse he gave to the " Grace Testimonial Fund " last year, are appropriate examples of his having done the right thing in the right way, and what the nation as a whole would have had him do, had it been previously polled on the subjects.

The Prince very much objects to exaggerated sentiment and adulation of any kind. At a notable mansion not a thousand miles from Grosvenor Square, a certain baronet when being presented, attempted, in excess of zeal, to kneel to the Heir-

Apparent, who, it is said, was by no means pleased with the ill-timed and inappropriate effort.

Servants entering the Prince's service for the first time, are, as a rule, well-grounded in the art of deportment towards Royalty, and are told that it is not their place to make the obeisance reserved for the gentlemen of the household, but to remain "at attention" when their Royal Highnesses pass by. On one occasion, however, a youthful footman, over confident, and unmindful of his more experienced comrade's injunctions, departed from this rule to such an extent that the Prince could stand it no longer, and one day suddenly turning upon him, exclaimed, "What are you doing that for? Do you think you are paid to stand there bowing and scraping?" Thus did the unlucky offender realize the inadvisability of being too zealous even in the demonstrations of respect to a superior.

At the theatre it is well known the Prince likes to enjoy the play quietly, to be treated like the rest of the audience, and not to have attention specially drawn to himself, as happened on one occasion, when an over-patriotic conductor, spying His Royal Highness in his box, instructed his orchestra to strike up the well-known air "God Bless the Prince of Wales."

Like his Imperial nephew, of Potsdam, the Prince expects a frank straightforward answer from the person to whom he puts a question. He cares not for those who stand obsequiously bowing before him and avoiding his glance, in which respect he strongly resembles the Empress Frederick, who loves nothing better than to be looked straight in the face, and to have her queries answered unreservedly yet respectfully.

Rightly, the Prince objects to the practice of "tipping" still prevalent, though less so than in the last century, when, according to Professor Lecky, a foreign minister dining with a nobleman of highest rank, usually expended in fees and vails, as much as ten guineas. Sometimes, however, this kind of blackmailing was manfully protested against, as in the case of Sir Timothy Waldo, of whom it is said, that after being entertained by the Duke of Newcastle, the domestics pressed forward as usual for their fees. Arriving at the cook, Sir Timothy presented him with a crown-piece, which was returned with the remark, " I do not take silver." " Don't you indeed?" said the baronet, putting the coin into his pocket. " Then I do not give gold."

His Royal Highness is always an advocate for social reform in every direction that his good judgment tells him it is needed. In fact, with his liberality and breadth of views, he moves with the times.

He is decidedly witty, possessing largely the Royal facility for making *à propos* remarks, and vastly appreciates this art in others. He is full of fun, and can freely relax when the occasion justifies it, particularly in the privacy of his family-circle.

"Uncle John," a certain much-beloved relation, used frequently to stay at Marlborough House; but as he could speak little English, it was arranged that he should be coached by certain members of the family in some of the more familiar and necessary every-day phrases. His Royal tutors pointed out to him that certain strong expressions in our language are used occasionally to give force and emphasis, but they omitted to mention that only under peculiar circumstances were such expressions at all excusable. The Royal party, therefore, were highly amused one day at dinner, when the Prince, upon enquiring of "Uncle John" how he liked a certain *plat*, received for answer, delivered with the utmost gravity, " I thank you It is —— good." The prefix to this adjective was a word which Captain Corcoran, of *H.M.S. Pinafore*, indignantly declared he never, at least, "hardly ever" used.

The Prince speaks French, German and Italian, excelling in the former, but he does not converse in Danish. He is fond of a game of whist, and was instructed in the science of billiards by the father of the present famous John Roberts.

His Royal Highness's skill at shooting-parties is well known, but perhaps everybody is not aware that his preference seems to be for overhead shots at "rocketers," during the battues at Sandringham, and that he generally uses a hammerless breech-loader.

For fishing, the Prince has never evinced much taste, though the lordly salmon must often have been landed by him in Scotland and elsewhere. One day in the year, he, with the Princess and their children, used to extract a good deal of fun from Virginia Water, where trimmers were set over-night for pike—"the tyrants of the watery plains"—and a kind of fishing tournament was held. But His Royal Highness's disposition is too active to urge him to emulate the contemplative trout-fisher, much less the patient disciple of Izaak Walton, who hour after hour at some well-baited "swim"

"hopes the scaly breed,
And eyes the dancing cork and bending reed."

In the confession-book of a Norfolk lady, it is said that Her Royal Highness the Princess of Wales has left a record in her own hand-writing of two most interesting facts—one, that her favourite art is millinery, the other that her favourite employment is "minding her own business." Ever since she came to dwell amongst us amid unexampled national rejoicings, when Tennyson broke into joyous song of Vikings and their illustrious descendant, the Princess of Wales has steadily carried out the principle so pithily expressed in her confession.

To maintain with dignity and grace the proud position of second lady in the Empire, to abstain from the least interference in politics, to give offence to none, and to retain the admiration and respect of a great nation, is no slight achievement, and is an evidence of the firmness of purpose lying *perdu* beneath the winning grace and charm of manner that long ago captivated all hearts.

No Royal person has, perhaps, been so much run after as *the* Princess. Before her great sorrow, country-cousins and all sorts and conditions of men and women were seen day after day in the park, striving to catch a glimpse of her well-known carriage, with its fine bays, or her graceful victoria, with its high-stepping grey horses. No trouble was too great, and no amount of personal discomfort, damped the enthusiasm of those who were determined to see the Princess drive by; and it was not unusual for visitors to the metropolis, in writing to their friends, to boast of having contrived in one way or another to "view" the Princess of Wales as many as fifteen or twenty times in one week.

Most people read in the daily journals of the presence of Her Royal Highness at State functions, theatres, and *fêtes*, etc., and they also imbibe a vast amount of utterly false information concerning her, from certain weekly papers. But they hardly realize how thoroughly domesticated and simple is the life of the Princess at Marlborough House, and especially in the retirement of the Norfolk home she loves so well, and where she is seen at her best.

A fellow-feeling with weakness and suffering developing into that most womanly of all instincts, the nursing of the sick, is predominant in the Princess. Some time ago, when Mrs. Jones, who came from St. Bartholomew's Hospital to nurse the Princess during her tedious illness in the year 1867, and to whom Her Royal Highness became much attached, calling her by the pet name of "Johnnie" —fell seriously ill, no one could dissuade Her Royal Highness from sitting up with her for some nights—until the end came.

A few days after the sad event, a modest brougham might have been observed proceeding to the Brompton Cemetery, where at the last resting-place of her favourite attendant, the Princess with her own hands, sorrowfully placed a memorial wreath. Later on, she caused a beautiful monument to be erected on the well-known eastern terrace, whose entire wall is clothed with a perpetual mantle of flourishing ivy. It bears this inscription :—

IN
MEMORY
OF
ELIZABETH JONES.

Who died May, 13th, 1881. For 14 years the faithful servant and friend of Alexandra, Princess of Wales, by whom this monument is erected.

Another example of the Princess's thoughtfulness for others, even in the midst of an overwhelming personal grief, comes to me from the highest source. During that sad period four years ago, the Memorial Chapel at Windsor was the scene of numerous special services, in addition to the ordinary ones at St. George's. Her Royal Highness before she left, enquired if another and final service could be arranged late in the evening. Her desire was at once acceded to, and

> "Hearing the holy organ rolling waves
> Of sound on roof and floor
> Within, and anthem sung."

doubtless the Royal mother's grief was somewhat stayed. With tender solicitude, she did not forget the extra work entailed upon the little choir boys—fourteen in number—who might possibly go supperless to bed, or at any rate, have but their usual fare, so on her return to the Castle she at once gave instructions that chickens and other good things beloved by juveniles should be sent to their residence in the cloisters, personally satisfying herself that her orders were carried out; and they had —as they characteristically expressed it the next morning to a high church dignitary — a "jolly good feed."

With inborn kindliness, the Princess likes to hand to her household and servants at Christmas-time, the gifts—principally of silver—that it has been the custom for years past to bestow upon them at Sandringham. Those who have been there a long time have become gradually possessed of what one might term a service of plate; and as a register is kept of these gifts, no one runs a chance of receiving a duplicate.

When Mr. Blackburn, the present house-steward, was married at Sandringham in 1874 to Mary Wagland, the second nurse at Marlborough House, the Prince, Princess, and young Princesses were present at the ceremony, and afterwards went into the vestry to sign the register. The Princess kissed the bride and congratulated her, while the children clung to her, crying bitterly at having to part with their beloved "Marie"—"my good Mary" as she was generally called by the Princess. Very tender associations naturally entwine themselves around the personality of old and trusted servants, experienced in a special manner by Royalty, debarred as they are from many of the ordinary friendships of life."

Bereavement is a sacrament which levels all ranks, during which we kneel side by side without respect of persons. I was struck by an exemplification of this in an incident related by Mrs. Martin, the housekeeper at St. James' Palace, who, in her younger days had been nurse to the infant Princes. Mrs. Martin, when describing her first meeting with the Princess of Wales after the death of the Duke of Clarence, touchingly added "Her Royal Highness said not a word, but embracing me, silently wept."

Not only to say the right thing at the right time, but to do the right thing at the right moment, is a talent in itself, and very conspicuous in the Princess. Her Royal Highness has, too, the gift of fluency of speech; in fact she is—like H.R.H. the Princess Louise—an excellent speaker. In the minor as well as in the more important functions of life the Princess's delicate perception is very evident. She has a kind word for everybody, and if when in going out, she passes through the offices at Marlborough House, she never fails to bestow a smile of recognition and a word of enquiry upon each and all of the messengers and commissionaires who happen to be in the way.

But, as I have said, it is at Sandringham that the Princess feels most at home, and freer to indulge her philanthropic propensities.

Attached to the charming châlet which does duty as a model dairy, is a boudoir—a beautiful room decorated with choice and quaint china—where in one of the cabinets is kept an earthenware milk-jug of a kind used by the very poor. This humble piece of pottery had been given to the Princess by a young girl, who died of consumption, and was a token of gratitude for the kindly attention with which the Mistress of Sandringham had soothed her last days. The Princess greatly treasures this simple gift.

Her Royal Highness is constantly in the cottages round about Sandringham House, talking freely and familiarly with the inmates. Often she may be met walking in the lanes unattended, or at most with only Miss Knollys as escort. Then is the opportunity for some dejected-looking tramp to approach, and accosting either the Princess or Miss Knollys—who is equally tender-hearted—to pour forth a dismal tale of destitution more or less genuine. If none of the equerries are about, the applicant goes on his way rejoicing, with substantial relief in his or her pocket. Evidently the Charity Organization Society has no terror for the good Princess, who, doubtless believes in the doctrine sanctioned by the Highest Authority that relief should be instant and precede inquiry.

By the way, these applications to Her Royal Highness will be rendered somewhat difficult should she patronise the new motor carriage of which the Prince of Wales made personal trial at the Imperial Institute. This machine would probably displace the tricycle at present used by the Princess, adopted, it is said, because the " Royal Premier " so well liked by her daughters, was found to be unsuited to Her Royal Highness, who, in testing it, more than once experienced a rather undignified tumble, much, however, to her own amusement.

So widely known is the Princess of Wales' disposition to give, that she is made the subject of endless appeals. It may be remembered that not long ago, an old lady named Thomas attained her hundredth year at Buryport, when the gift of one hundred shillings was thoughtfully sent to her from

Marlborough House. Since then, it appears that the Princess has been literally overwhelmed by applications from all the old women in the kingdom, who in spite of the dictum of the late Sir George Cornwall Lewis, insist that they are centenarians, the result being that all further donations —even in the case of the latest applicant, who professed to be 104 years old—have had to be reluctantly stopped.

A propos of the Princess's zeal in doing good, even to the undeserving, there is rather an amusing story. In the days of the late Mr. E. Beck, who ruled as Agent and Steward at Sandringham, a certain "ne'er-do-weel" had the audacity to pitch upon a spot of unoccupied waste land—part of the outlying estates of the Prince of Wales. Forgetful that England is not Australia, he became a "free selector," and ran up a shanty just sufficient to shelter his wife and children from the rain and wind, but more fit for an animal than for a human being. He existed partly on charity, and partly by wildfowling, eked out, no doubt, by an occasional bit of poaching, in spite of the vigilance of the numerous keepers. In fact, he was the *bête-noir* and despair of the parish, and his mode of life a scandal to the Princely estate. Why he was ever suffered to remain is a mystery. But probably, there was some technical difficulty in the way of an eviction, and the kindliness of both Prince and Princess precluded any violent means being adopted.

Her Royal Highness took up the man's cause, and determined that he and his family should at least have a decent roof over their heads. Mr. Beck was appealed to, but he could not conscientiously see his way to recommend the building of a cottage for a man who would not work, and whom he knew to be irreclaimably idle.

However, the Princess was not to be deterred from her beneficent purpose. Her one thought was of the suffering to which the man's wife and children must be exposed, so Mr. Beck was finally summoned into the presence of the Prince and Princess, when her Royal Highness's wishes were once more made known to him. He used all his powers of argument to demonstrate that the Princess's charity was misplaced and would not be appreciated, but the Prince cut the interview short by saying "Now, Beck, you have heard all that the Princess desires, there is nothing more to say on the subject."

The cottage was duly built in the style for which throughout England the Prince's estate is famous —as comfortable and snug an abode for a labourer as might be found anywhere. But the "ne'er-do-weel" requited the kindness of the Princess with the extraordinary inconsistency of his class, and although he knew perfectly well the advantages of a decent home, flatly refused to permantly occupy it, and reverted to the more congenial pig-stye he himself had constructed.

When Gibson, the sculptor, was engaged at Marlborough House shortly after the marriage of the Prince and Princess, in modelling a bust of Her Royal Highness, he found, as did Frith, that he had a very indifferent sitter to deal with, and the latter relates how the young bride on being good-humouredly reproved by her husband, turned charmingly round upon the two artists and exclaimed "You are two bad men!" but from that time forth gave them no cause for anxiety as to the result of their labours.

A somewhat similar and thoroughly characteristic incident happened at Sandringham when the Princess was new to the place, and to the residents in the neighbourhood. Her Royal Highness had set her heart upon paying an informal and unannounced visit to one of the county families, and her Comptroller had respectfully pointed out to her that it was hardly advisable to bestow such an honour without previously making known her intentions, and delicately hinted that it might be inconvenient for the recipents to entertain so exalted a guest at a moment's notice. Another fact complicated the position, namely, that the country-seat was some distance, and would entail a prolonged absence from Sandringham House. Still the Princess professed her inability to see why she should not do as she wished, playfully advancing the crushing argument that if the luncheon were the difficulty, she would "take her own with her." At last better counsel prevailed, and—though rather unwillingly—she abandoned her project, but for the next three days pretended to be quite vexed with her faithful Comptroller, hardly interchanging a word with him. When she thought he had been suffi ciently punished, her kindly disposition re-asserted itself, and she no longer had the heart to feign an obduracy foreign to her nature, so one morning, as the gallant warrior in question was passing along the chief corridor, the Princess, without the least warning, darted out from her apartment, and giving him a playful push, announced her reconciliation, and submission to his superior judgment, by smilingly uttering these words, " You are a brute!" The charming way in which this little scene was enacted, and the pretty accent and emphasis on the final word, is quite indescribable.

Almost fatherly, one may say, is the way in which Sir Dighton Probyn looks after the Princess's interests, and endeavours to shield her from every possible harm or mishap. If, while in the grounds at Sandringham, she remains talking at any length, say, to some authority on horses, and becomes so absorbed as to forget the wind that blows about her keenly, as on the coast of Norfolk in the winter it knows so well how to do, a respectful but firm observation on the risk she is running is sure to proceed from her vigilant guardian, to whom Her Royal Highness, to do her justice, instantly submits with the prettiest grace imaginable.

Her Royal Highness has absolutely no sense of fear, and, if such an expression may be used in speaking of so exalted a lady, she is the quintessence of pluck, as will be seen from the following incident which occurred some years ago. Since her serious illness, it is well known that her saddle has had to be peculiarly made. This arrangement to suit the stiffness of her knee, once proved the indirect means of saving her from a very serious catastrophe. Riding home from a certain meet of hounds, closely followed by Sir Dighton Probyn, splendidly mounted as he usually is, the Princess was making her horse show off its best paces, when, for some unaccountable reason, it bolted; she lost all control over it, and was flung violently backwards, with her foot fast in the stirrup, her body and head hanging down, her whole weight, in fact, being momentarily supported by her foot, and the clutch she still retained of the reins. Sir Dighton was alongside in a moment, frightened for once in his life, yet, as in India, full of energy and resource. Catching hold of the bridle, by sheer force of arm he brought the runaway down upon his knees, and to a dead stop. The Princess's life was saved, or at the least, some dreadful disfigurement avoided. With consummate self-possession Her Royal Highness, true descendant of Vikings, turned to him, and smilingly acknowledged the service rendered to her, not a trace of alarm upon her face at her very narrow escape.

But a lesson had been learnt, and in future the

Princess was careful never to gallop hard, even when so skilled and brave an attendant was close at hand.

Sir Dighton Probyn and the Princess once had a most amusing experience together. Finding themselves, after a fatiguing run with the Norfolk hounds, many miles from home, in a part of the country where they were not known, Her Royal Highness felt very tired so they drew rein at a humble but respectable-looking little wayside inn, and entering the parlour asked what refreshment they could have. Bread, cheese, and ale—all that the cottage could produce—were set before the gentleman. Then turning to the Princess, the hostess remarked to Sir Dighton, " Now what would this young lady, your daughter, be pleased to take ? I can make her a cup of tea in no time." The offer was accepted, and to this day the old dame is doubtless ignorant of the exalted rank of the " young lady."

But anecdotes could be given without end, every one of them adding to our knowledge of the universal goodness and kindness of the Prince and Princess of Wales.

We are constantly hearing of some new but impracticable scheme, that is to annihilate even the most tenacious of evils, while suggestions keep pouring in from all quarters for the amelioration of humanity, destined in the opinion of their originators to rapidly bring about a state of social perfection that will land us in the Millenium. Yet after all, are not their Royal Highnesses of Marlborough House, by force of example, the truest reformers?

As the leaders of society, they effect incalculable good by making it fashionable to think of and help the poor, the sick, and the sad. As future rulers over three hundred millions of human beings, they are regarded with feelings of no ordinary kind by Great Britain, India, and the Colonies—that indissoluble "Triple Alliance" of the Queen's "World Domain."

Magnificent the inheritance coming years will bring to the Heir Apparent, glorious the national traditions, that in due time will be personified by him, and infinite the possibilities of good for his gracious consort.

What more splendid destiny can be conceived than to lead such a race as ours, drawn up by a common peril into close order, ready for anything that may happen, animated to stand by their rights at all costs, and upon whose shield is emblazoned this ineffaceable motto:—

> "*Come the three corners of the world in arms,
> And we shall shock them.*"

CHAPTER XII.

SOME INTERESTING GHOSTS ROUND AND ABOUT MARLBOROUGH HOUSE—A GLANCE AT PALL MALL, AND A VISION OF ITS DIM PAST.

GHOSTS are the peculiar heritage of well-aged cities. One can hardly associate them with the mushroom towns of Australia and the far West, where no historical phantoms can exist. If ghosts are there, they must be those of dispossessed aborigines or of the coyotes and kangaroos that once roamed upon their sites. But they abound in London; and from Marlborough House we need not go far to meet some of the most highly respectable specimens of this interesting genus.

Could Thomas Thynne, Esq., of Longleat, Wilts, have had any premonition of what the day would bring forth when, on the morning of Sunday, the 12th of February, 1682, aided by his valet, he leisurely dressed himself in all the finery of the Restoration period at his lodgings near Charing Cross, hard by those of his boon companion, the Duke of Monmouth? There had been an eclipse of the moon the night before, watched by the astronomer, Flamsteed, with his imperfect instruments as patiently and keenly as it would be to-day by the highly-trained staff at Greenwich; and Thynne had gazed with ignorant amazement at the unfamiliar sight of a shadow inexorably creeping over the moon's silvery face, turning it to a deep olive. The age was a singularly superstitious one, fruitful of signs and wonders ; and it would not have been surprising had he therefore conjectured that the omen was meant for himself, and that some dark shadow was about to eclipse his life. Yet the occurrence made but a fleeting impression upon him, and he remained in London.

He spent more time than usual on his toilet, for, besides numerous other engagements, he had to pay a visit of ceremony to Lady Northumberland, through whose influence he had been recently married to the child-widow of the Earl of Ogle, the great heiress of Northumberland, thus adding a mighty fortune to his already ample revenues.

Just upon the stroke of eight that evening, the sentries in front of St. James' Palace, in their red uniform, with the rose and thistle embroidered on their coats back and front, and halbert in hand were, as usual lounging listlessly by Holbein's gateway longing for the relief guard which should set them free to visit the sutler's house hard by, where they might smoke their walnut-shell pipes, and grumble to their heart's content at sundry soldiers' grievances of the day.

In the Roman Catholic Chapel close by, the incense floating up before the altar and losing itself in the roof above, announced that vespers were just over; and Queen Katherine of Braganza with her maids of honour, after devoutly listening to the Portuguese priests, had returned to the old palace.

In many a City church, staid citizens with some difficulty had followed the new form of prayer, essaying to derive some crumbs of comfort from the platitudes of duly ordained rector or vicar. At the Moravian Chapel in Fetter Lane, the saintly Baxter had eloquently pleaded with the crowded congregation, moving them to tears and repentance, and many a fool " who came to scoff, remained to pray."

But now, throughout the great city, over which had settled down a stillness unknown to this generation, all honest folk were safe indoors enjoying the last meal of the day. Lights twinkled in the stately pile of buildings at Whitehall, where Charles and his dissolute courtiers gambled and caroused. Filmy clouds floated gently over the heavens, but slightly obscuring from time to time the light of the moon, which, being only a little past full, rendered superfluous the torches carried by the running footmen of Thynne's lumbering coach, as, drawn by six big horses with flowing tails, it rolled uneasily over the cobble stones of St. James' Street and turned into Pall Mall, past the future site of Marlborough House.

What was that solitary horseman after, who had been hovering about the neighbourhood since the clock struck half-past seven? wondered the guards at the Palace Gate. And why did he take from his bandolier a charge of fine powder wherewith to renew the priming of his wheel-lock blunderbuss? Stranger still, why, at the first gleam of the approaching torches, did he gallop up Pall Mall towards the Haymarket?

But the sentinels—grizzled old warriors who had fought on many a battle-field since that of Marston Moor—soon forgot all about the great coach and the mysterious horseman, and if they thought at all, it was of supper.

Presently a sound came ringing down the street, making their ears tingle with its associations, waking the echoes, causing the dogs far and near to bark loudly and nervously, windows and doors to be thrown open, and people to come out to listen and peep. To the soldiers there was no mystery as to what that loud report was, for often enough had they heard it in the past.

Then came a confused noise of shouting, and wild plunging of horses. Had they been a little further up Pall Mall, they might have heard the hoarse command of "Stop!" as three ruffians rode up to Thynne's coach, and have seen the flash and cloud of smoke from the weapon fired straight through the window at poor Thynne, sitting all unconscious of impending evil.

"I am murdered!" was all he could faintly whisper.

The assassins, frantically, but vainly, pursued by one of the footmen, disappeared. Thynne's coach quickly bore him home, and on his gaily-decked bed they laid his stricken form and waited for the surgeon to say if his wounds were mortal or not. In hot haste, a message was sent to the Duke of Monmouth, who, with others of his set, sped at once to his friend's bedside. All the gold he possessed could not avail to keep him alive. Two of the cruel slugs had shattered his spine and two others had lodged in the lower part of his body. Already the signs of dissolution had set in. His skin was cold and clammy, his eyes were sunken, while he trembled like an aspen leaf; his pulse was barely perceptible, and his breath came short and quick. About midnight, the watchers by his bedside, thinking the end was near, hastily offered him a cordial which he eagerly swallowed ; but Monmouth and his friends were presently startled by the sudden change in poor Thynne's looks. His eyes brightened, a flush of crimson stole over his cheeks, his pulse became perceptibly stronger — there might be hope, after all ! But soon he began to mutter incoherently, and no longer recognised the faces of those around him ; his voice, got weaker and weaker, and at last ceased.

Slowly the night dragged on, and just upon the stroke of twelve—ere the tardy dawn of a new day —a grey shadow stole over the suffering face, and all was over in this world for Thomas Thynne, foully done to death at the instigation of his rival, Köningsmarck, who—more lucky than the actual murderer—escaped the gallows to find, four years later, a soldier's death when fighting the Turks in Greece.

Up Pall Mall from Whitehall, with phantom step comes King Charles II., a monarch who, unconsciously, had a good deal to do with the Marlborough House of the future. For by Letters Patent under the Great Seal, dated September 20th, 1683, at the request of "his dearest consort, Katherine," he granted to her a ninety-nine years' lease of the identical ground upon which Sir Christopher Wren was afterwards to build the great Duchess's town mansion. And it is very certain that Nell Gwynn's garden in her Royal friend's time, constituted a part of the existing grounds of Marlborough House.

Therefore, King Charles can justify his ghostly presence here. But he is hardly a phantom; for, like his Secretary of the Admiralty, he still lives. In Westminster Abbey and Crutched Friars' Church, their dusty mortality is, no doubt, securely sealed up, but in the spirit, they are round and about us as when the clatter of their high-heeled shoes could be heard in Palace or Navy Office.

Unhappy Charles! for all time, object-lesson of lost opportunities. Of all weary souls in the nether world, he should experience the truth of these pathetic lines:

"That of all saddest words of tongue or pen
The saddest are those ' It might have been.' "

If ever restless spirit

"brake the band
That stays him from the native land,
Where first he walk'd when claspt in clay."

it must be that of him, the once-called " Merry."

In St. James' Palace, where he was born and where he reigned, in the Mall and Park, at Whitehall, in the old London City that lent him its spare cash to be flung with careless, joyless prodigality to worthless followers, the pale shade of Charles II. should be often seen, vainly contemplating the evil that his indolence and inability to say "No" had wrought directly and indirectly on individual and nation.

Beloved and trusted by a people wearied of Puritan austerities and hypocrisies, that loved lavish kings and hated meanness in a ruler were he as wise as Solomon, Charles started with the ability and desire to reconcile all parties in distracted England, and was willing to be, as he confessed, "the man of his people." Gifted with immense common sense, educated by bitter experience in a thorough knowledge of mankind and their weaknesses, and possessing a natural and irresistible charm of manner, no Prince ever had so many things in his favour. For his extravagance and love of ease, he had indeed the excuse of having suffered much, and having long borne the hardships of exile and poverty. But just as the fidelity of his friends had saved him during his wanderings after the battle of Worcester, the " set " which surrounded him at Whitehall, and to whom he indolently surrendered himself, was the cause of his moral ruin.

But we left him just now coming up Pall Mall—whither bound ?

Not to the Palace, nor for a stroll in the neighbouring pleasant meadows and orchards, but to a certain house of modest dimensions on the south side, where Nell Gwynn was expecting him in her long garden at the back, under the shade of the elm-trees, where she had laid out a table well-provided with the French wines preferred by him to Malmsey or sack. (Dom Perignon, the pious monk and cellarer of the Benedictine monastery at Hautvilliers, alas, had not yet discovered champagne). Here she may many a time have twitted the good-humoured King for having originally given her only a lease of the ground upon which, on receipt of its fee simple, and not until then, had she built her new house. It is a curious fact that the site of her residence is to this day the only one on the south side of Pall Mall that is not Crown property, though it is said the original title-deeds have never been discovered. After her death in 1687, the dimensions of the garden must at some period have been considerably curtailed. The site of her old home, No. 79, now the office of the Eagle Insurance Company, terminates with a high wall, and overlooks the stables of Marlborough House, which are upon a lower level, the ground at this point and all along the south side of Pall Mall, having originally sloped towards the Park. There have been three houses where Nell Gwynn's house once stood, the last of which has been recently restored and completely altered by Mr. J. M. Anderson, the well-known architect, and the attenuated garden in the rear, built over. Two elms of considerable size formerly grew right against the dividing wall, a fair evidence that *there* at least was not the original boundary of Nell's garden. Nor is it reasonable to suppose that in her days, when land was not so valuable as now, she would have been content with a pleasance but 70 feet in length, wherein to disport herself.

That the land all about her house was covered with plantations, is shown in Van Wyck's painting of Charles II. and his courtiers walking through the tilt-yard at Whitehall towards the decoy ponds; the landscape to the north, *i.e.*, in the rear of Pall Mall, being covered with trees, amidst which no building is visible save the Queen's Chapel at St. James'. Therefore, it may be assumed that the late Mr. E. M. Ward, R.A. was correct as usual in locating the scene of his well-known picture—Nell Gwynn talking to King Charles from her garden-wall—at a spot in the extreme south-eastern corner of the Marlborough House grounds, which was kindly pointed out to me by Mrs. Ward herself, whose husband had shown it to her years ago.

Thus the large dining-room and the Royal visitors' rooms at Marlborough House overlook the identical spot where many a time poor Nell must have walked and talked with the swarthy-complexioned, harsh-featured, bushy-eyebrowed, eagle-eyed King, in black suit and flowing peruke.

When digging out the old garden during the recent alterations at No. 79 Pall Mall, though no discoveries were made, an ancient watch was turned up, and of course pronounced to have belonged to Nell Gwynn, perhaps a present from her Royal master, and carelessly dropped, or flung away in a moment of temper. Might it not be—suggested the antiquarians who read of the find—one of David Ramsey's beautiful productions made for King James I.? Or even an "Edwardus East"? so-called after the famous maker in Pall Mall.

Alas! conjecture was at fault; as was the case last December when an English watch with two seals attached was discovered in a chimney in Newton Street, Holborn. It was supposed to have been once the property of Lord Lovat, but as the date on the time-piece was found to be that of forty years *after* the execution of the Jacobite Peer, the question was settled to the contrary.

The Nell Gwynn watch on examination proved to be only an outer case of 18th century work; and all hope of coming upon any new trace of the fair, but frail, little actress vanished. She will never be forgotten. Yet out of the multitudes who pass St. Martin's Church, how few are aware that Nell Gwynn sleeps beneath the familiar edifice, and that the good and charitable Archbishop Tenison preached her funeral sermon.

In 1769, her house in Pall Mall was purchased by Dr. William Hebarden, a well-known physician of his time, from Dame Denise Hart, of St. James' Palace, who, doubtless had it from the St. Albans family.

In the documents relating to this transaction it is stated that the house was formerly in the occupation of Sir Peter Leicester, Bart., and more recently in that of Maria, Countess Dowager of Waldegrave. Subsequently, the descendants of Dr. Hebarden conveyed the property to the Eagle Insurance Company in the year 1866, after it had been for some years tenanted by the Society for the Propagation of the Gospel in Foreign Parts.

Although that part of the West-end now comprising St. James' Square and the north side of Pall Mall was pasture land and orchards up to within five years of Charles II.'s death, as general prosperity increased it began to be built over ; nearly all the nobility leaving the city and taking up their abode along the Thames between Westminster and Temple Bar thus commencing to move westward in earnest.

Distinguished strangers very quickly discovered

the incomparable advantages possessed by this fine thoroughfare close to palace, park, and playhouse, and to innumerable coffee and chocolate-houses, to say nothing of the fashionable taverns wherein the best of company was to be met.

It was in one of these latter—the " Star and Garter," where the Nottinghamshire Club met— that the poet Byron's ancestor (William, fifth Lord), on January 26th, in the year 1765, killed his relation, Mr. Chaworth, in an *encounter*, for one could hardly call it a duel. They had dined together at the fashionable hour of four, and, as was customary, had sat long over their Burgundy, following up that generous wine with punch. As the evening began to merge into night, they had both reached that dangerous stage of conviviality when argument only evokes irritability and a disposition to take offence. The subject of game preservation and the game laws was introduced, and Lord Byron maintained that under his system, he could always show on his estate a bigger total of fur and feather than any of his neighbours. To this Chaworth took exception, and swore that he had more game than anyone in the County of Notts; and the dispute quickly developed into a decorous, but bitter, quarrel. With significant gesture—after bidding the drawer prepare an adjoining chamber, and telling him that they wished to settle some private business there— they both left the room. Lord Byron entered the apartment first, and as Chaworth, who followed, was closing the door, he saw his antagonist had already half-drawn his sword, as if to attack. Instantly whipping out his own weapon, he made a swift lunge at Byron, piercing him as he supposed through the side, but he had merely penetrated his long-flapped waistcoat—unbuttoned for ease during the long sitting—and which, in the gloomy light of a single tallow candle, deceived him. Disregarding Chaworth's expression of regret, Byron closed, and shortening his sword, plunged it with great violence into Chaworth's abdomen — a blow which proved mortal, though he lingered in great agony until the morning, after doing all he could to exculpate Lord Byron from blame in the sad business.

At another tavern, the "Queen's Arms," the infamous Lord Mohun, who lodged hard by in St. James', supped on the night preceding the famous duel in Hyde Park, of November 15th, 1712. One can think away the present, and picture the past, as the scoundrel peer, who had broken up the Kit-Cat Club (of which the great Duke of Marlborough was an original member), sat with his companions in guilt, boasting and carousing until the small hours of morning—his last on earth—and it was time to seek some rest before the dreadful business should begin in the quiet glades of Hyde Park. How the combatants in that desperate duel could have gone on fighting after mutually receiving such fearful wounds, is a mystery! An eye-witness declared that they seldom parried, but continued to thrust at each other until both succumbed. It was a fitting end for so depraved and violent a character as Mohun's, in the poisoned atmosphere of whose career his contemporaries might well exclaim :—

> " Religion blushing, veils her sacred fires,
> And, unawares, Morality expires."

About the latter half of the 18th century, was founded the famous house of Christie, the auctioneer. The original Christie started business in Pall Mall, and in and out of his premises went all the celebrities and *virtuosi* of the day, amongst them the famous Lord Chesterfield, who became his patron and staunch friend.

At Schomberg House (built in 1650), on the south side of Pall Mall, lived William, Duke of Cumberland, hero of Culloden, whose physician was a certain Doctor Gastaldi, renowned for his gourmandizing propensities, and who, dining with the Archbishop of Paris, in spite of the prelate's remonstrance, partook three times of a dish of deliciously-cooked salmon, which brought on a fit, and caused his death in a few hours. In one of the second-floor rooms of Schomberg House, expired Gainsborough, whose passion for buying musical instruments was so marked. His apartment was literally filled with violins, viol-de-gambas, hautboys, and theorbos, upon which he performed but indifferently. He it was whom the beauty of the lovely Duchess of Devonshire fairly baffled in his endeavour to do full justice to her perfect features. It was at Schomberg House, too, that the first idea of the *Beggar's Opera* was conceived, which made " Gay rich, and Rich gay," and which Mr. Sims Reeves considers to be "really a comedy with songs, rather than an opera."

The present War Office was erected for the Duke of York, brother of George III., and was called after him. He died, unmarried, in the year 1767. It became a subscription club-house, and was designated the Albion Hotel—the forerunner of the stately edifices that now make Pall Mall almost an avenue of club-houses.

Clubland is a tempting subject to dwell upon, but the modern club is too recent an institution to possess genuine ghosts. In the year 1800, there were but White's, Brooks', Boodle's, the Cocoa Tree, Graham's, and a few others in existence, mere tavern-clubs not counting. Reference to one club only, the " Marlborough," is necessary in a work on Marlborough House. No. 52, Pall Mall is quite an unpretending two-storied, narrow-frontaged building, with stone facings and bay windows, and with glazed door of oak, generally kept closed. It is larger than it looks from Pall Mall, as it runs back a considerable distance into Crown Court. This club consists of a small *coterie* of His Royal Highness's special friends, and is, one need hardly say, a most select and exclusive concern, numbering about eighty members, amongst whom are Prince Edward of Saxe-Weimar, Lord Colville of Culross, the Marquis of Conyngham, Lord Templeton, the Duke of St. Albans, Lord Suffield, Sir Edward Lawson, General Stanley de A. C. Clarke, one clergyman — the Rev. Charles Martyn — and, closely associated with the locality, Sir John Thynne and the Duke of Marlborough. Inside, it differs somewhat from the gorgeous edifices of a like character, so common now-a-days, being quite plainly furnished and without any pretension to decorative grandeur, but sufficiently comfortable, well warmed and lighted, and with a *cuisine* and service of the best. There is the usual card-room, and a capital billiard-room; and at the rear there used to be an American bowling-alley. As there is a magnificent one at Sandringham—specially built—one concludes the Prince is fond of bowls. Curiously enough, there is no billiard-room at Marlborough House (the mighty Windsor Castle has, I believe, but one, and that is poked away in the basement). There used to be one where Mr. Long's office and the waiting-room adjoining are now situated, but it was done away with years ago; and if His Royal Highness desire a quiet game, he goes over to the "Marlborough," whither from his own private sitting-room he has to walk only a few yards. The club is a convenient place for the Prince to meet his very intimate friends, and to receive and reply to his private letters, etc.

Now as to the origin of the name Pall Mall. In King Charles II.'s time, it was sometimes called Katherine Street, and in the year when Marlborough House was in course of building, was known as Pall Mall Street. As early as James I.'s reign, the game of Pelle Melle was recommended as an excellent field exercise for the King's son Henry; and there can be little doubt that later it was played in the long alley near St. James' Palace, popularly called Pall Mall; and when this long alley became a street, Charles II. caused the portion of the Park, known to us as The Mall, to be laid out and reserved as a place where the "quality" might indulge in the popular game.

There exists a "Pall Mall"—a wretched little street—in Liverpool, and why it is so named is a mystery. But with the famous London thoroughfare there can, I believe, be little difficulty in determining whence its peculiar appellation is derived. Paille-maille; Palla (a ball) and Maglia (a mallet) supplies the key. The Italian game of "palla," or "ball," has been popular since the days of Nero, though the plaything itself has for centuries been increasing in size and weight. "Mall," in the Icelandic signifies an "avenue," or "walk covered with shells"; and *Anglice* a "public walk," or level, shaded resort, where ball could be played with malls (*malleus*, a hammer). Therefore, the street is probably so named after the game; just as in future times some thoroughfare in Wimbledon, Hurlingham, or far-distant St. Andrews, built over past all recognition, will be known as " Golf " or " Polo " Avenue.

In 1731, the great sewer along Pall Mall was being arranged, and at the corner of Warwick Street, twenty-eight feet beneath the surface, a remarkable antediluvian forest was unearthed, together with the remains of some kind of mammoth. Being in the neighbourhood, and pondering over this discovery of more than a century and a half ago, and the contrast between the misty past and the tangible present, I failed to notice that the rattle of street traffic had gradually subsided, and that Pall Mall was deserted. Presently, it began to grow dusk, and the houses on each side seemed to recede until they altogether disappeared. Strangely close and damp became the atmosphere, curious vegetation—sequoias and fan palms—appeared in groups around the spot on which I stood; yet no sign of human habitation, nor voice of man, broke the monotony of the view or the death-like silence. There seemed to be a vast estuary beyond the trees, and by the half light I saw elephant forms with immense tusks toiling up from the stagnant water, which they shook in glistening drops from their mighty sides. Herds of heavy short-legged, three-hoofed monsters with large heads and long snouts, laboriously wallowed in the distant mud, and like tapirs, grunted with delight as they rolled in the slime whereon innumerable tortoises crawled like the land crabs of the West Indies. As if at a given signal, these awful creatures suddenly paused in their occupation, raised their uncouth heads, and looking straight in my direction, simultaneously charged! Not waiting for their onset, but utterly unnerved by these and other ghosts of the past, I precipitately fled, presently to recover my senses, and find myself in the hospitable 19th century smoking-room of the United University Club close by.

CHAPTER XIII.

FACTS HISTORICAL, ANTIQUARIAN, AND ARCHITECTURAL CONCERNING MARLBOROUGH HOUSE—MODERN ALTERATIONS AND ADDITIONS, AND A SUGGESTED NEW SITE FOR MARLBOROUGH HOUSE.

"AB ovo usque ad mala," that is to say, everything in orderly sequence, was the excellent rule at the old Roman banquets, and a similar principle may well be observed in dealing with the antiquarian history of the spot on which Marlborough House stands.

Far back in the past, when the river Thames, encircling Thorney Island at Westminster, and, unrestrained by dyke or embankment, periodically enriched the land along its course, certain meadows pleasantly diversified by coppice and tangled undergrowth of bush and briar, lay to the west of Charing village a kind of no man's land, but admirably situated, thought certain pious citizens of London, for the purpose they had in view—the building of a refuge for poor women afflicted with leprosy, that most awful form of all incurable diseases.

Stone by stone, the quaint little structure rose from the ground, and duly provided with refectory, chantry and chapel—for the spiritual as well as bodily wants of its inmates had to be thought of—

the modest charity started upon its beneficent career.

During more than four centuries the brethren and sisters were left in peace on property legally theirs—even in the absence of Royal grant—by right of long possession. For generations past, had the original donors "slept with their fathers." The fourteen "poor females" of the foundation had been succeeded again and again by others similarly afflicted. At Hastings, the great battle had been fought and won; William the Conqueror became King, and in course of time Magna Charta was wrested from his descendant. Slowly the infant Parliament of England struggled into life, and under Henry the Fifth, France became a province of Britain. The Wars of the Roses deluged the land with blood; Bosworth was a thing of the past, and the first Tudor King dying at Richmond was borne to a splendid tomb in the Abbey which, during these four hundred years, had slowly risen to grandeur on the banks of the Thames.

By this time, the Hospital of St. James' had grown to considerable dimensions; its gardens and orchards were fair to look upon and wonderfully productive. But more attractive still in the eyes of the new sport-loving monarch, Henry VIII., were the adjacent coverts and marshy land belonging to the old establishment. They swarmed with game, and especially with wild fowl. At the present day, standing on the little peninsula at the eastern end of St. James' Park, it is not so hard to realize that there was a time when flights of wild duck, and dark, wedge-shaped masses of teal, might be seen hurrying up from the saltings and desolate creeks at the river's mouth, to pitch down with mighty splashing on the solitary pools that here abounded. Look steadily through your field-glass at the weeping-willow, whose curved branch just dips into the water. Two grebes are hard at work constructing a summer residence; a slight movement of the hand, and they instantly disappear. Geese—Canadian, Chinese, Egyptian, and Magellanic — are solemnly looking after their eggs. Ducks of all sizes and colouring are around in profusion—the mallard, with his speculum of rich shining purple; the Carolina, tufted and pochard; the common and the Chilian pintail; the shoveller, widgeon, and the dainty mandarin duck. Herons stand motionless on one leg; the ruddy sheldrake, resplendent in his wedding dress, slumbers on the sward, while peacocks and cock-pheasants, leaving all domestic cares to their sober-hued partners, complacently strut about, as if the park were entirely theirs.

It did not take covetous King Henry long to discover that a hunting-lodge in this identical locality, " far away from the town," was an absolute necessity, whence he might start upon pleasant excursions for hawking and coursing, towards the woods at Kensington, or the breezy uplands of Hampstead. An "exchange" was, therefore, arranged between the Crown and the Hospital of St. James', whose representatives received certain lands in Suffolk by way of compensation. The sisterhood was pensioned off, and their helpless leprous charges were turned out into the world, to find what shelter they might. Almost every trace of the original building vanished, and at the touch of Holbein, St. James' Palace sprung into existence.

All is now tolerably plain sailing in dealing with the history of the locality. Stuarts succeeded to Tudors; St. James' gradually became, in lieu of Whitehall, a centre of English Court life; Charles II. was restored to his throne and his country, and on the 21st of May, 1662, in a private room at Portsmouth, according to the rites of the Roman Catholic Church, Katherine of Braganza linked her life with that of the fickle Charles Stuart. A chapel had been erected in the time of the Martyr King for his consort, Henrietta Maria, on some ground adjoining the Palace used as a kind of preserve for half-tame pheasants and partridges. For the new Queen's convenience this was restored and put in order, its altar and Popish decorations having during the Commonwealth been ruthlessly demolished, and the fabric itself allowed to become dilapidated. In addition to this, Katherine of Braganza was permitted to build suitable "lodgings" for her Portuguese priests next to the chapel, and also to erect cloisters at the rear which completely enclosed a "green court," wherein, according to ancient usage, persons belonging to the religious establishment *might* be interred with proper ceremonial, but a burial-ground was likewise provided.

There exists a curious plan of St. James' Palace printed in London 1689 for Simon Burgis, to prove the possibility of a child having been secretly conveyed into the Queen's bed-chamber, and consequent illegitimacy of James II.'s son, the Pretender (the Warming-pan plot). This plan shows a "burying-place" exactly in front of the Queen's chapel—now the German chapel; yet, when the present roadway at Marlborough Gate was constructed by the Board of Works in 1856, no human remains were found.

An interesting discovery was, however, made at this place about the year 1862, favouring the theory which I advance "without prejudice," that when the Portuguese priests were brought over by Queen Katherine of Braganza, there still lingered a faint recollection of the old Hospital buildings, and the position of its original consecrated ground for interments, thus accounting for the priests' burying-place being there. The "find" in question occurred when the cellarage attached to the residence of the Clerk Comptroller of the Royal kitchen was being enlarged, and it was necessary to excavate beneath the Palace walls. At a depth of about six feet from the surface, an ancient stone coffin was disclosed *outside* the palace wall lying with its feet to the east at a spot beneath the colonnade, exactly opposite the German chapel, and there were traces of others. With good taste, Sir F. C. B. Ponsonby Fane would not permit it to be disturbed in any way, nor was its existence made known ; therefore the public, as they pass to and from Pall Mall and the Park, are unaware that any relics of mortality lie beneath their feet.

So enamoured became Katherine of Braganza with the " Friary " as it began to be called, that Charles II. granted her a lease of the premises for ninety-nine years at the nominal rent of five shillings annually.

In 1701, during the reign William III., the Earl of Albemarle, apparently unaware of the existence of this grant, applied to the Crown for a lease, intending to re-build the dwelling-houses ; and the Surveyor-General reported that the property was worth £150 a year, or a fine of £2,250 for a fifty years' lease. But the fact of King Charles' grant afterwards coming to his knowledge, caused further negotiations to be abandoned by the Earl.

Then came the year 1708, when the Duke of Marlborough was at the height of his fame, and the Queen could refuse nothing to the hero of Oudenarde. Therefore at the recommendation of Godolphin, that honest minister eulogized by King William III. as " never in the way, or out of the way," and on the petition of the Duchess, a fifty years' lease of the Friary and grounds attached, was granted to her under the Great Seal, in the name of certain trustees, at a yearly rental of five shillings, in consideration of the payment of £2,000, the lessees having power to erect certain buildings to be approved by the Surveyor-General; but they were prohibited from putting up any tenements in the existing garden.

This was in August of 1708, and the legal formalities being at last satisfactorily settled, the Duchess was at liberty to think about the plans for her new house. She wisely consulted Sir Christopher Wren, who, though in his 76th year, was in as full possession of his mental powers as when St. Paul's Cathedral beneath his guiding hand rose phœnix-like from its ashes.

To the delight of the Duke and Duchess of Buckingham, between whose families and the Marlboroughs there had been considerable coolness, Sarah Duchess selected their town mansion as a model for her own.

The first thing done after deciding upon the design, was to demolish the old structures except, perhaps, the priests' "lodgings" next to the chapel, and to prepare the basements of the mansion; and on Tuesday, May 24th, 1709 (O.S.)—a fine, warm day—the foundation stone of Marlborough House was laid without any ceremony, the event creating so little stir in fashionable society that it was not so much as mentioned by the "Tatler." The stone, quite a small one, about 3 feet long, bears the following inscription :—

" Laid by
Her Grace the Dutches of Marlborough
May ye 24 ⎫
June ye 4th ⎭ 1709."

Facing the north-west, it must have originally been visible from the quadrangle just above the ground, as there used to be a grating close to it, evidently for ventilating purposes. No longer forming part of the outer wall, the stone, since the extensive additions to the north front of the house, is now to be seen close to a staircase in the passage beneath the corridor. The Duchess, as will be noticed, had the old and new styles of dating inscribed upon the foundation stone, thus showing herself ahead of her times, as the new mode of reckoning did not come into general use until 1752. Doubtless her constant correspondence with the Continent, where Pope Gregory's reform had for some years been in force, influenced her action in the matter.

With great rapidity the work proceeded; and three months later, *i. e.*, in August, it was commonly reported about town that the Duchess's house had advanced prodigiously, and was already "a covering," which meant that the basement was completed and boarded over. By the February following, people were able to form some little idea of what the mansion would be like, and the general opinion seems to have been that it would be one of the most perfect in England.

As the building progressed, the Duke, who was still abroad campaigning, received from the Duchess sundry commissions, one of them showing the "frugal mind" that characterized them both. In a letter from Sir Christopher Wren to the Duchess, dated October 31st, 1710, he says, "The rooms will take up about 12,000 tiles, and the chimneys about 2,200." This letter was sent on to the Duke endorsed by the Duchess to the effect that she could give him no better instructions regarding the tiles she required, which were "cheap" in Holland, and "coming with him" would "cost less and be less trouble." They were to be quite white without the least painting upon them. No doubt the greater number were intended for a sort of dado in the hall and kitchen, such as can be seen to this day in old Dutch houses; but her intention was never carried out, as no trace of the tiles can be found at Marlborough House or at Blenheim.

When Sir Horace Rumbold, Bart., G.C.M.G. British Minister at the Hague, was kindly making some researches for me on the subject, he—like Saul, the son of Kish—came upon something of deeper interest; for although he could find no record of tiles in the State archives, he discovered some documents relating to a request made by the British Secretary of the Legation for the free export of six large looking-glasses for the Duke of Marlborough, evidently intended for the embellishment of Marlborough House, the permit to ship them from Rotterdam being dated March, 1710. This is the English rendering of his application and the reply :—

" HIGH AND PUISSANT GENTLEMEN,—The undersigned Secretary of Her Majesty the Queen of Great Britain, humbly prays your Highnesses to grant their Passport for six great mirrors which have to be sent from Antwerp to Rotterdam for the Duke of Marlborough, in order that they may without hindrance pass by Lille and other places, and be shipped from Rotterdam to England.
" SA D'AYROLLE."

To which those "potent, grave, and reverend Signiors," the States General, graciously replied as follows :—

" Resolution of the States General, 3rd March, 1710—

" In answer to the Memoradum of the Secretary, D'Ayrolle, it has been resolved, after previous deliberation, that a Passport shall be forwarded for the exportation of six great mirrors on behalf of the Duke of Marlborough from Antwerp to Rotterdam to be exported from there to England free and without payment of any duties, and a copy of the Resolution of their Highnesses will be sent to the Admiralty Board of Zeeland which has been ordered to see that the above-named mirrors be passed through their offices free, without hindrance and without any molestation.

"Minute book of the States General,
"1709/10."

"Passport in reply to the Memorandum of the Secretary D'Ayrolle praying to export six great mirrors on behalf of the Duke of Marlborough from Antwerp to Rotterdam, and from there to England.
"Given at the Hague,
"March 3rd, 1710."

Dutch bricks were undoubtedly used in the construction of Marlborough House, rather smaller than those made in England, redder in colour, and decidedly cheaper. They were brought over as ballast in some of the numerous hired transports constantly coming and going between Holland and Deptford, where they were usually paid off. High-sterned, bluff-bowed merchantmen, such as the *Elephant*, *Expedition*, or *Margate* — names that frequently occur in the Transport office records of 1709-10—might well have had as cargo the raw material of the house then building in Pall Mall, whither the bricks could easily be carted from Westminster, the nearest point of discharge, where lumbering barges with gaily painted stems and sterns much like those to be seen any day on the Thames, had carried them from Woolwich or Deptford Yard.

Sarah Duchess had long realized that the space at her disposal in the Friary grant, was not sufficient to provide so large a garden as she had mentally planned, to say nothing of the offices and riding-school she had calculated upon having. Accordingly, in 1709, a new lease of fifty years (in the name of the same trustees) was obtained from the Crown under the Great Seal, cancelling the original one, and including the piece of land next to the Friary, formerly in the possession of Mr. Secretary Boyle, and known as the Royal Garden. It was about two acres in extent, thus bringing up the total of the Duchess's leasehold property to its present area of about four and three-quarter acres. The consideration for this new lease was a ground rent of £14 for the two pieces of ground, the lessees agreeing to lay out in the course of three years a sum of not less than £8,000 in improvements and building, while retaining full permission to pull down and alter any existing houses.

The laying out of the garden was duly taken in hand, and accomplished at a cost of something under £500, at the sacrifice—so it was said at the time—of many fine old trees, while the work of clearing away and levelling proceeded. Uninteresting and uniform was the result, as may be clearly seen in Kip's bird's-eye view of St. James' Palace and Marlborough House. One shilling and eight-pence per diem was the wage paid to the labourers engaged upon this work, not such bad pay considering the different value of money and the comparative cheapness of provisions; the general rate throughout England in the 18th century for agricultural labour being according to Professor Lecky, ten and ninepence per week within twenty miles of London, decreasing in proportion to the distance from town, until, 170 miles away, the wage dwindled down to but six shillings and three-pence.

At Midsummer, 1711, the house was finished, and occupied by the Duke and Duchess. It did not present any very imposing appearance, being merely a fair-sized, very plain one-storied building, little more than one-half the height it is at present, with long narrow windows—not unlike its neighbour, the Palace—and without any portico entrance, but its situation in the midst of the rapidly growing west-end was undeniably excellent. Its weak point was the approach from Pall Mall—inconvenient and cramped as it is to this day—and must often have excited wonder that an abode so important could have been so defective in the matter of avenue and entrance gates.

A certain curate of St. James' Church, Piccadilly, the Rev. M. E. C. Walcott, who wrote a handbook to his parish in 1854, gives the following plausible

JOHN KIP'S BIRD'S-EYE VIEW OF ST. JAMES'S PALACE AND MARLBOROUGH HOUSE.
Circa 1720.

Facing page 236.

explanation of this anomaly, which has apparently been accepted by almost every writer on the subject since. It was the Duchess's wish, he says, "to make an entrance for her house, then called Priory Court, into Pall Mall, but Sir Robert Walpole, having quarrelled with her, bought the house in front of it in the main street, and so frustrated her purpose."

That the Duchess intended to improve the approaches after Sir Robert Walpole's resignation and retirement in 1742 is evident from a block plan in existence at Blenheim, dated 1744, which shows the proposed enlargement of the entrance by 111 feet, to be obtained by the demolition of four narrow houses which stood in the way in Pall Mall: but her death ensuing in the same year, the idea was obviously abandoned, and the requisite crown lease never applied for. Far from desiring to frustrate her purpose, Sir Robert Walpole — although he may have "fallen out" with her—was willing to further her designs, for in one of her letters she writes of him that he had on several occasions told her that he could do most things at the Treasury upon his own authority, and regretted that she made no use of his influence, except to obtain the lease enabling her to make a way into Marlborough House. In the same letter, she states that Marlborough House had cost the Duke and herself close upon £50,000. This information is taken from the few papers and documents referring to Marlborough House that are preserved at

Blenheim. These records also show that the Walcott report originated in the fact that—presumably at the instigation of Sir Robert Walpole—the Duchess was refused the privilege of going from her residence through St. James' Park in her coach, a favour she had enjoyed during Queen Anne's reign. In complaining of this treatment, she said, that although she had no desire to see St. James' Park transformed into a street, she thought, considering the situation of her house, and the little use she had made of the liberty granted to her, the privilege might have been continued. She drew attention to the fact that the approach from Pall Mall was through a narrow passage, and that in consequence of the encroachments (evidently the buildings that had been erected), a coach and six horses could hardly get out from Marlborough House. If the Duchess's intention had been carried out, the approach from Pall Mall would now extend from Marlborough Gate to about the extreme end of the Guard's Club House.

Another popular tradition was that in order to secure speedy and constant access to Queen Anne at the time of her ascendancy over the Sovereign, the Duchess caused a covered bridge to be constructed between Marlborough House and the Palace. This could only have been effected from the coach-houses adjoining the German chapel, where the width across the footpath from Pall Mall was only 10 feet; but the Duchess in proceeding to this isolated building for the purpose of reaching the Palace, would have been seen by everyone in the place. No authentic record can be found at Blenheim, nor is there a trace in any existing print, of this bridge.

Queen Anne's "lodgings" in the Palace were on the south side, facing the Mall; and all that the Duchess had to do was to take the nearest way, *i.e.*, through the side gate in her own garden, and crossing the road—which here was as wide and unbridgeable as it is at present — go through the "iron gate" of the Palace, when she could readily, and almost unobserved, get access to the back-stairs' entrance leading to the Queen's apartments. All this can be easily proved on inspecting any of the contemporary prints of the locality.

By the Duchess's will, dated August 11th, 1744, the residue of the crown lease was left in trust for George, second Duke of Marlborough. Now ensues the record of bewildering succession of surrendering and renewing of leases on the part of trustees of the crown—splendid legal pasturage on which conveyancers of the old school may graze to their heart's content, but maddening in their complication to ordinary intellect. In 1784, the Surveyor-General reported that a lease of 50 years could be granted, and stated that the substantial brick mansion and offices were in good repair, and could be valued at a rental of £600 per annum, a considerable advance upon the estimate of 1709.

Accordingly a final lease of 50 years for the mansion, offices and gardens was granted by the Crown in 1785, expiring in 1835; but for a portion of the premises called the "front court," another lease terminated in 1817, and was not apparently renewed, although the rent continued to be paid into the Land Revenue Offices until 1835. This gave rise to the impression, formed at the time of the Princess Charlotte's marriage, that the Duke of Marlborough's lease lapsed altogether to the Crown in the year 1817.

Meantime, sundry additions and improvements went on at Marlborough House after Sarah Duchess's death. A second storey, low and incommodious, and with small square windows, was added by Charles, the third Duke—who succeeded to the title in 1733—and the ground-floor apartments were improved.

A large riding-school was built on the site of the present stables, by George, the fourth Duke, who succeeded in 1758, and the fabric thenceforth remained practically unaltered until its occupancy by the Prince of Wales in 1863.

As the Prince's family began to increase, it was discovered that the old upper rooms, which had been devoted to the children's use, were somewhat unhealthy and unsuitable; and the fire that took place in the year 1865 had revealed the fact that the timber was in anything but a sound condition, therefore steps were at once taken to re-model this portion of the mansion, and to build an additional story to the sides, but not to the centre of the house. Under the direction of Mr. J. Taylor, one of the surveyors of Her Majesty's Board of Works, this operation was skilfully and satisfactorily executed in the year 1870. At the same time Sir Dighton Probyn's room and the school-room were built on the north front.

In the course of the alterations, it was ascertained that although the lower walls were thick the upper portion would hardly bear the burden of an additional story, without some further support, which was judiciously afforded by means of iron girders concealed in the brickwork.

Scamping is no mere product of the intense competition of the 19th century. Though not so universally practised, it was perfectly well known in the past, as evidenced by part of the masons' work in the old top story (*temp.* George II.), which was found to be largely made up of rubbish *secundum artem*. Even some of Inigo Jones' work, or rather that of his designing, has been proved to be not quite above suspicion in this respect. In fact, Mr. J. Taylor met with an example of ultra refinement in the art of scamping when the new New United Service Institution was building at Whitehall, for on the top floor, luckily in a position where no harm could arise, a portion of the south wall was disclosed, filled up, not with rubbish, but with *hay!*

These extensive alterations to Marlborough House added considerably to the comfort of its inmates, the original top floor being heightened to the proportions of that beneath it, and the new top-most one affording excellent accommodation for the servants. Sir Christopher Wren's style was adhered to as much as possible, and on the garden-front, the new story was embellished with stone medallions of the Prince of Wales' feathers. Altogether it was much improved in appearance. Indeed, few houses look more charming than does Marlborough House in the summer, its rather monotonous garden-front broken by the conservatory, and by its flower bedecked windows, beautifully draped within and shaded without by gay-coloured sunblinds.

The Prince of Wales' sitting-room—on the first floor, facing the quadrangle—was built in 1874-75; and a corresponding room was added on the east side of the building, so that the elevation should be symmetrical. A story was also added in 1885 to the east and west wings of the office buildings. In plan Marlborough House is almost a square, with the saloon in the centre. The ground floor is devoted entirely to the state apartments; the first floor to the private rooms of the Prince and Princess of Wales and Royal visitors; the second floor to those of the young Princesses and Miss Knollys; while the third floor—which extends on two sides of the square only—is occupied by servants. Including the domestic offices there are about one hundred and six rooms in the house, and it may be stated for the benefit of those who love exactitude, that the ground covered by Marlborough House and garden, including its approaches, is nearly 4¾ acres, also that the dimensions of the grounds are 542 feet east and west, and 364 feet north and south. There are three carriage entrances, one in Pall Mall and two in Marlborough Gate, where there is also a private door by the side of the German chapel. These are the only means of entry and exit. It may be noted that, as a result of the way in which the house is planned, it has three garden-frontages.

Most of the older mansions in London had very primitive arrangements for drainage, and it is not astonishing that outbreaks of malignant fever periodically killed off their inhabitants. Primitive as the system was, it was not very bad so long as the connecting drain-pipes remained level, or nearly so; but in the course of time as the earth beneath them subsided, the pipes dipped, and the natural outflow from the house was diverted, especially after heavy rains, in the opposite direction, actually filtering *backwards* under the basement, and imperceptibly producing a shocking state of insanitation. This was the case at Marlborough House until 1877-78, when everything was set right, and a system in accord with the advanced science of the day, was carried into practical effect.

The old sewer running from St. James' Palace——with which the Marlborough House system is connected—is substantially built of brick, and of considerable antiquity. It used to lead direct to the river by way of the Horse Guards in Whitehall, and Mr. J. Wilkie, the obliging Clerk of the Works at St. James' Palace, to whom I am indebted for much valuable information, tells me that it is large enough for a man to walk through with his hat on. During spring tides, the water used to be forced up the sewer, filling it to the top and frequently flooding the basement of the Palace, but now that it is connected with the main drainage this is rendered impossible.

St. James' and neighbourhood is noted for its healthiness, partly attributable to its gravel soil and to the open ground round about the Palace and Marlborough House, and in neither of these abodes are cases of sickness often known.

Her Majesty's Board of Works may be regarded in the light of benevolent landlords of Marlborough House. They do everything that is required in the way of making good all structural defects, effecting repairs, and keeping things in general in order, not even forgetting the cleaning of windows and the sweeping of chimneys. One thing, however, this paternal department cannot do for Marlborough

House, and that is, pay the parochial rates, which are heavy enough, in all conscience.

Buckingham Palace being an actual, though only occasional residence of the Sovereign, pays no rates, About one half of St. James' Palace is occupied by the Queen's official servants, and they are therefore exempt from parochial taxation ; for the remaining half of the Palace and precincts, Her Majesty by "grace and favour" contributes to the St. Martin's rates £450 every year.

Marlborough House, however — regarded as a private residence—is assessed by St. Martin's parish at £4,439 ; and taking the average rate to be 6s. in the £, the amount payable yearly by His Royal Highness is the respectable sum of £1,331.

Soon after George III.'s accession to the throne, a certain Mr. John Gwynne, architect, published an elaborate description of how London, and especially the West-end, could be altered and beautified. His work, excellently illustrated, was dedicated to the King, and sold at Mr. Dalton's, in Pall Mall. Mr. Gwynne suggested that the nation should erect a splendid palace for the Sovereign, in the middle of Hyde Park ; or, as an alternative to this ambitious scheme, that the entire block bounded by a portion of Piccadilly on the north, Cleveland Row and Clarence House on the south, St. James' Street on the east, and the Green Park on the west, should be devoted to a palatial residence in lieu of St. James' Palace.

Loyal John Gwynne's idea suggests a similar one. If at any future time it should be thought desirable to provide a new home for the Heir Apparent to the British throne, a magnificent edifice, up to date in every respect, and forming an architectural feature of the renewed metropolis, could easily be erected in that eastern portion of the Green Park which faces Devonshire House and other mansions up to Bolton street. The frontage would be splendid, the position unrivalled, and the view from its windows, of gardens and terraces across the rise towards the Surrey hills, magnificent. The appropriation of this slip of Park would incommode nobody, as this particular part is never used save by a few nurse-maids with their charges, and by tramps reclining upon the grass in the hot weather. As a matter of exchange, the gain to the national exchequer would be considerable; the cost of the new building and laying out of its grounds would be much more than covered by the ground-rents accruing from the site of Marlborough House. Ground-rents in Pall Mall are quoted at present at about 9s. 6d. per foot; therefore, with proper management the $4\frac{3}{4}$ acres of ground occupied by Marlborough House would represent an income enabling my suggestion to be carried out financially with the greatest ease.

CHAPTER XIV.

THE DUKE OF WELLINGTON'S FUNERAL-CAR AT MARL-
BOROUGH HOUSE—THE VERNON COLLECTION AT
MARLBOROUGH HOUSE.

THAT a funeral - car should ever have been exhibited at Marlborough House seems strange to the present generation; but every middle - aged individual must recollect the unsightly shed in the quadrangle, where for several years the Wellington car, deprived of many of its adornments, used to be seen on payment of a small fee.

In the middle of September, 1852, the great Duke of Wellington, the "hero of a hundred fights" succumbed to the

"single warrior
In sombre harness mailed,
Dreaded of man, and surnamed the Destroyer,"

who

" did not pause to parley or dissemble,
But smote the warden hoar."

Great Britain having decided that the funeral should be on a stupendous scale, the preparations were necessarily prolonged, and two months elapsed before the crypt of St. Paul's Cathedral received the ashes of the Duke. A magnificent funeral-car had from the first been decided upon as the central feature of the imposing procession, and the carrying out of the idea was entrusted to the School of Design, a modest institution originally accommodated at Somerset House, and after the death of the Queen Dowager, in the upper rooms of Marlborough House. All the technical arrangements for the funeral were left to Messrs. Holland, an old-established London firm, who proved fully equal to the arduous task set before them. They had previously gone down to Walmer Castle to take charge of the Duke's remains, and convey them to London. Both the plain little room in which he expired as well as the principal apartments in the Castle, had been hung with finest black cloth—expense not being considered on such an occasion—and when the Duke's body had been started upon its last journey, a regrettable wrangling arose as to the possession of these sable hangings. They were claimed as perquisites by the Duke's attendants, but their claim was ultimately disallowed, and the draperies were sent back to Messrs. Holland by the chaplain.

This incident need occasion little surprise, as Court history is full of such disputes, requiring the most delicate adjustment on the part of officials to prevent an open breach of the peace. For instance, at the coronation of Charles II., after the banquet at Westminster Hall, when the King had left, the Royal footmen "got hold of the canopy," under which, accompanied by Barons of the Cinque Ports, who upheld it by its six silver staves, the King, with the crown on his head, had entered the Hall. It was a prize worth having, no doubt, and a furious contest seems to have raged between the barons and the footmen for its possession, until the Duke of Albemarle wisely caused the bone of contention to be placed in the hands of Sir Robert Page, pending an arbitration thereon next day. Even at Buckingham Palace during the Georgian period, in fact, until the late Prince Consort initiated a system of much needed reform in the domestic arrangements, it was a common practice after a grand ball there, when perhaps some 800 tapers had been used, for the most unseemly scramble to take place amongst the pages for the candle ends.

Quite forty-seven years had elapsed since a car at all resembling Wellington's had been seen in the streets of London ; and, needless to say, this was at the state burial of Lord Nelson, when the pageant was one of the most impressive ever witnessed. This funereal but triumphal chariot was supposed to represent the " Victory." There was a figure-head in front, and at the stern floated the hero's ensign, half-mast high. The coffin (without pall)—made out of the mainmast of *L'Orient* after the battle of the Nile—rested in the centre, beneath a lofty catafalque supported by draped palm-trees at each corner, with the significant motto, "*Palmam qui meruit ferat*" above, and the name of one of Nelson's greatest victories, the "Nile" in front, while the words "Trafalgar" and "Copenhagen" figured on each side of the hangings below, which partly concealed the base of the car and its four massive wheels.

Another historic funeral-car—that used at the state obsequies of Napoleon the Great—had to be considered ere the design for the great Duke's could finally be decided upon. Early in the morning of December 15th, 1840, to the accompaniment of thundering salutes, and with much incense, the great Emperor's coffin, surrounded by a vast crowd, was landed from the barge lying near the Invalides, and transferred by the sailors of the *Belle Poule* (which had brought it from St. Helena) to the Imperial car. This was hardly artistic, being little better than a huge, cumbrous machine, rolling, as best it might, upon four wheels of antique shape. Upon the platform thus supported, adorned with banners, laurels, eagles, and velvet hangings, were twelve gilded statues, upholding with raised arms an enormous shield whereon rested the coffin. An Imperial crown, partly concealed by violet crape, was placed on the top of all, and at a given signal, horses in splendid trappings, led by grooms in Imperial livery, drew the vast structure slowly, and with difficulty, to its destination.

The Wellington car differed materially from both of these. Its main feature, like the two

The Duke of Wellington's Funeral Car as it appeared Nov. 18th, 1852.

From an original Sketch in possession of His Grace the Duke of Wellington.

just described, was necessarily a platform calculated to bear a considerable weight, but a trophy at the four corners consisting of real helmets, guns, flags and drums, produced a sense of reality and fittingness, contrasting favourably with the semi-theatrical adornments of the vehicle upon which the body of Napoleon was borne to the Invalides. Wellington's bier, covered with a splendid velvet pall, diapered with the Duke's crest and baton across, fringed with laurel leaves, the whole worked in silver, rested upon this platform; and upon the bier beneath a canopy of rich tissue, supported by halberds, lay the coffin, uncovered by pall, and bearing upon it the old warrior's sword and plumed hat.

(By the way, the great Duke was always supposed to be somewhat below the ordinary height of man; but this, like many other popular illusions, has recently been dispelled—and in a very simple manner. A suit of clothes worn by the Duke of Wellington, was tried on by the present Duke's butler, a man of medium stature, and proved too big for him.)

A carriage-framing, fitted with six ponderous bronze wheels of antique design, supported the whole. It was richly adorned with bronze figures of " Fame " upholding palm branches, with panels of " Fame," lions' heads, and the Duke's Arms. As there was not sufficient time to cast some of these figures—lions' heads, etc.—in metal, they were temporarily constructed in *carton pierre* and bronzed over, but the effect was the same. Shields, bearing the names of the endless engagements in which the great Commander had taken part, surrounded the platform. Altogether, the impression produced was one of grandeur, simplicity, and dignity combined. The entire edifice—for such it was—had been draped and beflagged by Messrs. Holland; and, in order to give an air of *vraisemblance* to the car while on exhibition in the courtyard of Marlborough House, some of this drapery was allowed to remain. In its present condition in the crypt of St. Paul's Cathedral, it is shorn of all its pomp and circumstance. A few years ago, the Council of the Institute of British Carriage Manufacturers made an application to the Dean and Chapter for its restoration and removal to some more suitable spot; but nothing came of it. Possibly, the most appropriate place wherein to exhibit this memorial of a great military leader, would be the Royal United Service Institution's new premises at Whitehall, not many yards from the Horse Guards, issuing from whence, the Iron Duke, clad in blue frock-coat, white trousers, and neck-cloth, the whole surmounted by a narrow-brimmed hat, was a sight familiar enough to a past generation.

Visitors to the Vernon Collection at Marlborough House, who *en route*, inspected the funeral-car in the courtyard, quickly realized the difficulty that

Marlborough House. 253

had been experienced in moving this ponderous vehicle. It was one thing to construct, quite another matter to haul the construction along the line of route to the Cathedral; and when a rehearsal was decided upon the day before the funeral, ordinary undertakers' horses were found to be utterly powerless to draw their load. An official in the Lord Chamberlain's department was, however, equal to the occasion, and promptly pressed into service the dray-horses of a well-known London firm of distillers. These splendid creatures, covered from head to foot with sable trappings, and led by trusty drivers, clad in mourning, with whose voices they were familiar, easily surmounted the difficulty, and added materially to the stateliness of the spectacle.

In the year 1860, the association of Marlborough House with this historic car finally ceased, as it was then made over to the care of the Office of Works, by whom it was transferred to St. Paul's Cathedral.

But what *was* the Vernon Collection referred to as being accommodated in Marlborough House?

When Marlborough House was settled upon the Prince of Wales, the Marquess of Lansdowne explained to the House of Lords that " it might be desirable to appropriate it to the object of displaying the collection of pictures which, by the munificence of the late Mr. Vernon, had become the property of the country. While in the House of Commons during the ensuing debate, the Chancellor of the Exchequer explained that it was not proposed to keep up any establishment at Marlborough House for the purposes of the Vernon collection. "There would," said he "merely be porters at the door, and door-keepers to take care of the pictures within."

Wandering through the spacious courts and galleries of the present edifice in the Cromwell Road, wherein are contained some of the most magnificent art objects in the world, rivalling even those of the Louvre or the Hotel de Cluny, and in many departments even surpassing these collections, it is hard to imagine that the first adumbration of this splendid institution was to be seen in seven or eight comparatively small rooms of a disused old mansion, where some porcelain and a few ill-hung pictures represented in the year 1850 economical John Bull's faint appreciation of a higher culture.

An amusing article entitled "A house full of horrors" appearing in "Household Words," humorously describes a visit paid to Marlborough House by a certain Mr. Crumpet, who, until his inspection of the ideal patterns and designs of the Practical Art Department, had always considered himself the happiest and most contented man in existence. Ever after, he became haunted by the most horrid shapes. "I could have cried, Sir. I was ashamed of the pattern of my own trousers, for I saw a piece of them hung there as a horror! I dared not pull out my handkerchief while anyone was by, lest I should be seen dabbling the perspiration from my forehead with a wreath of coral. I saw it all when I went home. I found that I had been living among horrors up to that hour."

In 1853-54, a splendid opportunity arose for the nation to acquire at a reasonable cost a most valuable addition to its art collection; but as is too often the case, the purchase was deprived of completeness through the parsimony of the then existing Government (the Earl of Aberdeen's). The facts were these: Mr. Bernal, Chairman of Committees in the House of Commons, had for several years been creating an extensive collection of *objets d'Art* (porcelain, etc.) which had cost him some £20,000. Nothing could have been more desirable than that Great Britain should possess it; and when Colonel Sandham, son-in-law and executor of Mr. Bernal, wrote to Mr. Henry Cole, offering it for £50,000 on the condition that a reply should be given within ten days from date, Prince Albert was consulted, who, with his usual clear insight into the merits of a thing, and with keen artistic perception of the excellence of the proposed transaction, at once pronounced in favour of the purchase. Lord Granville also was well disposed towards it, and a meeting of the Commissioners of the 1851 Exhibition was held on February 8th, to consider the matter. As to funds, there was not the slightest difficulty, for a large surplus had, as everybody knows, accrued from the World's Grand Show in Hyde Park. Mr. Disraeli was for buying the collection; Mr. Gladstone, with constitutional "open-mindedness" was both for and against such a course, giving no doubt eloquent reasons for taking this view of the matter.

Ultimately it was agreed that £20,000 only should be expended, the Department of Practical Art (now converted into the Science and Art Department) to contribute £12,000, and the British Museum, £8,000. Mr. Gladstone managed to impose a condition which proved rather calamitous, viz. that the Department was to limit the price of every object, and that any balance remaining after the purchases were effected was to be refunded, and not used in acquiring other articles, however desirable, if exceeding the official sum; the result being, that some of the most beautiful specimens were lost.

All this time the Vernon Gallery of paintings, which included some by Turner and many other great British artists, were on view in the lower rooms of Marlborough House, and were well worth seeing, many of the works now so familiar to visitors at the National Gallery being in those days quite new to the general public.

Almost simultaneously with the installation at Marlborough House of the objects purchased at the Great Exhibition, it became evident that special facilities for advanced instruction in art and science, should be afforded the School of Design students at Somerset House, and it was not long before they were installed at Marlborough House, which from the year 1852, became the head-quarters of the new " Normal Training School of Art."

But a permanent home had to be found for all these purchases. The fact had to be faced that when the Prince of Wales should attain his majority, the premises at Marlborough House would have to be vacated. Again the Prince Consort was ready as ever with an admirable plan, the result of much foresight. He suggested to the late Sir Henry Cole— to whose work on " Fifty years of Public Work " I am indebted for some of these facts—that a company should be formed to erect suitable buildings on a quadrangular piece of ground adjoining Holy Trinity Church, Brompton, to be used as temporary galleries for the Marlborough House Museum, the Educational Museum, and the British Museum. His Royal Highness sketched on blotting-paper, a ground plan and elevation of the proposed buildings, and desired Professor Semper to at once make finished drawings of the same. The Prince's ideas, however, proved to be rather too grandiose for the purpose, and something less expensive had to be thought of. Lord Palmerston asked Parliament for £15,000, a sum deemed sufficient to provide covered space for the artistic treasures mentioned. This amount was voted without a division, and a group of iron buildings, which earned for themselves the name of " Boilers," were erected by Sir W. Cubitt, whither the entire collection was transferred from Marlborough House, July 3, 1856.

Meantime, Mr. J. Sheepshanks had bequeathed to the nation his magnificent collection of modern British paintings; and, as no accommodation could be found for them in the Brompton sheds, the Government, willy nilly, had to authorize for their reception, the construction of a permanent gallery at Brompton, from the designs of Captain Fowke, R.E.

At 9.30 p.m. on June 20th, 1857, Her Majesty the Queen and Prince Albert opened this new gallery, which ceremony taking place after dark, necessarily involved its being lighted by gas—then a novelty in the administration of museums or public galleries—which was permanently adopted, and universally approved.

A suggestion had been made to the Prince Consort to designate the new Institute, the " South Kensington Museum," of which the Queen and His Royal Higness signified their approbation on the occasion of its opening.

Thus the Art-baby, nursed as the Vernon collection in the restricted space of Marlborough House, ultimately found plenty of room at South Kensington to develop into an artistic giant.

CHAPTER XV.

PAST OCCUPANTS :—PRINCE LEOPOLD.

ONE of the most interesting occupants of Marlborough House, was Leopold George Christian Frederick, third and youngest son of the Duke of Saxe-Coburg Saalfeld, brother of the Duchess of Kent, and therefore uncle both of Her Majesty the Queen and of H. R. H. the late Prince Consort.

Naturalized as an English subject, created Duke of Kendal, and united to the ill-fated heiress of the British Crown, to whom he was tenderly attached, the association of Prince Leopold with England cannot fail to be of a peculiarly close and touching nature, while the success of his after career as head of the Belgian nation, and his position as beloved and confidential adviser of our Sovereign and Prince Albert, will always entitle his memory to be held in the highest respect by the nation at large. At the outset of his military career, owing to the marriage of his sister to the Grand Duke Constantine, he speedily attained to the rank of General in the army of the Emperor Alexander of Russia, and was present when that monarch held his memorable interview with the great Napoleon at Erfurt. Then came Lützen, Bautzen, and Leipsic, at all of which battles he greatly distinguished himself; especially

17*

at the latter, when, during the four days of severe fighting, he performed prodigies of valour. He entered Paris with the allied monarchs on the 31st March, 1814, and also accompanied them to England in the following June, when London was crowded with historic personages, and fête succeeded fête in rapid succession on a scale of unprecedented magnificence.

It was during these festivities that the youthful Prince met for the first time the Princess Charlotte, then a bright and charming girl of eighteen, who had already received a good deal of attention from many eligible suitors, but had evinced no striking partiality for any of them. Prince Leopold had little indeed to recommend him in the way of fortune, for although on the staff of the Czar, his income probably did not at that time exceed £400 per annum, and he lodged at a modest establishment in High Street, Marylebone, it being not until much later that he removed to the more aristocratic Stratford Place. He possessed, however, qualifications of a very high order, and his manly, handsome personality left nothing to be desired. In both parents he was singularly fortunate. His father was cultured, intelligent, and of great political sagacity; his mother, a combination of strength of character, refinement of taste, and rare elevation of mind. Thus it was hardly surprising that their offspring should distinguish himself—as Leopold eventually did—amongst all the Princes of Europe, by his varied accomplishments and attainments in art, literature, and science.

The young Princess was not slow to discern the sterling worth of such an admirer, and with characteristic independence of character, she no doubt secretly made up her mind that upon him would she bestow her hand and exalted fortune, or upon none. A strong and mutual attachment sprung up between them, and ultimately, in 1816, the Prince was invited to England by the Foreign Secretary, Lord Castlereagh, as a possible suitor of the Heiress Apparent of Great Britain and Ireland.

In the early part of the year, the Prince Regent, acting in the name and on behalf of the King, gave his consent to the marriage; and in response to the gracious message announcing this fact, an Act of Parliament was passed, April 11th, 1816, granting an annuity of £60,000 to the Princess during her lifetime, and—in the event of her pre-decease—the sum of £50,000 per annum to her husband until his death.

Thus, so far as income was concerned, an ample provision was made for the due maintenance of their dignified position.

As regards their future residences in town and country, nothing was definitely settled before the wedding. But amongst the London mansions suggested was Camelford House—now the residence of Lord Hillingdon—at the corner of Oxford Street and Park Lane, then, of course, a much more retired spot than at present. It was frequently inspected by the happy young couple, who eventually pronounced it to be incommodious and inconvenient, and decided against it.

It is said that negotiations were also begun with the Duke of Marlborough, with a view of renting his historic house in Pall Mall, but his Grace asked £4,000 a year, which was considered excessive —and, for the time, all expectation of residing there was relinquished.

After their wedding, the estate of Claremont was purchased for them, under an agreement dated June 15th, 1816, entered into between the Commissioners of Woods and Forests, and Charles Rose Ellis Esq., whereby the latter disposed to them of his freehold manors of Esher and Milbourne, together with the mansion called Claremont, and its furniture—in all, some 516 acres—for the consideration of £66,000.

An Act for ratifying this purchase passed both Houses of Parliament on the 1st of July following, and the estate was settled upon the Prince and Princess for their joint lives; the survivor to possess the property during his or her lifetime, with reversion to the Crown. It was also provided that in the event of the Princess succeeding to the throne during the lifetime of Prince Leopold, the estate should immediately after her decease become part of the Land Revenues of the Crown; and in the event of the Princess surviving the Prince, and

afterwards succeeding to the Crown, Claremont should upon her accession be similarly disposed of.

A more auspicious day than Thursday, May 2nd, 1816, as regards weather, could hardly have been imagined. It was simply perfect. The sun shone brightly; the trees in the parks were clothed in virginal apparel of tender green; and the softness in the air, hinting at coming summer, tempted multitudes of Londoners to assemble at a very early hour in the neighbourhood of Carlton House, where the marriage ceremony was to be performed in semi-privacy.

Prince Leopold had been residing for the past three days with the genial and popular Duke of Clarence, and throughout the previous day—with the exception of two hours during which he drove out in his plain green chariot—he good-naturedly made his appearance on the balcony of the first floor three or four times an hour, from ten o'clock in the morning until five in the afternoon, thereby securing the good-will of the crowd beneath, who gave him a hearty welcome His easy, though modest, demeanour showed that he felt at home with his adopted countrymen. His manly appearance, intelligent and good-natured face, and simple, unaffected bearing, together with the plainness of his attire—blue coat, buff waistcoat, and grey pantaloons—mightily hit the public taste as being indicative of "all that was considered most respectable in the English character."

At ten o'clock, ten grey horses—the Princess's favourite colour—were paraded before the Prince, who expressed his unqualified approval of them, and they were sent on forthwith to Oatlands Park, the Duke of York's seat, where the honeymoon was to be spent.

That evening, at 8 p.m., the Prince-Regent, in honour of the coming event, gave a grand dinner, whereat H. M. Queen Charlotte was present, having driven from Buckingham House with the bride and with her daughters, the Princesses Augusta, Elizabeth, and Mary; the Queen and Princess Charlotte of Wales occupying the back seat. They arrived at Carlton House by the garden-entrance, and were very affectionately welcomed by H. R. H. the Prince Regent.

Late at night, the Queen and her daughters returned to Buckingham House, leaving the bride with her Royal father. We can easily picture the father's tender words of advice and blessing, and the daughter's half-regret, half-shy exultation at the thought of the new life of independence that would dawn upon her on the morrow; and we can readily imagine that the parting must have been peculiarly trying.

On the eventful day following, Queen Charlotte and Their Royal Highnesses, the Duke and Duchess of Orleans, and Prince Leopold, were, on their arrival at Carlton House, at once conducted to the Prince-Regent's private apartments, where they cordially greeted the bride. Her Majesty and all the female branches of the Royal Family then proceeded to the west ante-room, and thence into the great crimson saloon specially prepared for the occasion. Here, Her Majesty was led by the Prince-Regent to a chair of state, whereon she sat throughout the ceremony on the right of the temporary altar, which was covered with magnificent crimson velvet, the cushions and splendidly-bound prayer-books having been brought from the Chapel Royal, St. James'—whose sergeant was in attendance in his office as verger. Upon the altar also were the massive candlesticks and other church plate from the military chapel at Whitehall, where at that period the Guards regularly worshipped.

A procession—formed of all the great personages present—had been previously marshalled by the Lord Chamberlain, and ushered through the suite of state-rooms to the grand saloon. Lord Chancellor Eldon, the two Archbishops, most of the Bishops, and a long array of the nobility were present.

When all was ready, and the prelates had taken their places at the altar, the Lord Chamberlain returned to the Prince's private apartments — where the young couple had all this time been waiting — and conducted the bridegroom to the altar. He bore himself under the trying circumstances with great *aplomb*, and was attired in full British military uniform, wearing the insignia of the new Hanoverian Order of the Guelphs, together with other emblems of knighthood from Saxony, Austria, Russia, the Netherlands, Prussia, Bavaria, Wurtemberg, and Denmark, He also wore a magnificent sword and belt mounted with diamonds and studded with various gems. Having performed this function of his high office with great success, the Lord Chamberlain, who seems to have had a very prominent part to play in the day's proceedings, went back to fetch the bride; this time accompanied by the gallant sailor Duke of Clarence, in his naval uniform as Admiral of the Fleet.

The glances of all present in the saloon turned towards the Princess Charlotte, "the star of the goodly company," as she entered, leaning on her bachelor-uncle's arm, accompanied by her five bridesmaids — the Lady Charlotte Cholmondeley, Lady Caroline Pratt, Lady Susan Ryder, the Honourable Miss Law, and Miss Manners, the Archbishop of Canterbury's daughter. Slowly they advanced to the altar, where the Prince Regent, dressed in full regimentals, and wearing all his orders — conspicuous being the Austrian Order of the Fleece in brilliants — greeted the bride, and gave her away.

At the conclusion of the ceremony, the happy couple returned arm-in-arm, and received the hearty congratulations of all present, and shortly afterwards set off in a travelling-carriage to Oatlands Park.

When they had left, the guests were magnificently entertained, and the health of bride and bridegroom was enthusiastically drunk.

On the St. James' Park parade and at the Tower, the guns firing Royal salutes, announced to the expectant crowds that the marriage was *un fait accompli*. In the evening, all the Princess's tradesmen in honour of the event illuminated their places of business with rows and festoons of lamps and the letters " P. C." in blazing light.

Finally, be it recorded, that the bride's wedding dress was designed by a Mrs. Triaud, of Bolton Street, London, a noted dressmaker in those days. It is described as being of " magnificent silver lama or net over a rich silver tissue slip with a superb border of silver lama, the embroidery at the bottom forming shells and bouquets; above the border, an elegant fulness tastefully displayed in festoons of silver lama, and finished with a very brilliant rolio of lama. The body and sleeves to correspond, were trimmed with beautiful Brussels point lace. The mantle of rich silver tissue was lined with white satin, trimmed round with a superb silver lama border in shells corresponding with the dress, and festooned in front with diamonds. Head-dress, a wreath of rose-buds and leaves composed of brilliants. Her travelling-dress was of rich white rep silk, with flounces at bottom of Brussels point lace, with corresponding ruff and cuffs."

Her trousseau included a gown said to have cost 800 guineas, "a very superb Brussels point lace dress," worn over a slip of rich white satin.

The first anniversary of their wedding-day had come and gone, and the summer of 1817 had imperceptibly merged into autumn. Their devotion to each other had become deeper than ever as the expectation strengthened of a new and tender bond that should link them, if possible, even more closely together, and ratify the nation's hope that the succession to the throne might be assured in the direct line.

Favourable reports of the Princess's health continually arrived from Claremont; and so little apprehension was felt, that Queen Charlotte towards the end of October went down to Bath for rest and change of air as usual.

On Monday, November 3rd., the Princess was taken ill, and the next day at 3 a.m., the Princess's medical attendant, Sir Richard Croft, informed Prince Leopold that the expected event in his domestic life was imminent. The following day, all was still going on well, save for a certain amount of delay; and a bulletin to this effect was "with great propriety," as the papers said, issued to the public.

At last, on the evening of November 5th at nine o'clock, a baby prince was brought into the world, still-born. The mother, however, was reported to be doing extremely well, and as she fell into what was considered a refreshing slumber, anxiety was for the moment banished, and the Prince, who from the first had watched by her bedside with unremitting attention, was persuaded to retire to an adjoining apartment and endeavour to take some repose, a matter of necessity with him, for he was completely exhausted.

At midnight, when the Princess awoke, it was observed with the deepest concern by her attendants, that she experienced a difficulty in swallowing some gruel, and that she complained of feeling chilly, and of a sense of oppression in the chest.

Prince Leopold was immediately sent for, and instantly came to her bed-side. The three medical men present applied every possible remedy, but it was not long before it became too painfully evident to their practised intelligence that all hope must be abandoned.

At 1 a.m. violent spasms set in, succeeded by ominous exhaustion, which no restorative could overcome. All the time the sweet young Princess retained consciousness, and never once removed her tender eyes from her poor husband, who vainly endeavoured to conceal his own agony of grief. Frequently she extended her hand, which he clasped in speechless despair.

Between one and two o'clock she grew rapidly worse. Restlessness, difficulty of breathing, and signs of fatal collapse supervened; and just before the minute hand of the clock marked the half-hour after two a.m., she faintly whispered "Is there any danger?" to which the doctors could only reply that it was essential H.R.H. should compose herself. She breathed one last gentle sigh, and passed away to the other and better life beyond.

On receipt of the fatal intelligence, Lord Sidmouth, the Home Secretary, without a moment's delay, sent off a despatch to the Queen at Bath. The messenger arrived at her residence in Sydney Place at a quarter to six o'clock the same day, and found Her Majesty at dinner with the Princess Elizabeth, the Countess Dowager of Ilchester, General Taylor and others.

As the despatch was addressed to the General, he was summoned from the dining-room, and read the message with the deepest emotion, and decided that the news had better be broken to the Queen by some one else. Lady Ilchester, who was then sent for, undertook the painful task, and she and General Taylor both returned to the dining-room. On their entry, the Queen, conjecturing from their manner that something unusual had happened immediately changed colour, and with evident alarm, exclaimed "I know some fatal event has happened!"

When the full extent of the terrible calamity had been disclosed Her Majesty's agony was extreme. She covered her face, gave one convulsive sob, and retired to her private apartment, where her devoted daughter did all she could to mitigate her parent's distress and sorrow—of which, indeed, throughout her life she had experienced her full share.

Mother of fifteen children, with many and peculiar causes for family anxiety and trouble, this last and crowning sorrow—recalling the early death, seven years before in the same month, of Princess Amelia, the afflicted King's favourite daughter—completely broke up her health; and on November 17th, exactly a year afterwards, at the age of seventy-four, she followed her beloved granddaughter to the grave.

There is hardly a parallel in our time to the consternation which descended upon this country when the fact became known that the heiress to the Crown was dead, and that her infant had never lived.

In all historic cases where the heir-apparent had not survived—the Black Prince, Prince Arthur, Prince Henry of Wales, (1612,) etc.—the loss was a single loss. But the gap in the succession caused by the death of both parent and child, affected futurity in a much deeper and more important sense.

So deeply was the Prince Regent afflicted, that it was deemed necessary to bleed him twice, besides cupping him; after which drastic remedies he felt relieved bodily, but his mental suffering was as great as ever. In the midst of his own trouble, however, he, with characteristic thoughtfulness at once sent a special messenger to his son-in-law, urging him to stay at Carlton House while the melancholy preparations for the funeral were being made at Claremont.

Prince Leopold's grief was terrible to witness. He seemed like one bereft of all comfort, and for the time was deaf to the partial consolation afforded by Christian faith in a bright hereafter. His health became alarmingly affected, and he had to be "let blood" and otherwise prescribed for.

All that was mortal of the amiable Princess underwent the process of embalming, and on the nineteenth of the November following, she was laid to rest in the Royal Tomb House, Windsor. The funeral took place at night, and it was remarked as a strange coincidence—as though Nature herself had joined in the universal signs of mourning—that although it had been a very fine moonlight evening, the sky became suddenly overcast, and unusual darkness set; or so it seemed to the thousands of spectators assembled in the Royal Borough to see the mournful procession pass by.

By nine o'clock, in almost death-like silence, a sad congregation had assembled in St. George's chapel around the beloved form, borne thither by torchlight on the shoulders of six Life Guards, and followed by the agonized husband as chief mourner. The sublime service of the Church of England fell upon the dulled senses of Prince Leopold, who, utterly absorbed in grief, never once raised his eyes. But at that supreme moment when the coffin, containing all that was once his greatest happiness, was slowly lowered by a windlass into the dark vault below, his self-possession and powers of endurance almost failed him, and he became so distressingly affected that the Royal Dukes of York and Clarence, who affectionately supported him, became fearful lest he would sink beneath the burden of his terrible affliction.

All was over by ten o'clock, and, oppressed by a sorrow that nothing could mitigate or divert, the Royal family, together with the numerous spectators of the melancholy scene, slowly dispersed to their respective homes.

Not only in the metropolis, but throughout the kingdom, the effect produced was indescribable, culminating on the day of the funeral. For fourteen days, the public journals had been edged with deep borders of black, and teemed with advertisements relating almost exclusively to the general mourning, the signs of which were absolutely universal ; and it was remarked that the poorest of the poor managed somehow to become possessed of pieces of crape, or scraps of other black material, wherewith to testify their sympathy and respect.

Counting-houses and shops were everywhere closed, and even the coffee-houses and licensed victuallers put up their shutters! Business was entirely suspended at the Government offices, the docks—where every flag was half-mast-high—and elsewhere. Little groups and knots of people were seen in every direction discussing the latest details with tearful and eager interest. It seemed as if some great and terrible blow had fallen from on high over the entire land—as indeed it had. Throughout the dismal day, the blinds of all private dwellings were closely drawn down; the guns in Park and Tower, and bells high hung in tower and steeple, so pathetically associated with the joyfulness of a brief year and a half before, minute by minute boomed forth a solemn requiem, or chilled all hearts with their mournful and significant tolling. Such universal grief had not been witnessed since the news of Nelson's death had arrived in England by the schooner *Pickle* on November 5th, 1805, at Spithead, announced in the *Gazette* on the following day

Twice only during the Victorian era, has the nation so universally mourned: thirty-five years ago for a Royal Consort full of honours—but alas! not of years—and again for an eldest son, like Milton's Lycidas, " dead ere his prime."

Though more than three-quarters of a century has elapsed, so familiar to us is the story of poor Princess Charlotte, her marriage with Prince Leopold, the birth of her child, and her own untimely death, that, as we gaze at Wyatt's famous cenotaph in the nave of St. George's Chapel, touchingly representing the Princess's apotheosis, and the fine statue of her husband, appropriately placed close by, we feel linked in a peculiar and personal manner with the times in which they lived;

and the "one touch of nature" which "makes the whole world kin" enhances our sympathy with the Queen's beloved and trusted "Uncle Leopold," deepening our regret for the sad experience of his early days in this, the country of his adoption.

Upon Prince Leopold this bereavement fell with overwhelming force, and, for the time, he retired absolutely from society of any kind, and lived in the strictest seclusion at Claremont, the scene of his greatest happiness. He paid off all the workmen who had been employed in effecting the various alterations and improvements in which the Princess had taken much interest.

Gradually, like one who had been stunned, the Prince recovered consciousness of the fact that his own life had to be lived out to its allotted space, and that duties, however distasteful, had to be faced; but it was several years before he felt equal to the excitement of a London season. During his retirement at Claremont, he endeavoured to divert his mind from incessantly brooding upon the past, by making a journey to Scotland, where he visited Sir Walter Scott—then at the height of his fame—at Abbotsford, who describes him in a private letter as "melancholy, yet evincing a capacity for humour," and he goes on to say that the Prince, once alluding to the crowds that followed him everywhere, mentioned some place where he had gone out to shoot, but, said he, "I was afraid to proceed for fear of bagging a boy."

During the year succeeding Prince Leopold's marriage, and before anything had been decided about a residence, attention was freely drawn by the newspapers to Marlborough House as a particularly suitable abode for the "heiress of the British throne." But as we have seen, the negotiations for the rental of it fell through for the time being. However, in 1824, the fourth Duke of Marlborough sub-let Marlborough House to Prince Leopold, and he lived there when in town until he became King of the Belgians in 1831.

Prince Leopold's Comptroller of the Household was Sir Robert Gardiner, who had been selected for that position after his return from Waterloo and Paris, and whose son General H. Lynedoch Gardiner, Her Majesty's Groom-in-Waiting in Ordinary, has kindly given me some very interesting facts connected with Prince Leopold's occupancy of Marlborough House.

Naturally of a sociable disposition, Prince Leopold, on his return to London society, soon began to assume the *rôle* of entertainer, for which he was eminently qualified, and invitations to his dinner-parties were eagerly welcomed and appreciated. They were very elegantly served, with a refinement of taste by no means universal in those days. The marvellous floral decorations we are accustomed to were then unknown, while heaviness was the feature of the *cuisine* even in the best houses, in spite of the efforts made by such *bon-vivants* and connoisseurs as the Earl of Dudley and Ward, and the Earl of Wilton (the latter of whom had the best *cuisine* in London) to popularize "foreign kickshaws."

Lady Louisa Tighe, now in her ninety-third year, exemplifying the well-known fact that very aged people recollect events which have happened at the beginning of their career very much better than the occurrences of yesterday, distinctly remembers dining at Marlborough House in March, 1825, with her mother, the Dowager Duchess of Richmond, when Prince Leopold congratulated her heartily on her approaching marriage with Mr. Tighe, of Woodstock, Inistioge, Ireland, and added with great affability and feeling, "I hope you will be very happy." This good wish was most amply fulfilled, as the lady throughout her married life considered herself the happiest woman in existence. Lady Tighe vividly remembers that the plate used at the dinner was extremely handsome.

It was also the custom of Prince Leopold to give concerts at which the leading operatic singers of the day took part—Sontag, Pasta, Curioni, Donzelli, and a host of others. These delightful entertainments were given in what was then the hall, but is now the saloon; and no apartment could have been more suitable for the purpose. It was considered a great privilege to be a guest at Marlborough House during Prince Leopold's genial reign, and the delivery of the magic cards commencing "Sir Robert Gardiner is commanded by H. R. H. Prince Leopold to invite, etc.," always caused quite a flutter of excitement at their aristocratic destination.

Greece having obtained her independence after the battle of Navarino, and the three powers—Russia, France and England—deciding that the classic little country should be made into a separate kingdom, the crown was offered to, but declined by, Prince John of Saxony. Prince Leopold was approached on the same subject in the year 1830, and after many consultations—amongst others, with the Earl of Aberdeen—and much consideration, the Prince provisionally accepted the throne offered to him, but eventually relinquished it, his announcement of this fact being dated from Marlborough House.

His London residence was destined soon afterwards to be the scene of still more important historical negotiations, as Belgium, emerging from the trouble and confusion entailed by her final separation from Holland, sent over to England certain deputies empowered by the provisional government to sound Prince Leopold as to the probability of his accepting the crown of Belgium. They met with a very courteous reception from the Prince at Marlborough House, and received a diplomatic and carefully-thought-out reply to their enquiry.

On the fourth of June, after some formidable

riots had taken place at Liège, Antwerp, and Brussels, the National Congress, at the conclusion of a prolonged debate, elected Prince Leopold to be their hereditary monarch, by an overwhelming majority. Directly the result was known, Mr. White, Lord Ponsonby's secretary, set off from Brussels with the news, and reached London only to find that the Prince had gone down to Claremont. Following him thither, he communicated his highly-important intelligence to the King-elect, who received it with much gratification. On the twenty-sixth, preliminary agreements relating to the acceptation of the exalted position were signed at Marlborough House, and at nine o'clock in the evening of the same day, a deputation from the Belgian Congress presented the National decree calling upon Prince Leopold to become King of the Belgians.

As newly-elected King, the Prince, on the 12th July following, received the representatives of the five great European Powers, who came to offer their formal congratulations, to which he replied in very suitable terms, and on the 16th he finally left London, entering Brussels in Royal State on the 21st.

Thus closed this amiable Prince's residential connection with our country, extending over a period of fifteen years. But until his death in December 1865, he frequently came to England, and on one occasion, after the decease of the

Duchess of Kent, he spent five weeks with Her Majesty the Queen, to whom he was able to afford very special comfort and consolation.

With a noble appreciation of the fitness of things the Prince, on becoming King of the Belgians, placed his income of £50,000 per annum in the hands of Trustees, and directed them to keep up Claremont in the same manner as during his occupancy of it, and after providing for the salaries of the officials, Sir Robert Gardiner and Sir Edward Cust, and the wages of the servants, to pay the balance into the National Exchequer, as he did not consider it right that a foreign sovereign should spend English money abroad.

Claremont, the King placed at the disposal of Queen Victoria whenever she felt inclined to make use of it; and she was in the habit of spending her birthday there in perfect retirement with the Prince Consort until the Revolution of 1848 drove the Orleans family from the Throne of France, to find a refuge and a home for many years in this quiet country-seat of lovely Surrey.

Sir Robert Gardiner, as Comptroller to Prince Leopold, used to occupy "Little" Marlborough House, as it was called, which stood against the north wall of the German Chapel, and extended halfway up the entrance roadway towards Pall Mall, leaving just room for carriages to pass to and from the gates. General Gardiner says that he well remembers long before the South

Western Railway was made, coming up to Marlborough House from the "Bear Inn" at Esher in his father's carriage with grey post horses, and himself and his brother being always turned out to play in the grounds where the Prince of Wales' garden-parties are now given.

Well, may the present ruler of Belgium, during his pleasant and unostentatious visits to England, associate Marlborough House with his Royal father, upon whom, as King, no higher eulogium could be bestowed than that which at his death was transmitted by telegram from the Emperor Napoleon III. :—" The Empress and myself sympathise most deeply in the affliction that has befallen you. Your august father always displayed great affection towards me, and I always entertained for him the same feeling. King Leopold was renowned for his great intelligence and wisdom. He was one of the most justly revered monarchs of Europe. I hope that on the throne you will follow the great example bequeathed by your illustrious predecessor. On every occasion, I shall be happy to give you proof of the affection I feel for you."

CHAPTER XVI.

PAST OCCUPANTS:—QUEEN ADELAIDE.

ONE of the first matters that engaged King William's attention on his accession to the throne, was that of settling by Act of Parliament upon his Royal Consort, an annuity of £100,000 in the event of his predecease, with the delightful provision which all rate-payers will appreciate, that every part of it should be "free and clear from all taxes, impositions, and other public charges whatsoever." In addition to this it was enacted, in case she should survive the King, and also for her better accommodation, that Marlborough House should under the Great Seal be given and assured to her for her sole enjoyment and benefit during the term of her natural life.

Not content even with this practical manifestation of his regard, King William appointed her as "Keeper and Custodian of Bushey Park," at the same time bestowing upon her the office of "Housekeeper and Custodian of the Honour of Hampton Court" for life, and subsequently made her "Perpetual Ranger of St. James' Park."

Apart from the King's attachment to her, there must have been something peculiarly trustworthy and attractive in the character and disposition of the

Royal Consort, to merit so striking an example of the King's favour.

After her demise, at Bentley Priory, in 1849, the great preacher, Frederick Robertson of Brighton, evidently in reference to her remarkably simple funeral, wrote to a friend :—

"Mr. A. told me some interesting things about the unaffected simplicity of the Queen Dowager and the deep religiousness of her character. Certainly it is a wonderful thing to remember how she steered through one of the most tangled portions of our history, giving no offence, dismissing all pomp, refusing to hold a court, and, by the simple power of spotless goodness, commanding an enthusiasm which has been rarely given to the most splendid achievements. I do not know that I have ever heard anything so real as her funeral directions since the account of the death of Arnold."

The hand that penned this eulogium, and the eloquent tongue that from the pulpit subsequently dilated upon the "Good Queen's" virtues, are still in death. But the following verbatim and interesting summary of Queen Adelaide's character comes to me from a lady still living, who, through her connection with the Court, had unusual facilities for forming a correct judgment.

She says that "when Queen Adelaide became a widow, her life was retired and mostly spent at Bushey Park or Marlborough House. Her time was occupied with acts of kindness to all who came within her reach. She was not beautiful, but very graceful, and her large grey eyes were full of expression, and could look either very stern or very tender. The motive power of her character was a deep sense of duty, down to the minutest details, and it was through her example and influence that many adopted the practice of family prayers before breakfast. The service was performed by her domestic chaplain, the Rev. John Ryle Wood, afterwards Canon of Worcester Cathedral. Her generosity was great, and was manifested in the most delicate manner. Her patience and anxiety to save trouble to others was shown in many ways. She spent the tenth of her income regularly in charity or in forwarding any work for God. No one who knew her could fail to be raised in the tone and conduct of their conversation. Her judgment was so much to be relied on that it was sought by many. She lessened the work of the cooks on Sunday, and refused to go a Ball given in her honour in Germany, on that day which she always observed with reverence. She died beloved by all who knew her good and simple life."

By the death of Princess Charlotte, the succession to the British throne was placed in a state of considerable uncertainty, and it was no wonder that steps were quickly taken to remove, so far as human foresight could prevail, the unsatisfactory state of things that existed.

Two of the Royal Dukes—Cambridge and Kent

HER MAJESTY QUEEN ADELAIDE.
After the oil painting by H. Dawe.
Facing page 284.

—were married in Germany during the month of May, 1818. As regards the Duke of Clarence, the sagacious Queen Charlotte had some time previously, with motherly foresight, selected his future wife in the person of Adelaide Louisa, eldest child of George, ruler of the independent little kingdom of Saxe-Meiningen, a duchy comprising not more than 1,000 square miles—at the present moment absorbed with its quarter of a million of inhabitants in the mighty German Empire.

This Duke George, whose wife was Princess Louisa of Hohenlohe-Langenburg, was gifted in a marked degree mentally and morally. During the revolutionary wars he had fought like a hero, and when peace was assured within his own borders he offered a refuge to men of letters and politicians who had been driven into exile from the surrounding States. He loved to gather round him scholars, artists, poets and philosophers, and amongst those with whom he mixed in unrestricted social intercourse, were Schiller and Jean Paul Richter. Unlike his predecessors, who were given to formality, ceremony, and the strict observance of etiquette, Duke George condescended to visit the burgher families in his duchy, and went so far in his levelling ideas as to cause his own mother to be interred in the common church-yard. " She was worthy," he said, "of lying among her own subjects," most of whom were simple country folk, at whose rustic festivals the Duke would willingly partake of the creamy beer that on such occasions they regaled themselves with.

Besides Princess Adelaide, Duke George had another daughter, Ida, interesting to us because she ultimately married, and became mother of our popular and well-known Prince Edward of Saxe-Weimar.

George III.'s wise consort, could have made no better selection for her middle-aged sailor son than that of a Princess possessing all the virtues combined with an unusual wealth of common sense.

Surmounting many obstacles, chiefly of a pecuniary nature—which at the time seemed to threaten failure—the preliminaries of this marriage were at last arranged; and one July evening in 1818 as darkness was setting in, the Duchess of Saxe-Meiningen with her daughter Adelaide, then aged twenty-six, drove up to Grillon's Hotel in Albemarle Street. But by some mistake—probably because they arrived earlier than was expected, or from some other miscalculation of time—there was no one present to accord them the welcome naturally looked for under such circumstances. The Prince Regent was dining at Carlton House, and the Duke of Clarence was out visiting.

After the Duchess and her daughter had dined, and somewhat recovered from the fatigue of travelling, the Prince Regent having been apprised of their arrival, quickly came to pay his respects. Later on, the bridegroom elect drove up in a carriage drawn by four horses ; mutual acquaintance speedily ripened, and with much informal hilarity, the visit was prolonged well into the small hours of the morning.

On the eleventh of the same month they were quietly married at Kew Palace, the Prince Regent giving the bride away. At the same time, and in the same place, the Duke and Duchess of Kent— who had been united onthe 29th of May at Coburg, according to the rites of the Lutheran Church —were re-married in accordance with the Church of England ritual.

After the ceremony, the Duke and Duchess of Kent took their departure, but the bride and bridegroom remained, and took part in a very lively *al fresco* tea-party, held in the well-known grounds near the Pagoda. They afterwards drove away to St. James' Palace, the Prince Regent with good spirit leading the hearty cheering that proclaimed their happy " send-off."

After a brief residence at the Palace, and afterwards at Bushey Park, they went to Hanover, where a daughter was born, who survived but a few hours. In December, 1820, another Princess was brought into the world, but, to the great sorrow and disappointment of the parents, the little one lived only until the following March. Chantrey, with exquisite skill, reproduced in marble the form of this lost child, which has its place to this day in the famous corridor at Windsor Castle.

Returning to England, they had apartments allotted to them in St. James' Palace, where they were anything but comfortable, the rooms being small and very inconvenient. They also lived at Clarence House.

When the intelligence was conveyed to the Duchess that by the death of George IV. she had become Queen of England, she burst into tears, and bestowed upon the bearer of the tidings, a prayer-book she held in her hand. It seemed to her an appropriate gift; but probably a less spiritual *largesse* would have been more appreciated by the recipient of the new Queen's favour.

Amongst the members of the new Royal Household, were the present Earl Howe's father, who was appointed Lord Chamberlain, and remained in office for some years—to whom Queen Adelaide was so devoted, that when political differences with the Government compelled him to resign, the Queen steadfastly refused to have anyone nominated in his place—and Earl Denbigh, Master of the Horse, also a great favourite, and grandfather of the present Earl. The daughters of both these Peers were frequently at Queen Adelaide's Court.

On sharing the throne with William IV. Queen Adelaide's mode of life does not seem to have much changed. It was simply that the sphere of her good actions became greater. She was cheerful and hopeful as ever; her evenings were spent very quietly, generally given up to tapestry-work, in which she was an adept. Certainly, the Court could not be said to possess much grandeur. It was essentially homely, as were the habits of the Royal couple, whom nothing pleased better than to look on at some thousands of the poor being feasted in Windsor Park, or to do some quiet shopping at Brighton, where the Queen once picked up a reticule dropped by an infirm old lady, a kindly action made much of at the time, and doubtless never forgotten by the bystanders.

It is said that King William and his Consort paid more private visits to people of all ranks than any Sovereign before them, and this is probably true. As Duchess of Clarence, the Queen when at Chatham, had usually been entertained by Commissioner Cunningham's daughters on terms of perfect freedom and unrestraint. On her accession, the young ladies were invited to Bushey, and at their first meeting they naturally bent down to kiss the Queen's hand. "No, no," said Her Majesty, "that is not the way I receive my friends. I am not changed." And so it was always; whenever she met with old acquaintances, they were greeted affectionately, kissed, and treated without the least appearance of affectation.

The year following the King and Queen's accession, Princess Victoria appeared for the first time in the Royal circle, the occasion being that of a Drawing-room held on February 24th, 1831, in honour of Queen Adelaide's birthday. Standing on the left of her aunt, the youthful Princess—then in her twelfth year—dressed in white satin, and wearing a pearl necklace, with her fair hair held back by a diamond clasp, was the observed of all that brilliant throng.

Towards the year 1837 the King's health had begun to fail, and in the month of June, it became evident that he had not long to live. Queen Adelaide nursed him unceasingly. On the eve of his death as Archbishop Howley, having concluded the solemn service for the sick and dying, pronounced the benediction, the old monarch turned his eyes upon his sorrowing wife, and with the characteristic heartiness of his former profession, and in a voice as cheerful as his failing strength would permit, bade her "bear up, cheer up." Until all was over, the Queen remained by his bedside; then, laying his unconscious head, which she had been tenderly supporting, upon the pillow, she withdrew from the room.

She was present throughout the ceremony of the King's obsequies at Windsor, being the only Queen of England who had ever actually witnessed her Kingly Consort laid in the tomb. In the following month, she left the castle for Bushey while Marlborough House was being got ready for her; but as there had been nothing done to it in the way of substantial repairs for many years, considerable delay was involved.

In the year 1836, a sum of £3,700 was voted— on the general estimates for Royal palaces and public buildings—to be spent in repairs; in addition to £1,728 received from the Duke of Marlborough. The next year, £4,000 more were provided; and, later on in the same year, an additional sum of £21,000 was voted upon a separate estimate for preparing the house for its occupation by the Queen Dowager, who came up from Bushey to see what was necessary in the way of alterations and repairs, Lady Clinton being in attendance upon her, and amongst her suite, Earl Howe, Earl Denbigh, Sir B. Stephenson, Lady Bedingfield, Miss Hudson, and the Rev. J. Wood. As it was her first visit to the Dower House, the Marquis of Conyngham was present in his official capacity as Queen Victoria's Lord Chamberlain.

In forming the new establishment at Marlborough House, the Countess of Brownlow and Lady Barrington were included as Ladies of the Household, and the minor offices were filled up from the old servants at Windsor Castle, most of whom had been discharged with pensions on the accession of Queen Victoria. Out of twelve footmen thus selected, eight were placed at Marlborough House, and the organizing of the household proceeded.

But it was not until March the following year that the *Court Journal* was able to inform the world that the Queen-Dowager had arrived in Town from St. Leonards, where she had passed the winter, and had taken up her residence at Marlborough

House; also that the Duchess of Cambridge and other members of the Royal family had visited her, and that the apartments had been fitted up with "great elegance," but the workmen were not yet out of the house.

On April 7th, 1838, Queen Victoria paid a visit to her widowed aunt for the first time at Marlborough House, though they had frequently met at Windsor and Bushey. During the season, Queen Adelaide gave several small and very select dinner-parties.

On Her Majesty the Queen's memorable Coronation-day, the Queen-Dowager was in residence at Marlborough House, and at 9 a.m., she drove along the line of route to be taken by the procession, in order to view the preparations for the approaching ceremony—a remarkable instance of the good-feeling existing between the two exalted ladies, and the entire absence of jealousy on the part of the elder. Queen Adelaide was loudly cheered by the crowds already at that early hour assembled. A covered balcony was erected at Marlborough House, and placed at the disposal of a number of ladies and gentlemen connected with the household.

One of the first special entertainments given by Queen Adelaide in London was that on the 8th of June, 1839, when her brother-in-law, the Grand Duke of Saxe-Weimar, was the chief guest; Count de Beust, M. de Wyner, Earl and Countess of

Mayo, Earl Howe, and Viscount Curzon, amongst others being present.

But the Marlborough House festivities of that year, culminated on the twenty-ninth of the same month, when Queen Victoria dined there, attended by a large suite — the Countess of Burlington (Lady-in-waiting), the Earl of Uxbridge (Lord Chamberlain), the Earl of Albemarle (Master of the Horse), Lord Gardner, the Hon. Colonel Cavendish, and the Hon. W. Cowper. The Queen's half-sister, the Princess of Leiningen, accompanied her on this occasion, and the guests invited to meet Her Majesty included the Duchess of Gloucester, the Duke of Sussex, the Duke and Duchess of Cambridge, and Princess Augusta, the Princesses of Hohenlohe and Prince Edward of Saxe-Weimar. After dinner, there was a small party, Her Royal Highness Princess Sophia Matilda, and the ladies and gentlemen of the different Royal households, joining the circle.

On the occasion of Queen Victoria's marriage the following year, another grand dinner was given by the Dowager-Queen, in honour of the joyful event, when several members of the Royal Family and many dignitaries were present.

Queen Adelaide's entertainments at Marlborough House were proverbial for their completeness and comfort, and Lord Brougham, during the debate in the House of Lords in 1850 upon the bill for securing Marlborough House to the Prince of

Wales, recorded his experience of the late Queen-Dowager's kind hospitality of which he had so often been the recipient.

Prince Edward of Saxe-Weimar says that in those days the interior arrangements of Marlborough House were very different from what they are now, and were probably identical, or nearly so, with those of the Duchess Sarah's time. Before me is a very interesting " Plan de l'Hôtel de Marlborough à Londres," published in Paris in the eighteenth century, and in it the principal rooms on the ground floor are placed much as they were in 1837-1849.

The present large drawing-room was divided then into three separate apartments; the dining-room was the drawing-room; the present tapestry and painting-rooms combined, formed the dining-room; spiral staircases communicated with the first floor in the south and south-west corners of the house; and in the same portion of the building, were small apartments, one of which, during his Royal aunt's time, was set apart for Prince Edward's use, ever a welcome visitor, and whose recollection, therefore, of Marlborough House in the past, is probably more extensive than that of any living person, except the Queen.

Queen Adelaide's private sitting-room, or boudoir, was on the first floor, and identical with that used by the Princess of Wales, while her bedroom—now the reception-room, was next to it. The present household dining-room formed two rooms ; and the saloon, as we have before noticed, was the hall where the footmen sat, and where callers of no great social importance waited. A long covered passage reaching half-way down the quadrangle gave shelter to visitors as far as the front door, which was approached by steps as at present.

In the inner hall—the modern saloon—the Queen Dowager used to give delightful concerts at which Malibran, Miss Stephens, Braham and others charmed their hearers. Ballets also, says Prince Edward, were performed here with great success by Viennese dancers, who were especially patronized by the Court leaders of fashion. Referring to these relaxations, got up and arranged by the good Queen Dowager chiefly, we may be sure, with a view of giving pleasure to others, the lady referred to in the opening of this chapter says : " I remember several delightful evenings at Marlborough House. Once Madame Rachel recited in the drawing-room unaided by scenery or actors, which only displayed her genius the more ; but the exertion was so great that she fainted away. Another evening of rare enjoyment was on the occasion of a concert in the Hall of the House, when Jenny Lind and all the greatest artistes took part."

The Queen Dowager, although a most devout woman, had no trace of rigid Puritanism in her disposition, and liberally encouraged the musical and dramatic art of the day ; for Blanchard Jerrold in his "Life of George Cruikshank," mentions the fact that in 1837, a "Fairy Album," edited by L. E. L. was dedicated by special permission to Queen Adelaide. This periodical was of microscopic proportions; even to read it at all, requiring the use of the magnifying glass which accompanied it. Bound in vellum and gold and enclosed in a blue velvet case, its pages were enriched with fairy music, and it was illustrated with tiny portraits of Pasta, Malibran, and other noted singers.

In Messrs. Broadwood's books there is an entry recording that H.M. the Dowager Queen possessed a grand piano made by their firm. In the same ledger, appears a record that Her Majesty hired an upright piano on September 13th, 1836, which was dispatched to Portsmouth to be placed on board H.M.S. *Hastings*. In the following year, there is the interesting entry that a hired cottage-piano was returned from Marlborough House.

Exceedingly simple were the Queen Dowager's tastes and habits, and she was very saving as regards her personal expenditure. Both King William and herself made it a rule never to exceed their income, the result being that at the year's end there was often a considerable surplus to devote to charitable purposes.

The crown used for Queen Adelaide at her coronation was very diminutive. It was most brilliant, however, and was composed of her own jewels, in order to save expense. Indeed the entire ceremony curtailed as it was in many of its features, and minus the grand banquet at Westminster Hall was altogether on an economical scale, and cost certainly less than a fifth of the sum expended upon George IV's coronation. A curious incident occurred in connection with this toy-like crown. Queen Adelaide's hair was arranged in the prevailing fashion in a knot at the top of her head. The Archbishop duly placed the diadem in its proper place, but necessarily so insecurely that the slightest movement would have precipitated the emblem of Royalty upon the floor of the Abbey, which, in conjunction with the dropping of the sword of state by Earl Grey on the same occasion, would have been regarded as a double omen of dire significance. Her ladies in waiting, however, quickly perceived the precarious position of the crown, and by skilful manipulation secured it safely upon her head. At the moment that the Primate crowned Queen Adelaide, a bright sunbeam darted through the windows, and fell full upon her diadem of jewels, lighting it up with wonderful effect.

This charming incident must have been recalled by the eye-witnesses years afterwards when they reverently listened to the words of hope with which the remains of Adelaide the Good were consigned to the grave, and thought of that other and imperishable crown she had won in the world above by the beauty and excellence of her life here below.

CHAPTER XVII.

PAST OCCUPANTS :—THE FIRST DUKE AND DUCHESS
OF MARLBOROUGH—CONCLUSION.

NOT long ago, a writer in the *Saturday Review*, remarking upon the influence of climate on the formation of character, gave it as his opinion that in the West of England "all asperities of thought, all acute prepossessions, gradually translate themselves into a vacuous indifference under the spell of the balmy atmosphere, and the voluptuous colours of the fertile hills. Devonshire is the grave of mental enthusiasms and physical angularities; its population absorb moisture and grows fat."

Whether, if Fate had decreed for John Churchill, a continual residence within the boundaries of this lovely county, he too would have lost his individuality, is a fit subject for one of those curious speculations that the elder Disraeli indulged in. Almost certainly the fate of many countries throughout Europe, and possibly that of our own land, would have been different had Winston and Elizabeth Churchill's second son, born to them on the banks of quiet-flowing Axe, remained in his native district. True, that wherever his lot had been cast, John Churchill would have distinguished himself; but he might never have met with Sarah Jennings, the battle of Blenheim might never have been fought, and the mansion in Pall Mall, might never have been built.

To do more in one short chapter than sketch in outline the life of England's greatest general, and that of his remarkable wife, is obviously impracticable.

Up to the age of twelve, young Churchill was tutored by the Rector of Musbury, the site of a Roman camp commanding the valley of the Axe, and it is easy to imagine the future conqueror of Tallard imbibing from the old associations of the neighbourhood his taste for a military career.

Frequently must he have visited Lambert's Castle, some six miles to the east of Axminster, one of the pre-Roman hill fortresses abounding in the district—a strong entrenchment with triple mounds and ditches, covering an area of twelve acres, whence an unequalled view is obtained far and wide into Devon and Dorset. Doubtless, he wandered through the narrow lanes, and over the undulating hills leading seawards, and past the mill at Uplyme—since rendered famous by the author of "'Twas in Trafalgar's Bay"—down a combe, musical with the tinkling of murmuring streams, inexhaustible even in the droughtiest summers, and examined with rapt attention the head-quarters of Prince Maurice at Colway House, who in the year 1644 essayed to bring about the submission of Puritan Lyme Regis, but had eventually to withdraw, leaving the bodies of two thousand of his Irish and Cornish troopers to fatten the orchards that abound on the banks of the winding and babbling Lyme. Charmouth too, the boy must have been familiar with, and the Cavalier side of his nature was doubtless stirred deep as he listened to the tale of the King's attempt to escape from England after the battle of Worcester in 1651, and how on that very beach the exiled monarch had paced hour after hour with Colonel Wyndham, vainly waiting until long after midnight for Captain Ellesden to appear with his long boat, and convey him to Lyme Regis, and thence in his sloop to France.

All this and more, the handsome, thoughtful lad must have pondered over, and returning home along the lofty Charmouth cliffs, may have watched with awe the uprising in the south-west of some great tempest, as masses of clouds piled themselves one upon another, dark and sullen, presently to burst with wrath and destruction upon the quiet bay beneath him. Little could he have imagined that a storm, the greatest ever known in this country, was to form the simile of certain immortal lines addressed to himself, the victor of Blenheim, and written by a most distinguished scholar and gentleman, named Addison.

But all this delightful wandering about at his own sweet will and pleasure was soon to cease. Crossing the wide sea for the first time, he sojourned with his parents in Ireland, and regularly attended the City of Dublin Free School. Returning to England at the end of a year, he was sent to St. Paul's School, there to become one of the 153 boys —representing the mystical fishes of St. Peter— out of "every nation, country, and class," for whose permanent classical enlightenment, old Dean Colet had so liberally provided in the previous century. Young Churchill, however, was destined to go forth into the world insufficiently equipped — so we should regard it—with scholastic armour; for the Great Plague broke out; the school was temporarily closed, and with it, permanently, John Churchill's education.

At the early age of seventeen, he commenced his military life by entering the Foot Guards, and joined the English garrison at Tangiers, that unsatisfactory item in Katherine of Braganza's dowry. Always conspicuous for courage, he fought his first duel on attaining the legal age of manhood, and under the great Turenne obtained his first experience of Holland, a country he was fated to become very familiar with. He gained the favour of Louis XIV.—an autocrat in whose Court grace of manner, combined with a handsome presence, always won immediate attention. Singularly attractive must have been Churchill's personal appearance, and his gentle demeanour and gracefulness of expression captivating to all classes. A profusion of fair hair, long eye-lashes shading eyes of deepest blue, straight, well-moulded features, a tall, finely-proportioned figure and commanding bearing, enhanced by the picturesque dress of the period, combined to make the charming picture which we instantly recognize in existing portraits.

On his return to England, his marked success at the French Court soon bore fruit, for though but twenty-four years of age, he was made Lieutenant-Colonel of a foot regiment.

About this time, all unconscious of her destiny, a bright young girl, playmate of Princess Anne at St. James' Palace, was developing the qualifications of mind and body that would fit her to be the consort of the distinguished young officer. Needless to say, this was Sarah Jennings, who, at the age of sixteen, became engaged to John Churchill, and was married to him in the presence of Mary of Modena, Duchess of York, whose maid of honour she was when but a child. A glorious couple they must have been; he in the maturity of manly beauty, ten years her senior, and she, radiant as some half-opened rose with youthful freshness and loveliness.

And now, the future Duke's career may be said to have commenced in earnest; for with a helpmate whose ruling passion was ambition, no chance was missed, no opportunity lost, in the race that ultimately led to power, fame, and fortune almost "beyond the dreams of avarice." To James II. John Churchill was indebted for his rapid advance in the army; and during the opening years of that

THE FIRST DUKE OF MARLBOROUGH.

From a miniature in the possession of His Grace the Duke of Marlborough.

Facing page 303.

NOTE.—This interesting portrait of his illustrious ancestor has been very kindly selected for this work by His Grace the Duke of Marlborough from his collection of miniatures at Blenheim Palace. The figure to the right is probably that of James, the first Pretender.

monarch's reign, he had, by his victory over Monmouth at Sedgemoor, fully vindicated the King's confidence in his talents. Then came his desertion of the last of the Stuarts, when William of Orange landed at Torbay, and the expedition to Ireland, which, though lasting but five weeks, resulted in his brilliant capture of Cork and Kinsale. In 1692, Churchill was summarily dismissed by William III. from all his public offices, and commencing to intrigue for the restoration of James II., he was consigned to the Tower for some weeks, though on the false evidence of a man of infamous character. But the accession of Queen Anne brought with it substantial rewards to the Churchills for their faithful adherence to the once neglected Princess. His immediate creation as a Knight of the Garter, his appointment as Captain-General of the forces, a Dukedom, and a life pension of £5,000 per annum were the preludes to honours that were to fall fast and thick upon him during the seven glorious years from 1702 to 1709 when victory succeeded victory—Blenheim, Ramilies, Oudenarde and Malplaquet.

Whilst Marlborough was winning the last named battle with the allied army in Flanders, the Duchess was planning the building of the London mansion that should bear their name for all time, and be, as she fondly hoped, the head-quarters of her ambitious social campaign.

"My precept," says Cicero, "to all who build is

that the owner should be an ornament to the house, and not the house to the owner." No doubt, this advice, with many a complimentary personal application of it, after the fashion of the day, had been repeated to the Duchess as soon as her intention of building a grand town house became known, and although, when completed, it was pronounced by society to be "one of the most perfect models in England," there can be little doubt that its greatest adornment was its originator and owner herself.

Although the Duchess was close upon fifty in 1709, she was still a magnificent and fresh-looking woman. There was something queenly about her tall stateliness, akin to her disposition; for as the historic Hume remarks, she might at one time have been regarded as *de facto* the sovereign of England. In the rich fullness of her lips, her pretty mouth, languorous eyes, and nose slightly *retroussé*, there was discernible an indication of latent coquetry, but her style of beauty, at even an earlier period of her life, was more calculated to inspire a sentiment of respectful admiration than the tender feeling of love.

The Marlborough family reached the zenith of their fame in 1709, when, in the natural order of things, their influence at Court began visibly to decline; but their final dismissal by Queen Anne had to be postponed to a more fitting occasion.

Meantime, from the correspondence of Lady

THE FIRST DUCHESS OF MARLBOROUGH.
After Sir George Kneller.

Wentworth, we get some interesting glimpses of the part played by the Marlboroughs in the constantly shifting social drama, and the jealousy and envy to which they were necessarily subjected, partly no doubt because of their arrogance and self-sufficiency.

Prince George of Denmark, the easy-going consort of Queen Anne, died on October 28th, 1708, and the Court went into deep mourning. At the expiration of six months, these outward signs of respect were partly abandoned by certain ladies, led on it was said by the Duchess of Marlborough's daughters, who had the bad taste to appear at the Chapel Royal before the Queen, dressed partly in colours, necessitating the interference of the Lord Chamberlain. But the Duchess herself had previously evinced her contemptuous disregard for etiquette and proper feeling by waiting upon the bereaved sovereign shortly after the death of her husband, with powder on her hair and a patch on her face!

All this seems paltry enough, but the downfall of Marlborough was as much due to the utter disregard of tact and self-restraint on the part of his wife, as to the machinations of his avowed enemies. Already, the tide had begun to ebb. In the following year, Lady Wentworth writing to her brother, Lord Raby, at Berlin, said : " The Duke of Marlborough by all that sees and hears of his successes, is pronounced a happy man, but I am told by a gentleman that saw a letter from him to a Parliament man, wherein he said he was vext to the soul at the usage he received from the House of Commons in a year when he had not only all the success cou'd be desired, but that he had labour'd more than ever to serve his country."

As Lord Wolseley says :—" It is a melancholy truth that success breeds envy and detraction. Marlborough's rivals, English and Dutch, thought to disparage his achievements by attributing them to good luck; but, making every allowance for the envy and hostility of this class, it is a curious fact that courteous, affable, and pleasing as Marlborough was, he had no party, and few adherents at Court, or even in the army. A host of acquaintances, indeed, he had, but he was always too self-contained to have many intimate friends. In an age of jovial festivity, he was not convivial, and his temperate and simple habits were a standing reproach to the gambling and drinking men around him. His frugality had earned for him the reputation of penuriousness, and it was complained that he never entertained."

The latter accusation was not altogether correct. In the autumn of 1711, when Marlborough House was completed, it was stated in the fashionable world that the Duchess of Marlborough purposed during the coming winter, " to keep assemblies, and live after a most magnificent manner at her new house"; and again, at the opening of the next year, it was the talk of the town that the Duke of Marlborough, on the Queen's birthday, "intended to make a ball that night at his house ; but when he found how it was took as a sort of vying with the Court, he left it alone." During the past summer, the Duchess had kept open house at her place near St. Albans, but although her entertainments were "very noble and fine," they failed in reviving her position in society. "If you had lived so, two or three years ago," the Duchess was bluntly told by one of her guests, "it might have signified something, but now it would signify nothing." In fact, all the efforts of Duke and Duchess were too late. Even the levées, held by the Duke, were comparative failures. "His house is very fine," was Society's verdict, "but 'tis not filled so much with company as when he was in lodgings."

In the midst of all the political intriguing and struggling to retain their lost power, we occasionally get a glimpse of the Marlborough habits, and of the softer side of their character, a mere glimpse, however, for, as Lord Wolseley says, there is in existing authorities little to be found which bears upon Marlborough's domestic life.

We hear of a great ball given by the Duke of Devonshire, at which the Duchess of Marlborough was present. The supper is described as "very handsome," but it would hardly have been up to our standard :—" At the upper end of the table cold chickens, next to that a dish of cake, parch'd almonds, biskets, next to that a dish of tarts and cheesecakes, next to that a great custard, and next to that another dish of biskets, parch'd almonds and preserved apricocks, and next a quarter of lamb " (sic).

In later years, too, when she resided at Wimbledon, there were pleasant and kindly interchanges of civilities between her and Pope, the poet sending her a present of pine-apples grown by himself, and receiving in return a fat buck, wherewith he regaled his friends, when they, no doubt, toasted Her Grace. To the Lord Mayor and Sheriffs, the Duchess was in the habit of sending venison, and used to receive the deputation from the City, who came to thank her for the gift, sitting up with stately dignity, after the custom of the day, in bed.

Although a thorough man of the world, with many failings, and hardened, one would think, by his dreadful trade of war, the Duke was very tender at heart, full of sympathy for the sorrows of others, an affectionate father, and a most devoted husband, as the secret drawer revealed to his wife after his death, where amongst his treasured possessions, she discovered her own beautiful light, gold-coloured tresses that she herself had cut off in one of her fits of passion, to vex him.

Mentally harassed, and in failing health, Marlborough did not live long to enjoy the grandeur of his London house. Not on the battle-field, like many another warrior, nor by the hand of an assassin, nor even in the mansion that bore his name, was he destined to find his final rest. The old war-eagle, listlessly moping in his eyry, secluded in the great forest at Windsor Park Lodge, died of paralysis, on June 16th, 1722.

The Duke had been partly paralysed for a long time, but on Monday, June 11th, came the final stroke, and he was taken alarmingly ill. Two "expresses" were sent to London for physicians; but on their arrival they could do nothing, and at four o'clock in the morning of June 16th, the great warrior breathed his last.

Much delay arose before the funeral could take place, and meantime the body, duly embalmed, was brought up to Town, accompanied by a detachment of Horse Guards, arriving at Marlborough House at 3 a.m., where it lay in state on a trestle, hardly three feet from the ground, beneath a canopy in the largest of the lower rooms, which was hung all round with rich black velvet.

They arranged matters curiously in those days, for we find that while the Duke's remains were yet above ground, his will was proved and probate granted; the executors being the Duchess, the Earl of Godolphin, the Duke of Bridgwater, and others. A little before his death, the Duke had given instructions that all his servants should receive two years' wages; and out of respect, and we may assume out of gratitude also, they took it in turn to watch by the corpse day and night while it lay in state, relieving one another every four hours.

At last all was in readiness. The four thousand silver memorial medals had been duly struck in the Tower, and on August 9th, a solemn procession set forth for the Abbey from Marlborough House, Lord Cadogan as Commander-in-Chief bringing up the rear of an imposing military escort. The Duke of Montague, being chief mourner, was behind the open car which held the coffin, whereon was placed a complete suit of armour, together with a helmet lying between two coronets; one of them was the late Duke's imperial diadem as Prince of Mindelheim, in Suabia, and the other his ducal coronet. A long train of carriages belonging to the nobility and gentry followed, including those of the King and the Prince of Wales.

At the service, an anthem by Signor Bononcini was sung, which had been rehearsed the day before; and, finally, in Henry VIII.'s chapel, in a vault which had at one time contained the ashes of the Duke of Ormond, and at another those of the usurper Cromwell, the Duke's were temporarily laid to rest. The pall, a magnificent and costly one, was stated to be, according to a very ancient custom, the perquisite of the Dean of Westminster. But a strange thing happened after the funeral—the pall disappeared! having been taken away by some person or persons unknown.

The Duchess remained at Windsor until all was over, and then returned to town. An imposing hatchment was affixed to the south side of Marlborough House, and represented a coat-of-arms, the crest a spread eagle with a large crown above it, and the family motto *Fiel pero desdichado*, "Faithful but unfortunate." The expense of the costly lying-in-state and the funeral, was borne entirely by the proud old Duchess.

Deprived of her husband, the Duchess lived on in semi-retirement, sometimes at Wimbledon where she possessed a mansion, occasionally at Windsor and Blenheim; and, lastly, at Marlborough House, where she closed her eventful life on October 18th, 1744, twenty-two years after the death of the Duke, having lived through four reigns and witnessed some of the most stirring events and changes in England's history. She sleeps at Blenheim beneath the private chapel whither the great Duke's body had been transferred from Westminster just before her death; and above them is the marvellous memorial by Rysbrach:—

"To the memory of John, Duke of Marlborough and his two sons, his Duchess has erected this monument in the year of Christ, 1733," her own name being subsequently added.

Their descendants occupied Marlborough House until the opening years of the present century. Then Prince Leopold, united for a brief period to the Heiress Apparent of the British throne, lived there for some years. Its next occupant was the gentle and amiable Queen Dowager Adelaide, who justly earned for herself the distinctive title of "Good." At her demise, an art collection, destined to develop into a noble museum of worldwide fame, found shelter beneath its roof. In the year 1863, it became the home of the Prince and Princess of Wales, and its old walls began to resound with the merry laughter of happy children.

Much has changed since it was built. England has developed into a mighty Empire, and a new era has dawned in every department of her national life. Unlike Marlborough's time, loyalty to the reigning dynasty, undisturbed by rival claimants to the throne, has now become universal in Great Britain and in that Greater Britain beyond the seas; a loyalty evinced on countless occasions to all the branches of the Royal Family, but never with greater enthusiasm than when the beloved and popular occupants of Marlborough House, emerging from their retirement, are seen in public by the Queen's subjects.

THE END.

www.ingramcontent.com/pod-product-compliance
Lightning Source LLC
Chambersburg PA
CBHW031432230426
43668CB00007B/505